Participation in Environmental Organizations

I0882114

For decades, social scientists have searched for factors that shape pro-environmental behaviour. However, only a few studies have investigated the causes and consequences of participation in environmental organizations. This book fills the gap by analysing in detail the determinants of environmental participation and its consequences in different parts of the world.

Benno Torgler, Maria A. García-Valiñas and Alison Macintyre seek the answers to several questions regarding who is working towards positive outcomes for our environment, what sort of social and institutional context will assist voluntary participation, what sort of attitudes are related to positive environmental behavior, and which countries are active on the intergovernmental stage. By focusing on voluntary participation in environmental organizations, we are able to determine the level of willingness to work towards a solution for environmental problems. This allows an insight into the motivations and attitudes of individuals and nations and how these factors can affect environmental cooperation.

Participation in Environmental Organizations sheds light on who is likely to participate and whose priorities and values are forwarded through voluntary activities, and discusses to what extent voluntary participation can become representative. Thus, the book provides a unique examination of citizens' willingness to participate in environmental organizations. The book will be of interest to economics students and researchers alike who seek a deeper understanding of the theory and practice of environmental participation.

Benno Torgler is Professor at Queensland University of Technology, Australia.

Maria A. García-Valiñas is a Junior Researcher at Toulouse School of Economics, LERNA-INRA, France.

Alison Macintyre studied at Queensland University of Technology, Australia.

Routledge Explorations in Environmental Economics

Edited by Nick Hanley

University of Stirling, UK

1. **Greenhouse Economics**
Value and ethics
Clive L. Spash

2. **Oil Wealth and the Fate of Tropical Rainforests**
Sven Wunder

3. **The Economics of Climate Change**
Edited by Anthony D. Owen and Nick Hanley

4. **Alternatives for Environmental Valuation**
Edited by Michael Getzner, Clive Spash and Sigrid Stagl

5. **Environmental Sustainability**
A consumption approach
Raghbendra Jha and K.V. Bhanu Murthy

6. **Cost-Effective Control of Urban Smog**
The significance of the Chicago cap-and-trade approach
Richard F. Kosobud, Houston H. Stokes, Carol D. Tallarico and Brian L. Scott

7. **Ecological Economics and Industrial Ecology**
Jakub Kronenberg

8. **Environmental Economics, Experimental Methods**
Edited by Todd L. Cherry, Stephan Kroll and Jason F. Shogren

9. **Game Theory and Policy Making in Natural Resources and the Environment**
Edited by Ariel Dinar, José Albiac and Joaquín Sánchez-Soriano

10. **Arctic Oil and Gas**
Sustainability at risk?
Edited by Aslaug Mikkelsen and Oluf Langhelle

11. **Agrobiodiversity, Conservation and Economic Development**
Edited by Andreas Kontoleon, Unai Pascual and Melinda Smale

12. **Renewable Energy from Forest Resources in the United States**
Edited by Barry D. Solomon and Valeria A. Luzadis

13. **Modeling Environment-Improving Technological Innovations under Uncertainty**
Alexander A. Golub and Anil Markandya

14. **Economic Analysis of Land Use in Global Climate Change Policy**
Thomas Hertel, Steven Rose and Richard Tol

15. **Waste and Environmental Policy**
Massimiliano Mazzanti and Anna Montini

16. **Avoided Deforestation**
Prospects for mitigating climate change
Edited by Stefanie Engel and Charles Palmer

17. **The Use of Economic Valuation in Environmental Policy**
Phoebe Koundouri

18. **Benefits of Environmental Policy**
Klaus Dieter John and Dirk T.G. Rübbelke

19. **Biotechnology and Agricultural Development**
    Robert Tripp

20. **Economic Growth and Environmental Regulation**
    Tim Swanson and Tun Lin

21. **Environmental Amenities and Regional Economic Development**
    Todd Cherry and Dan Rickman

22. **New Perspectives on Agri-Environmental Policies**
    Stephen J. Goetz and Floor Brouwer

23. **The Cooperation Challenge of Economics and the Protection of Water Supplies**
    A case study of the New York city watershed collaboration
    Joan Hoffman

24. **The Taxation of Petroleum and Minerals**
    Principles, oroblems and practice
    Philip Daniel, Michael Keen and Charles McPherson

25. **Environmental Efficiency, Innovation and Economic Performance**
    Massimiliano Mazzanti and Anna Montini

26. **Participation in Environmental Organizations**
    Benno Torgler, Maria A. García-Valiñas and Alison Macintyre

Participation in Environmental Organizations

Benno Torgler,
Maria A. García-Valiñas
and Alison Macintyre

Routledge
Taylor & Francis Group
LONDON AND NEW YORK

First published
2010 by Routledge
2 Park Square, Milton Park, Abingdon, Oxon, OX14 4RN

Simultaneously published in the USA and Canada
by Routledge
711 Third Avenue, New York, NY 10017

First issued in paperback 2011

Routledge is an imprint of the Taylor & Francis Group, an informa business

Typeset in Times New Roman
by Keystroke, Tettenhall, Wolverhampton

British Library Cataloguing in Publication Data
A catalogue record for this book is available from the British Library

Library of Congress Cataloging in Publication Data
A catalog record has been requested for this book

ISBN: 978–0–415–44631–0 (hbk)
ISBN: 978–0–203–84994–1 (ebk)
ISBN: 978-0-415-51689-1 (pbk)

To our families and our friends, who had to suffer many lonely hours without our presence and participation while writing this book; and to all those people who actively engage in environmental organizations.

Contents

Figures

Tables

Preface

This book began its journey as a working paper that we (Benno and Marian) wrote in 2006 entitled "Participation in environmental organizations: political interest and state capacity." The paper was accepted and presented at the 3rd World Congress of Environmental and Resource Economists in Kyoto (Japan), July 2006, and generated broad interest. It was published in 2006 in several working paper series such as the Yale Leitner Working Paper Series, the CREMA Working Paper Series, and the refereed CSERGE Working Papers where Professor Jouni Paavola, currently Professor of Environmental Social Science in the School of Earth and Environment at the University of Leeds and Deputy Director of Centre for Climate Change Economics and Policy (CCCEP), provided both encouraging comments and valuable suggestions.

We (Marian and Benno) first started to collaborate on questions regarding the environment after we spent some time together as Visiting Scholars at the Andrew Young School of Policy Studies (Georgia State University) in 2004. Our common interest in making a more thorough exploration of the factors that shape environmental social norms led to a joint paper published in 2007 in Ecological Economics. This paper was the beginning of our closer investigation of interesting international data sets such as the World Values Survey or the European Values Survey from an environmental perspective. We then became interested in exploring the link between informal and formal institutions and environmental behavior or environmental participation. As a consequence we wrote the paper on participation in environmental organization that was presented at the World Congress of Environmental and Resource Economists. Rob Langham, senior publisher at Routledge, contacted us asking whether we would be interested in submitting a book proposal based on this paper. At that stage, we had never thought of writing a book on this topic. We assumed that after the publication of Robert Putnam's seminal work Bowling Alone in 2000, many researchers would already have worked on a book on environmental participation. However, we were surprised to find that there are very few book contributions on this topic so we decided to follow Rob Langham's advice and submitted a book proposal to Routledge in 2006. Although we were not sure how reviewers would react to such a proposal, in the event, the reviews were quite positive, which motivated us to sign a contract with Routledge in 2007. Unfortunately, during 2007 the project stalled slightly and by 2008 we felt it necessary to substantially revise some of the sections. At that time, Alison Macintyre had finished her Honours dissertation work on environmental outcomes and the influence of institutions, receiving the university medal. She provided valuable comments and suggestions on the available draft chapters, and her engagement in the project was such that she naturally became the third author of the book. Her profound knowledge, enthusiastic nature and interest in the link between environmental outcomes and informal and formal institutions were key ingredients in substantially improving the book content.

In preparing the manuscript we received assistance and comments from several people. We would like to thank all those people who provided direct comments as well as all those who provided indirect support (such friends and family members). We would also like to thank Rob Langham, who has been patient and supportive throughout the entire process. In particular, we would like to mention three people who provided substantial assistance in bringing this project to completion. Markus Schaffner's work in the preparation of the macro data sets was invaluable, and special thanks are also due to Heather Loveband and Marco Piatti for carefully looking through the manuscript, correcting mistakes and suggesting improvements. There is no doubt that this book is the result of several years of effort, and all contributions and suggestions received during that time have helped give it the present form. We hope the reader finds the topic and the content as interesting as we do.

1 Introduction

> The development of modern society is not a story about war, conflict, and chaos. It is not about how individuals, groups, and countries fought endlessly with each other for the ownership of natural resources, as well as material and immaterial goods . . . If anything, the story of modern society is about large numbers of citizens cooperating with each other, trying to do something good for the welfare of their community and the broader society of which they are part.
>
> (Van Vugt *et al.* 2000: 3)

The question might (legitimately) be asked: what is so important or interesting about voluntary participation in environmental organizations that we would write a book devoted to the topic? We would like to suggest the alternative, and that is, why we do *not* see more books on this matter? If we reflect for a moment on the benefits of voluntary effort, we see that there are many desirable outcomes of volunteer behavior in general: volunteering is a form of leadership in our communities, it is a source of low cost labor, and is generally regarded as a positive and constructive activity. Volunteering in environmental organizations is particularly positive, as the costs of dealing with environmental damage may be reduced, and the likelihood of solving that vexed issue of generating environmental public goods may be increased. We all require that a certain level of quality of the natural environment be maintained for our very survival, and for the continued survival of subsequent generations. At the same time, we depend on the extraction of natural resources from the environment not only for our survival, but also to fulfill the "higher" aspirations of our species, such as acquisition, status, comfort, and security. It is no secret that current activities in pursuit of development and urbanization are imposing long-reaching and wide-ranging effects on environmental quality and ecological integrity. In the face of these competing uses for the environment, and the reported costs of switching to pro-environmental behaviors, the voluntary efforts of individuals, communities and nations deserve closer attention.

Our approach

Protection and preservation of the natural environment is an objective requiring some degree of cooperation at the individual, community, national and international levels, and the question of how this cooperation might come about is far from simple. We require a certain level of environmental quality, but how is this to be achieved? One way to approach this question is to investigate what is going "right," rather than focusing entirely on what is going "wrong." By exploring the characteristics of those already creating positive benefits through their voluntary actions, we can gauge the trends of participation and make comparisons across countries. Through our work in this book, we hope to say something about the relationships between voluntary participation, environmental quality, who participates, what the driving forces are behind participation, and whose preferences are being served. We also reflect on how voluntary participation within a society affects the kind of intergovernmental participation that is essential if we are to succeed in solving "global public good" problems or global externalities.

Rather than analyzing voluntary participation, we could have compared the standard of certain factors such as the level of pollution or deforestation. These outcome measures, while useful for determining the environmental "performance" of countries, do not tell us about the state of environmental morale in those countries. After all, it is environmental morale and environmental motivation that will determine whether individuals decide to engage in pro-social and pro-environmental behaviors, cooperating to solve current problems such as climate change, pollution, and loss of environmental amenity. By targeting our analysis towards voluntary participation, self-reported individual attitudes, and the engagement of nation states, we also avoid the difficulty of determining whether the environmental condition of a country is a result of factors such as the natural endowment or the location of heavily polluting neighbors, or historical levels of economic growth, or whether it is indeed a result of the conservation efforts of the citizens. The link between policy strategies or certain institutions and environmental outcomes is likely to be weaker as there is a substantial number of factors outside governments' control that impact the outcomes. On the other hand, such initiatives should have a direct impact on "environmental commitment," a characteristic that is less likely to be influenced by a large set of outside factors, or by the possibility of externalizing the problem upon the future and outside a country's frontier (Neumayer 2002). Thus, we may justify taking this approach that will "focus away from environmental outcomes and towards environmental commitment" (Neumayer 2002:145).

In the following chapters, we seek the answer to several questions regarding who is working towards positive outcomes for our environment, what sort of social and institutional context will assist voluntary participation, what sort of attitudes are related to positive environmental behavior, and which countries are active on the intergovernmental stage. By focusing on voluntary participation in environmental organizations, we are able to determine the level of willingness to work towards a solution for environmental problems. This allows an insight into the motivations and attitudes of individuals and nations and how these factors can affect environmental cooperation.

Environmental conservation

What is the problem that (we hope) voluntary participation in environmental organizations is able to address? Most people are aware of the potential for increasing environmental problems if we continue on the current trajectory. In recent years, the issues of climate change and environmental sustainability have become the focus of both the mainstream popular media and the academic literature. Reports on scientific findings regarding climate change and other deteriorating environmental conditions have prompted calls for government intervention, ratification of international agreements, education campaigns, and increased corporate social responsibility. Yet, how is the response to such issues to be organized? Should we demand new regulation from governments? Should we try to determine a monetary value for the environment? Should we impose a range of new taxes? (Will it be too little, too late?) The environmental sustainability discussion has generated a large set of publications ranging from the Stern Review (Stern 2007) to countless books from scientists, as well as many books from economists (e.g. Sachs 2008). Schuett and Ostergren (2003: 37) point out that the relationship between voluntary environmental participation and environmental concern has important implications for the managing of natural resources and stress that more "research should be pursued in exploring the link between attitudes about the environment and specific behaviors."

While the attention paid to environmental issues may seem to have increased considerably in the past five years, concerns regarding the unsustainable use of resources are not a recent phenomenon. Malthusian predictions of natural resource depletion and population collapse have sounded the alarm on environmental degradation since the late 1700s.[1] Proponents of the "no growth" movement have been active since the 1960s, and the current sustainability movement supports the idea of "slow growth," an optimistic view that it is possible to combine economic growth and environmental sustainability. This leads us to question what is being done at present and what can be done in future. Why do some people volunteer in environmental organizations and others do not? If voluntary participation is an effective means by which we can address environmental problems, can we hope for more of this type of behavior? Who among us devotes time to volunteering? What sort of determinants motivate people to participate and what sort of institutional context will assist cooperation and participation to solve this problem?

In asking the previous questions, there is one thing we are sure of: the classic economic assumptions of individual rationality and material welfare maximizing behavior are less helpful in analyzing this situation where we observe market failure in the provision of a good that is vital to and thus is (assumed to be) valued by every individual. This would hardly be news to many people – yet as we will discuss in the following sections, these classic assumptions are often still used when forming policy and predicting decision outcomes.

The environment as a public good: problems and solutions

The environment as a public good presents a social dilemma: it is a circumstance where individual rationality leads to "collective irrationality." While there is a minimum level of environmental amenity required to sustain human existence, if we use traditional economic analysis (as discussed later in the chapter) there is no clear motivation for individuals to incur private costs in providing such public benefits.

The problems

The problem with finding the motivation to take care of the environment is that, to a large extent, environmental quality is a non-private good. While private goods can be purchased, exchanged, owned and consumed by one person at one time, and it is possible to exclude others from consumption of the good, not all goods are private goods. However, if we are dealing with a non-private good, we cannot derive a market solution using monetary costs and benefits, or hope to discover an equilibrium price and quantity via the opportunity costs of demand and supply. Accordingly,

> environmental quality itself can be regarded as a public good, consisting of genetic diversity and a functioning ecosystem . . . Public goods exhibit the characteristics of non-excludability and non-divisibility, meaning that the socially optimal amount will not be supplied by the market.
>
> (Tietenberg 2000: 70)

Damage to the environment is a side effect of engaging in other activities, and certainly is not the desired end in itself. From an economics point of view, pollution and environmental damage caused by development, agriculture or as a result of emissions are all externalities.[2] Both externalities and public goods are classed as market failures: situations where the market fails to provide the efficient quantity of a good. Many instances of market failure arise from social dilemmas. This term describes a situation in which there is a conflict of interest between private interests of particular individuals and the broader public interest within a society (Van Vugt *et al.* 2000). The individuals receive a higher personal benefit from non-cooperative behavior with regard to the other people within a society, even if all individuals are better off when everybody cooperates (Dawes 1980: 191). Dawes concludes that "three important ingredients for enhancing cooperation in social dilemma situations may be: knowledge, morality, and trust." These ancient virtues were not pioneered by Dawes (nor by the United States government, which has invested millions of dollars in research grants over the years to have subjects play experimental games to replicate cooperation in social dilemmas). But the above analysis indicates that they may be the particular virtues relevant to the non-coercive (and hence efficient) resolution of the social dilemmas we face. As a public good that is destroyed by negative externalities, environmental quality presents a special problem for economists.

The solutions

There are several suggested solutions to the social dilemma associated with provision of public goods. This is the case both for public goods generally, and for problems particular to the environment as a public good. The four most commonly discussed solutions are property rights, regulation, market-based instruments, and (voluntary) cooperative action. Each of these solutions could have commanded our attention and resulted in a book – in fact, the first three have engaged many economists and environmental scientists in the past. It is useful to keep in mind that these first three solutions use incentives targeted at a different behavior or level than voluntary participation. We are not disregarding the possibility that these instruments can be effective in many situations. However, one should also note that the wrong intervention in the wrong context can make matters worse, bringing about iatrogenic effects (a disease that is caused by the cure). There are always advantages and shortcomings in any policy instrument or indeed in any approach to a problem. Dealing with environmental issues may require the use of a "set of instruments" to generate sustainable environmental improvements. In this section, we will examine the first three alternative solutions, looking at the pros and cons of using each. We will then explore the ways in which voluntary participation is a useful solution.

Well-defined property rights

The use of well-defined property rights may transform the "environment" (or at least parts of it) from a public good into a private good, thereby establishing private motives to take care of the asset. With defined property rights, the owner(s) can exclude others from enjoying or making use of the asset, and can capture the benefits of the asset for themselves. This approach has been implemented in body corporate situations and smaller areas of organized collective living. Well-defined property rights are most effective when the area under consideration can be segregated in some way, so it may successfully be applied to areas of forests[3] and can also be applied to isolated bodies of water. Yet this principle is difficult to apply when it comes to oceans, air, schools of fish, waterways, biodiversity, and ensuring genetic diversity. It is especially difficult to apply this principle in relation to the atmosphere and the well-publicized problem of greenhouse gas emissions. Carbon emissions may be the ultimate externality, producing effects that are dispersed across time and across geographical and political space. The inter-temporal and international nature of this negative externality constrains the ability for unilateral policies or actions to mitigate the overall problem (Levy *et al.* 1992). Essentially, well-defined property rights may not be the best solution to the public good and externality problems posed by the issues of environmental destruction and/or protection.

Regulation

Since it is not possible to attach clear property rights to *general* environmental quality, the state may be expected to provide incentives or to use policy interventions to protect and ensure provision of this public good. It has been suggested that there is an efficient role for government in providing these sorts of public goods (Tietenberg 2000). "While it is increasingly agreed that government actions are required to preserve our environment, the extent and form of those actions remain a subject of debate" (Stiglitz 2000: 215). If the state becomes involved in provision of public goods, the transaction costs of organizing individuals to solve these problems may be avoided, although considerable policing and enforcement costs may instead be incurred. The costs involved in organizing groups that voluntarily agree to internalize externalities can also be quite excessive, even for the state. Stiglitz (2000:223) mentions that the government could be seen as "precisely the mechanism that individuals have set up to reduce the welfare losses from externalities," which suggests that establishing a state with redistributive and legislative power is in itself an attempt to enable low transaction cost solutions to social dilemmas. Examples of this mechanism in action can be identified in the public programs of environmental protection, such as Local Agenda 21, an initiative proposed by the United Nations (UN) in 1989 and enacted by local governments to protect several facets of the environment. Additionally, there are national initiatives in many countries that aim to preserve water, air, and other natural resources.

There is a definite advantage in using regulation to provide public goods, since targeted policy can ensure provision of specific goods. This allows policy makers a degree of certainty in achieving desired outcomes. Direct regulations can be used to limit particular externalities; for example, by placing emissions standards on cars. If the state imposes a certain limit on the emission of air pollution, it can be targeted to specific industries and specific regions. State regulation of national parks and reserves protects those areas from exploitation and in some cases even covers such details as fires, camping, and littering.

However, it can be extraordinarily expensive to ensure (or enforce) compliance through policing behaviors. Moreover, when the government imposes rules on a situation, it runs the risk of choosing the wrong rules and the wrong method for implementation. Regulation might not only encourage or allow inefficient practices; it could also lead to crowding out of existing intrinsic motivations, resulting in less environmental protection.[4] This can also have spillover effects to other areas of life: a decrease in the willingness to voluntarily care for the environment as a reaction to poor regulation may decrease the willingness to engage in other community actions. Frey and Stutzer (2006) criticize the use of command and control techniques as they may actually damage the environment by changing the locus of control from intrinsic motivation and values to one of extrinsic motivation. However, just as there is the potential for negative spillover effects, there is also the potential for a positive side, and we will visit these effects in the discussion on voluntary participation.

Another argument against relying on regulation to solve problems around public goods and externalities is that government action is usually reactive and not proactive. A government can often be completely out of touch with the changes in attitudes or priorities of the voters. The Labor Party's victory over the conservative

Coalition in the last Australian federal election was popularly attributed to the fact that Coalition leaders had "lost touch" with the Australian public. Environmental issues were a focal issue in the 2007 election, and Kevin Rudd's promise to ratify the Kyoto Protocol was well-received by many voters (Beder 2009), contributing to the success of their campaign. A further example of an administration having "lost touch" was evident during the presidential elections in the United States. The fervor with which Barack Obama was received as a symbol of hope and change can be seen as an indication of how out of touch the Bush administration had become with the people it represented.

Market-based instruments

The argument for using market-based solutions in addressing environmental problems is driven by the principle of economic efficiency. However, the economically efficient outcome is based on the assumption that there exists some amount of money that will satisfactorily compensate people for the pollution of the air or water on which they depend for their health and survival. This demonstrates the potential for pricing mechanisms to encourage commodification of the environment. Throughout the discussions in this book we observe several instances of how the idea of determining a "price" for the environment can override previously held non-monetary values for the environment. Treating the environment as a commodity could result in unintended consequences for the willingness to preserve the environment.

Environmental taxes are an example of market-based instruments that have been developed to control pollution and emissions. Several specific taxes, such as those on electricity, transport, petrol, or emissions are considered to be "green" taxes, designed to influence individuals' decisions. However, for the taxes to be efficient, they must penalize polluters to the extent of the negative externality produced. This requires that the government determines the size and social cost of the negative externality, which is a very difficult process and is not certain to result in efficient taxation. A further complication is that sometimes taxes are created because governments need additional funds, and not to achieve environmental goals (Labandeira *et al.* 2006).

Market-based instruments also carry the potential to alter the intrinsic motivation to care for the environment, introducing iatrogenic effects.[5] It has been suggested that pricing mechanisms and tradeable emission rights have a strong crowding out effect similar to the indulgences of the Middle Ages; firms can essentially purchase a "licence to pollute" which jeopardizes any moral incentive to practice environmental stewardship (Frey and Stutzer 2006). A further complication in the use of pricing mechanisms is observed by Searle (2005), who suggests that even in the presence of social norms emphasizing environmental consideration, this would be lost on corporations, since these entities are set up to "create a set of power relationships without having the accompanying liabilities that go with those relationships when they are assigned to human individuals" (Searle 2005: 17). This raises an important point regarding corporations' liability in this situation, since a corporation cannot feel responsibility or obligation or duty to the environment. Only the individuals who own the company (shareholders) or the employees or the board of directors can feel such socially constructed morals. The aim of a corporation is to maximize shareholder wealth, therefore it is a legal entity that can enter into contracts with human legal entities while remaining free of those moral or social codes that regulate human behavior.

An emissions trading scheme rearranges both the incentives and property rights by creating an economic incentive to reduce carbon emissions and the targeted outcome is framed in economic efficiency and profit maximization. Hence, we have another solution that results in a monetary valuation for the environment. This has a further implication: by choosing the right discount rate, all future costs of environmental damage can be reduced to zero. In a cost-benefit analysis there would be no cost, only benefit, when working out the present value of a project. Therefore, while market-based instruments promise economic efficiency, the outcomes may vary, and economic efficiency does not guarantee other forms of efficiency or justice.

Of the possible solutions to the public good problem, there are problems with each of those discussed. Property rights, regulation and market-based instruments each have their advantages, but also their downfalls. Incentive-based instruments help to improve the natural environment, but favorable outcomes depend on particular conditions. Frey (1997: 65) stresses that incentive-based instruments "strongly influence behaviour but there are areas in which incentive instruments are much less effective owing to the countervailing effect of crowding out environmental morale."

In what may be termed as "low-cost" situations, voluntarism should be encouraged because external interventions in such areas might be problematic. Low-cost situations are those where "an individual decision is irrelevant for the individual himself/herself and for all other individuals, though the *collective* decision is relevant for all individuals (low-cost decision type I)" (for example, voting in elections), and where "an individual decision is irrelevant for the individual himself/herself, but the *individual* decision is most relevant for other individuals (low-cost decision type II)" (e.g., judiciary decisions) (Kirchgässner and Pommerehne 1993: 109). The problem is that in such low-cost situations, individuals may behave less responsibly, since "wrong" decisions are often without any short-term consequences for the decision makers. Moral rules or voluntary initiatives may help to reduce such a hazard, and may even be viewed as an indication that, over time, groups find ways to cope with such low-cost situations. "People who follow the standards of environmental ethics in their behavior because they find the underlying ecological issues fascinating, experience a severe loss of motivation when the same task is performed by an externally imposed policy instrument" (Frey 1997: 61). Separation of household refuse or the disposal of wastepaper and chewing gum in public places are examples of this phenomenon. On the other hand, in "high-cost" environments, environmental morale might not be activated as effectively due to the large burden placed on individuals and firms.

Consequences such as the "severe loss of motivation" alluded to by Frey (1997: 61), are not surprising to theorists who differentiate between the various types of norms and interactions involved in different sorts of relationships. Boulding (1985) distinguishes between threat relationships (e.g. police, armed forces), exchange relationships (such as auctions and stock markets), and integrative relationships (monasteries, church, and family). The extent to which a situation invokes a threat, exchange, or integrative relationship – and the relative importance of each of the three – will affect the norms, values, and expectations in that context. Each of the different relationships engender particular expectations and demands, as well as different responses. Using the principle of exchange in a relationship that calls more for an integrative response (e.g. offering monetary compensation for environmental damage) may be one of the reasons why commodification of the environment might actually affect willingness to engage in pro-environmental actions. Of course, the opposite can also be the case. Expecting someone to give their time voluntarily as if it was an integrative relationship, or threatening that person with physical violence when they require an exchange relationship (i.e. that they are paid in return for their labor), will also result in ineffective incentives.

Just as there are positives and negatives to property rights, regulations and market-based instruments, voluntary participation (collective action) also has its advantages and downsides. However, it is this potential solution with which the book is primarily concerned, and it remains a surprise to us that, so far, not many books have discussed the topic. The pros and cons, the benefits and drawbacks, and the underlying processes of voluntary participation will be explored in depth in the next section. In general, our perspective in this book is that a paradigm based *only* on a system of rewards for cooperation and punishment for non-cooperation might be too narrow.

Voluntary participation and collective action

Voluntary participation and cooperative behavior are terms we use to describe the action taken by individuals to collectively provide public goods and apply pressure to solve externalities. Unfortunately the transaction costs (that is, the costs of finding, learning to trust, and agreeing on a path of action) involved in organizing individuals around either provision of goods or solving externalities are very high. The following chapters of this book take a closer look at voluntary participation in caring for the environment; investigating questions of which institutional conditions will encourage participation, who is more likely to participate and take care of the environment and why. We also examine these differences at the regional and the country level. The book will analyze whose preferences are advanced by environmental conservation, which institutional and social conditions support collective action in respect to the environment, and what sort of macro conditions encourage voluntary participation.

Voluntary participation as a solution to the public good problem

Collective action leads to several significant benefits. First of all, it generates positive spillover effects to other areas of development and social interaction. The principle of community action and cooperation is transferable to the solution of other social dilemmas and may lead to greater engagement in other organizations. Social norms and environmental morale are both based on concepts of reciprocal fairness and may crowd in existing intrinsic motivation to take care of the environment. Positive spillover effects into other areas of life may be produced by certain ordinary activities, for example, the habit of recycling could make people more aware of the environment and therefore better at saving water in a drought.[6] In the short term, policy can support environmental morale through appeals and participation, and in the long term, environmental morale can be encouraged by education and by procedural fairness.

Focusing on environmental participation may also take into account that pro-environmental behavior is driven by a broader utility function that covers both self-interest and concern for others (interdependent preferences). Bamberg and Möser (2007) point out that:

> Pro-environmental behaviour is probably best viewed as a mixture of self-interest (e.g., to pursue a strategy that minimises one's own health risk) and of concern for other people, the next generation, other species, or whole eco-systems (e.g., preventing air pollution that may cause risks for others' health and/or the global climate).
>
> (Bamberg and Möser 2007: 15)

Moreover, provision of public goods through collective action contributes to and results from undistorted motivations (that is, not distorted by monetary incentives). As discussed above, policies aimed at Homo economicus could distort existing motivations to take care of the environment by trying to change what would be a value decision (possibly a bequest motive or intrinsic value) into a monetary one. In fact, as pro-social behavior is voluntary and heavily conditioned by norms of behavior observed in society, there exists a stronger chance to crowd in these behaviors than to persist in seeking the appropriate monetary value for the environment based on an individually stated willingness to incur private costs in order to supply a public good.

It is likely that behavior of individuals will be influenced by their perception of the behavior of other citizens. Torgler *et al.* (2009) show that perceived environmental cooperation (level of pro-social behavior) by the public is an important determinant in explaining environmental morale and environmental preferences of individuals. If a person believes that littering in a public place is common, then their environmental morale decreases. Alternatively, if an individual believes that others are abiding by social norms, then the environmental morale or environmental preference increases. Hence, community action on an environmental issue can reinforce positive social norms and values.

In many cases, collective action is cheaper and easier to organize than a regulatory regime. Voluntary environmental cooperation is attractive because it is not only cost effective but can be more effective in areas where law enforcement and market incentives fail (Torgler *et al.* 2009). Even though environmental morale can be unstable and unreliable, Frey and Stutzer hypothesize that it "is supported in the short term by appeals and participation, and in the long term by education" (Frey and Stutzer 2006: 17). Thus, environmental morale can be influenced by some kinds of social capital:

> These outside interventions strengthen consumers" self-determination. The locus of control remains with the individuals as these measures – at least if well done – emphasize their own responsibility. This crowding-in effect may be restricted to a particular area addressed by an intervention, but is likely to extend beyond that if individuals perceive a substantial degree of similarity of issue and content.
>
> (Frey and Stutzer 2006: 17)

Standard economic theory and voluntary participation

A traditional economic approach to volunteering would hold that volunteer activity is work performed without monetary rewards, therefore creating social output that would otherwise require paid resources. While this book takes the perspective that voluntary participation (collective action) is a mechanism through which the public good problem could be addressed, such a notion has not been popular with economists for the past 40 years. Yet, prior to 1965, it was assumed that groups would find their own ways to solve social dilemmas, through collective action arising organically from those groups.

This was challenged by Olson's (1965) seminal work on the theory of collective action, which found that "rational egoists will not act in their common interest but rather free-ride" because "interest groups trade in collective, or public, goods which are characterized by non-excludability" (Udehn, 1993: 14).[7] On the other hand, Olson (1965) also emphasized that his argument in regards to large, latent groups

> does not necessarily imply self-interested behavior, though such behavior would be completely consistent with it. The only requirement is that the behavior of individuals in large groups or organizations of the kind considered should generally be rational, in the sense that their objectives, whether selfish or unselfish, should be pursued by means that are efficient and effective for achieving these objectives.
>
> (Olson 1965: 64–65)

He points out that larger, more heterogeneous and less specialized groups, where people do not know each other as well, are less likely to develop the kind of social pressure that would help them satisfy their interest in a collective good. If we accept the rational egoist theory of human behavior, it follows that a rational, self-interested individual will free-ride in any situation, taking advantage of the benefits while avoiding any contribution to the costs of public good provision (Udehn 1993). This claim predicts the existence of far less collective action and cooperation than is actually observed (Udehn 1993, Torgler 2002, 2007, Ostrom 2000).

The concept of a "rational egoist" has influenced much of the policy and theoretical discussions over the past 40 years. This influence has been perpetuated by its featuring role in most textbooks (Ostrom 2000), and its legacy is evident in theories and literature concerning cooperation, public choice, and political science. If we are free-riding and self-interested individuals, it is rational to exploit the environment for personal gain and shirk from the cost of environmental protection. The destroyer will reap the benefits of exploiting the environment; they are unlikely to have to bear the costs of exploitation, yet they cannot be excluded from the benefits of any environmental amenity that is secured by the efforts of others. The costs are dissipated to others in society who do not benefit from the exploitation, and if they do form a group to solve the problem there is no way to exclude others from free-riding on the benefits of that solution (Frey and Stutzer 2006).

Even Olson recognized that the rational free-rider concept does not necessarily apply in this situation and that there must be some other mechanism at work. Yet, the use of fairly common policy mechanisms such as regulation, market-based instruments, and property rights are based on the rational utility maximizer. Taken out of context, Olson's arguments would justify the use of coercion and exclusion to solve the collective problems (Van Vugt *et al.* 2000). The assumption is that this maximizer will change behavior in response to the change in (mostly monetary) individual incentives. In our book we assume a more optimistic picture of humanity and will provide evidence that human beings are able to solve social problems. Ostrom (2000: 154) also raises the uncomfortable point that past policy based on payoff structures appealing to the rational egoists could have been misdirected, and introduced iatrogenic effects (as discussed earlier in this chapter). Interestingly, many common property resource problems have been successfully addressed by self-organization (Ostrom 1990), and in such a situation the outside intervention by government can generate disastrous consequences. One example of how a self-organized solution may succeed in ensuring sustainable use of a resource is demonstrated by the sharing of grazing land in Switzerland. While agricultural land is usually treated as private property, for centuries the grazing rights on the Alpine meadows have been treated as "common property." Specific rules that prevent overgrazing are enacted by an association of users and limit the number of livestock permitted on the meadow. The number of user families has remained stable over time, and rights and responsibilities have been passed from one generation to the next. This type of system and its underlying stability have led to a high level of trust and reciprocity, providing the foundation of a sustainable compliance over quite a long period of time (Ostrom 1990).

Basing policy on the wrong assumptions may work against the original intentions of the policy and crowd out the social norms that encourage cooperative behavior rather than encouraging collective action. It may be that the pre-Olson assumptions were correct. As has been noted by many authors already, several observable behaviors in everyday life, like paying taxes, voting, and volunteering, either in organizations as a collective aimed at a specific achievement or merely just to "help out," demonstrate the ability of groups to solve their own problems.

Why collective action can and does happen

The majority of Chapter 2 is dedicated to explaining how factors that are sometimes considered "frictions" (requiring collective action to overcome the failures of governance) can in fact explain much of the cooperative behavior that is observed. Yet, the neoclassical approach assumes individualistic preferences with zero transaction costs, regarding it to be "against human nature that people can make fair or efficient decisions on behalf of others" (Vatn 2004: 206). Recent empirical and experimental literature refutes this assumption, tending to support the understanding of human behavior as being socially constructed. The norms and inferred meanings on how one "should" act in certain situations then construct the background for choices. March and Olsen in Vatn (2004: 207) suggest that doing the right thing is so important that an "action is often based more on identifying the normatively appropriate behavior than on calculating the return expected from alternative choices." Under this framework, true rationality is doing what is socially appropriate. While assumptions of the rational egoist can be appropriate when analyzing interactions around a market situation (Boulding's exchange relationship), for example in analyzing auctions and competitive situations (Kagel and Roth 1992, Vatn 2004), it can be a mistake to transfer this assumption to situations requiring collective action (integrative relationship) or to derive policy implications entirely under such assumptions.

So, why would anybody make a voluntary effort to save the environment? One can argue that the majority of people cooperate because they are also concerned about others' outcomes. Cooperation is enhanced if individuals see themselves as part of a group. In addition, norms about fairness and justice in society also constrain self-interested behavior (Van Vugt *et al.* 2000). Thus, individuals may participate in environmental organizations because they care about what happens in their environment locally, nationally, and internationally. They may also feel good about themselves if they contribute to the environment, experiencing an increase in self-esteem. Alternative instruments that do not assume a narrow self-interested model may make massive and expensive punitive systems less desirable. "Psychologically, there may be something wrong, or at least self-defeating, with coercion because it threatens people's self-determination and creates an atmosphere of distrust among citizens. Accordingly, it inhibits people's self-respect, and the pride they take in their group membership" (Van Vugt *et al.* 2000: 13).

Structure of the book

Due to the significance of this topic, we analyze several dimensions of participation in environmental organizations, from both theoretical and empirical points of view. However, one should note that we are writing for a wider audience and therefore we tend to avoid too many technical details that could present an obstacle to the readers. While this chapter has provided a short introduction to the "puzzle" of environmental participation, comparing volunteering with the pros and cons of other solutions, we realize we have omitted more than we have included. Looking at the reasons why voluntary participation is such a "puzzle" would require the consideration of entire disciplines to analyze it in a satisfactory manner. We should also note there are some repetitions throughout the book. This is intended for several reasons. It helps to clearly identify priorities and links the arguments throughout the book. In addition, repeating the main points reduces the transaction costs to the reader if they wish to take a non-chronological approach to reading the book, as switching between chapters should not be too difficult.

Chapter 2 (social capital and institutions) links participation in environmental organizations to the network and civic dimensions of social capital and the influence of institutions. We look at the evidence for the influence of social capital and institutions, and discuss what this might mean for voluntary participation in environmental organizations. Generally speaking, social capital and institutions can reduce the transaction costs involved in organizing individuals to voluntarily address the public good problem. Transaction costs are incurred when we do not trust the people with whom we are interacting: it takes considerable effort and cost to gather the information necessary to determine whether we can trust others, and to establish mechanisms by which we can detect and punish free-riders. In fact, we might minimize our own efforts if we feel we cannot trust other people to reciprocate. In addition, if established rules of conduct are lacking, there will be a reduced quantity and perhaps also reduced quality of interactions. These established rules may be either informal rules at the social or community level or formal rules at the state or national level, and they can improve the efficiency of interactions, making activities such as trade and cooperation more likely. Thus, it is easier to organize voluntary participation and community action in a state or society in which there exists a higher level of trust, a well developed network of relationships, favors, reciprocity, social capital, and existing community action (which in turn contributes to the development of the previously mentioned elements). It is also more likely that this participation will evolve if there is a well developed institutional framework. Interestingly, our results also indicate that we find more community-level actions to preserve the environment in a deficient state characterized by corruption and dictatorship, but only if there is a rapid collapse of institutional structures producing a strong institutional, political, and economic vacuum that precludes private initiatives.

In general, to understand voluntary participation in environmental organizations we need to understand social capital and institutions. Chapter 2 attempts to shed some light on the phenomenon so that readers have a better understanding of how environmental participation is embedded within this complex notion of social capital.

Once we have analyzed the social capital framework, in Chapter 3 we conduct an overview of the available literature on volunteering, maintaining a particular focus on environmental participation. Such a review allows us to isolate the main factors that can be employed to explain voluntary participation in environmental organizations. The "costs" and "benefits" of participation are usually discussed in terms of their respective influence on an individual's final decision about whether to participate or not, and at what degree of intensity. Yet the decision to participate may not hinge on a simple cost-benefit analysis, and may especially not hinge on financial costs or benefits. One should note that we use a broad notion of "benefits" and "costs" covering not only material incentives, but also non-material incentives (or motivation). The established literature suggests several socio-demographic and socio-economic characteristics that may influence participation in voluntary organizations, and we point out that attitudes and ideologies also matter. A large set of variables described in Chapter 3 will be implemented in the empirical work in later chapters. We look to the previous literature in formulating the expected influence of these factors, and to guide the use of an adequate empirical model. We also seek to isolate new or underexplored factors.

After reviewing the main theoretical considerations, we search for some empirical understanding of participation in environmental organizations. Chapter 4 describes the databases used in the empirical work throughout the book – the World Values Survey and the European Values Survey. We present some descriptive statistics, reporting rates and levels of participation compared across countries, investigating which countries have the highest rates of engagement (whether active or passive) in an environmental organization. Differing levels of participation may be either membership in general or actively committing time and effort to an environmental organization. Looking at some relationships across socio-demographic and socio-economic strata, we can observe the evidence for such questions as whether females are more likely to participate, and the participation rates for different age groups and marital status. Additionally, basic correlations are presented, in order to detect some significant factors that can explain this collective action behavior, or the relationships among other pro-environmental or cooperative attitudes. We look at questions such as: if an individual is a member of another voluntary organization, are they more likely to also be a member of an environmental organization? Are there any correlations between environmental attitudes and environmental behaviors? We look at whether there is a tendency for those who state that they are willing to pay more for environmental quality to actually participate more regularly in environmental organizations. Furthermore, we could question whether there is any payoff to all this environmental participation: are there any correlations between environmental participation and better environmental outcomes? We compare some measures of emissions (CO_2 and PM10) to discover whether they are lower in societies that have higher rates of participation in environmental organizations and ask: what does this mean for the effectiveness of local action to solve local problems? We are aware that due to the explorative nature of the chapter (and the large number of tables that result), most readers will find it quite difficult to read chronologically from start to finish. However, it provides a good orientation to the dataset we have used in the following chapters, and the nature of the chapter should be such that a reader can skim those variables of less interest and take the time to read about the variables of greater interest.

There are three empirical chapters oriented towards the micro-analysis of participation in environmental organizations. To this end, Chapter 5 presents an initial approach to the key factors that influence participation. Controlling for commonly used factors in the literature, we include proxies for political interest and political involvement as possible determinants and then also include the perceived level of corruption to proxy the institutional quality at the micro level. Since very few studies have worked with such a "perceived corruption" variable at the individual level, we feel inclined to reduce such a shortcoming. Moreover, a further aim of this chapter is to characterize the kind of people who usually participate in environmental organizations from a microeconomic perspective. The results obtained from regressions covering a large set of countries in this chapter provide evidence for whose preferences are advanced by voluntary participation. We conduct this analysis across countries and across regions. We find that a higher perceived corruption is correlated with a stronger incentive to participate in environmental organizations. Interestingly, it seems that if individuals perceive a lack of administrative integrity, they seem to be willing to find alternative ways to pursue their goals. It seems we can argue that a higher quality of institutions encourages voluntary participation by facilitating collective action (Chapter 2), but at the same time we have empirical evidence in Chapter 5 that a lower quality of institutions (as measured by perceived corruption) also allows for voluntary collaboration to solve public good problems unless there has been a rapid collapse of the institutional structure leading an institutional vacuum.

What process are we observing here? Is it bearing out the pre-Olson notion that groups would cooperate to solve their own dilemmas? Or is this evidence of Olson's assertion that interest groups do not provide public goods; they only cooperate in order to seek to gain advantages for themselves. It is possible to argue that local groups that willingly cooperate to solve local problems – whether they are in the presence of a deficient state or not – are seeking to capture the benefits of a better environment for themselves.

From an institutional perspective, this seems to present something of a paradox. However, it may be argued that perceived corruption relates more to the current politico-economic conditions, where there is still some level of institutional regime in place. In this case, it is still possible for individuals to organize themselves to solve collective action problems. Moreover, "perceived corruption" is only one indicator of institutional strength, whereas when we measure "institutional quality" using a broader range of measures, we are measuring the institutional foundation at the constitutional level.

In addition, one of the key phrases is "unless there has been a rapid collapse of the institutional structure leading an institutional vacuum." If the institutional structures are changed completely, as they are in transition countries, there is a rapid reordering and replacement of institutions on a scale that precludes cooperation. The energy required for negotiating the ensuing chaos crowds out other forms of engagement. As explained by Kasper and Streit (1998: 3), "modern economic life depends rather precariously on numerous written and unwritten rules. If they are widely violated – as when society collapses after a lost war or in internal chaos – many of the human interactions on which we depend for our wellbeing are no longer possible . . . ”

This book also highlights the relevance of political discussion and political interest, variables that (until now) have largely been neglected in the environmental literature. We maintain that a higher level of political interest allows citizens to better supervise the government and may contribute to a stronger sense of civic awareness, hence leading to a higher environmental contribution or participation. Political interest influences the extent to which individuals go about collecting, processing, and interpreting political matters. This increased knowledge possibly augments the ability to acquire political information at lower costs, which in turn increases the individual incentive to be informed and to discuss political issues. This may enhance the perception and increase awareness of environmental problems. Thus, political interest may increase pressure on a government to perform in certain ways.

Next, Chapter 6 focuses on the influence that collective action has on individual attitudes to preserve the environment. We explore the possibility that the network component of social capital influences the justifiability of littering. In this respect, littering is a very clear behavior which contributes to reduction of environmental quality. So, the justifiability of littering by individuals is the “non ethical” behavior that we are going to try to explain in this chapter. Despite littering in public places being recognized as a major public health and safety hazard due to such dangers as water pollution, fire hazards, rodent and insect infestations, highway accidents, injuries suffered from discarded cans and broken bottles, and diminished aesthetic appearance of public places, few studies (particularly in the area of economics) have addressed this issue. Early sociology and psychology studies on littering and environmental attitudes used experiments, which have an advantage in being able to control for and manipulate the variables of interest. This allows the reduction of causality problems and thus provides good information not only about the relationship between two variables but also about the direction of the effect. Nevertheless, the survey data used in our book has the advantage of being able to include many socio-economic, demographic, and attitudinal variables which help to test a rich set of (new) theories while also comparing different countries and generating insights regarding how environmental participation changes over time. Taking the economics of crime approach, we would not expect that anybody would incur the cost of properly dealing with refuse, since the likelihood of being caught for littering is extremely small. Hence we look at what processes are at work to encourage this proper disposal of litter. The decision to litter or not litter is an observable, common, ubiquitous decision that almost everyone faces almost every day. If only for this reason, littering behavior is worth investigation. However, littering is also an interesting behavior because it requires a collective action to litter or not to litter. It is not just the action of a few firms, companies or individuals, it takes the actions of many individuals to either drop their litter or dispose of it properly. So what are the determinants of littering? What will stop people from littering? A politely worded sign? Conditional cooperation (“if you litter, I will litter, if you don’t, I won’t”)? Does it matter if the area is already dirty?

Our contribution presents new insights as we observe which factors influence the justification or acceptability of littering from an international point of view. Most previous studies have been carried out in small or medium-sized geographic areas. Comparing different areas of the world can give us some clues with respect to individual environmental preferences and morale, and allow us to characterize people who do not justify these behaviors. At the same time, we would like to check if the characteristics are the same for several environmentally friendly and cooperative actions, in order to draw connections between different behaviors.

Chapter 7 builds on the results obtained in Chapters 4 and 5. We seek empirical results regarding the effect of some pro-environmental attitudes on environmental behavior or the involvement in environmental organizations. Thus, we consider the willingness to contribute to the environment, by means of income and taxes, and also look at the willingness to free ride. This empirical exercise is based on a very simple theoretical model of volunteering which allows us to explore moral attitudes. In the previous chapters we have stressed on various occasions that there is a lack of studies which explore empirically whether some pro-environmental attitudes have a positive effect on environmental behavior or the involvement in environmental organizations. Thus, more empirical evidence is desirable to see whether environmental attitudes affect environmental actions, although the previous literature has generally shown that values and attitudes can affect individual behavior in a range of different areas. Our hypothesis is that a higher level of environmental motivation due to higher environmental moral standards leads to a stronger voluntary involvement in environmental organizations. In Chapter 7 we test the hypothesis using a large micro data set covering several European countries. Such breadth and depth of data allows exploration of the different channels through which individuals express their environmental motivation via pro-environmental attitudes. The motivation behind such an analysis, as discussed previously, is the observation that deterrence models fail to predict the relatively high level of compliance in various situations where a private cost is incurred in order to provide a public good. Environmental motivation, environmental morale, or pro-environmental attitudes are highly relevant to an understanding of why people have a higher willingness to be involved in environmental protection.

The previous chapters of the book were primarily motivated by the aim of providing a solid empirical micro-foundation. However, such a micro-foundation has its limitations; for example, it is difficult to link environmental participation to environmental outcome. Thus, it is useful to extend the previous chapters by adding a macro-analysis. The descriptive analysis conducted in Chapter 4 only gave us information about the "raw effects" and not the "partial effects" of the associations between our variables. In Chapter 8 we study the relationships in a multivariate context. We are interested in conducting a broad exploration of the factors that contribute to environmental participation to check whether the previous results remain robust at the macro level. In the micro-level studies, we determined that environmental motivation affects environmental participation in a positive way. This is also useful from a policy perspective. We indeed observe that environmental motivation is correlated with environmental participation, which is in line with the results of the micro-level analysis. The results at the macro level also indicate that people engage more actively in environmental organizations when they are situated in better institutional environments. Moreover, politicians and government have an incentive and the administration most likely has enough resources to translate these preferences into a stronger environmental commitment. The chapter also attempts an analysis of countries' environmental engagement at the intergovernmental level. In this analysis, we are broadening the scope from an engagement at the voluntary level to investigate involvement at the intergovernmental level. We explored whether societies with a stronger voluntary engagement at the individual level are also more engaged at the intergovernmental level. The results indeed support such a relationship. Thus, we can observe some sort of environmental participation culture within a country that is also visible at the local and also intergovernmental level. Finally, we also find support for the idea that there is a strong positive relationship between how effectively the countries are organized and the intergovernmental involvement in environmental issues.

However, we would introduce one caveat: it would be more appropriate to refer to observable correlation when discussing and interpreting our empirical results generated in this book. While regressions can be used to approximate experiments in the absence of random assignment (Angrist and Pischke 2009), in many situations it is quite challenging to deal with causal interpretations. We recognize that interpretation of our results is problematic, as is the habit of referring to observed correlations throughout all the empirical chapters as causal effects. We see the results as more precisely estimated partial correlations. For simplicity, we use the notion of "impact" or "effect" when discussing the results, the model and comparable papers in the literature review. Such results can provide a guidance to derive policy implications as long as one is aware that these are not fully precise estimates of the causal effect of interest.

We have focused on participation in environmental organizations as a way to protect the environment. Establishing the determinants of participation and the relationships with other attitudes and behaviors will help us to improve natural resource management, contributing to the solution of several current environment problems.

Notes

1 Malthus predicted that the increase of population is geometric, while increase in food production is arithmetic, resulting in inevitable famine and poverty (Malthus 1798).

2 Externalities are those costs and benefits of an activity that accrue to a third party not involved in the transaction. See Stiglitz (2000).

3 In fact, environmental groups are collectively purchasing tracts of land via their subscribers, see Abelson (2000).

4 In this respect, the Endangered Species Act has been one of the most controversial US laws ever passed. Lueck and Michael (2003) argue that the ESA has actually hurt the plight of the red-cockaded woodpecker by giving property owners an incentive to make their land uninhabitable to the bird. Recently, List *et al.* (2006) found a similar dynamic

in the case of the cactus ferruginous pygmy owl. In his book about market and governmental failures, Wolf (1988) referred to "governmental externalities" as those negative consequences due to the public regulation.

5 Similar to those "government externalities" (Wolf 1988) as discussed in the previous footnote (4).

6 Unlike the effects of regulation, which could crowd out intrinsic motivation in other areas as well. If extrinsic motivation is used and it crowds out intrinsic motivation, this may have spillover effects on other areas of cooperative behavior (Frey and Stutzer 2006).

7 See also Hardin's (1968) "tragedy of the commons."

References

Abelson, R. (2000) "Preserving the forest by leasing the trees," *New York Times*, September 24: P 3.6.

Angrist, J.D. and Pischke, J.-S. (2009) *Mostly Harmless Econometrics*, Princeton: Princeton University Press.

Bamberg, S. and Möser, G. (2007) "Twenty years after Hines, Hungerford, and Tomera: A new meta-analysis of psycho-social determinants of pro-environmental behaviour," *Journal of Environmental Psychology*, 27: 14–25.

Beder, S. (2009) "Token environmental policy continues in Australia," *Pacific Ecologist*, 18: 45–48.

Boulding, K.E. (1985) *The World as a Total System,* Beverley Hills: Sage Publications, Inc.

Dawes, R.M. (1980) "Social dilemmas," *Annual Review of Psychology*, 31: 169–93.

Frey, B.S. (1997) *Not Just for Money: An economic theory of personal motivation*, Cheltenham: Edward Elgar.

—— and Stutzer, A. (2006) "Environmental morale and motivation," *CREMA Working Paper* 2006–17.

Hardin, G. (1968) "The tragedy of the commons," *Science*, 162: 1243–48.

Kagel, J.H. and Roth, A.E. (1992) "Theory and misbehavior in first-price auctions: comment," *The American Economic Review*, 82: 1379–91.

Kasper, W. and Streit, M.E. (1998) *Institutional Economics: Social order and public policy.* Cheltenham, Glos.: Edward Elgar.

Kirchgässner, G. and Pommerehne, W.W. (1993) "Low-cost decisions as a challenge to Public Choice," *Public Choice*, 77: 107–15.

Labandeira, X., López, X., Picos, F., and Rodriguez, M. (2006) "Imposición energético-ambiental y financiación autonómica," *CLM Economía*, 8: 209–28.

Levy, M., Haas, P., and Keohane, R. (1992) "Institutions for the earth: promoting international environmental protection", *Environment,* 34: 12–36.

List, J.A., Margolis, M., and Osgood, D.E. (2006) "Is the Endangered Species Act endangering species?" *NBER Working Paper* 12777.

Lueck, D. and Michael, J. (2003) "Preemptive habitat destruction under the Endangered Species Act," *Journal of Law and Economics,* 46: 27–60.

Malthus, T.R. (1798) *An Essay on the Principle of Population.* Library of Economics and Liberty, 5 July 2009, <http://www.econlib.org/library/Malthus/malPop.html>.

Neumayer, E. (2002) "Do democracies exhibit stronger international environmental commitment? A cross-country analysis, *Journal of Peace Research*, 39: 139–64.

Olson, M. (1965) *The Logic of Collective Action: Public goods and the theory of groups,* Cambridge, MA: Harvard University Press.

Ostrom, E. (1990) *Governing the Commons: The evolution of institutions for collective action,* New York: Cambridge University Press.

——(2000) "Collective action and the evolution of social norms," *The Journal of Economic Perspectives,* 14: 137–58.

Sachs, J. (2008) *Common Wealth: Economics for a crowded planet*, New York: Penguin.

Schuett, M.A. and Ostergren, D. (2003) "Environmental concern and involvement of individuals in selected voluntary associations, *Journal of Environmental Education*, 34: 30–33.

Searle, J.R. (2005) "What is an institution?" *Journal of Institutional Economics,* 1: 1–22.

Stern, N. (2007) *The Economics of Climate Change: The Stern Review*, Cambridge: Cambridge University Press.

Stiglitz, J. (2000) *Economics of the Public Sector*, New York: Norton.

Tietenberg, T.H. (2000) *Natural and Resource Economics*, Reading, MA: Addison Wesley.

Torgler, B. (2002) "Speaking to theorists and searching for facts: tax morale and tax compliance in experiments," *Journal of Economic Surveys*, 16: 657–84.

——(2007) *Tax Compliance and Tax Morale: A theoretical and empirical analysis*, Cheltenham, Glos.: Edward Elgar.

——, Frey, B.S., and Wilson, C. (2009) "Environmental and pro-social norms: evidence on littering," *The B.E. Journal of Economic Analysis and Policy*, 9: art.18.

Udehn, L. (1993) "Twenty-five years with the logic of collective action," *Acta Sociologica,* 36: 239–61.

Vatn, A. (2004) "Rationality, institutions and environmental policy," *Ecological Economics,* 55: 203–17.

Van Vugt, M., Snyder, M., Tyler, T.R. and Biel, A. (eds.) (2000) *Cooperation in Modern Society: Promoting the welfare of communities, states and organizations*, London: Routledge.

Wolf, C.H. (1988) *Markets or Governments: Choosing between imperfect alternatives*, Cambridge: M.A. Press.

2 Social capital and institutions

He only says, "good fences make good neighbors."
. . . Why do they make good neighbors? Isn't it
Where there are cows? . . .
Before I build a wall I'd ask to know
What I was walling in or walling out,
And to whom I was like to give offense.
Something there is that doesn't love a wall, that wants it down.
He moves in darkness as it seems to me,
Not of woods only and the shade of trees.
And he likes the thought of it so well
He says again, "Good fences make good neighbors."

(*Mending Wall* by Robert Frost, 1915)

Introduction

How can we explain voluntary participation in environmental organizations? From an economics point of view, this activity incurs a private cost to secure a public benefit, presenting something of a puzzle for standard theory (as discussed in the previous chapter). Yet the reality is that people do cooperate to provide a public good,[1] a fact that has been covered by literature and experiments in several fields, including social psychology, demography, economics, and economic psychology. Recent literature addressing the "puzzle" of voluntary compliance has highlighted the quality of social capital and institutions as explanatory factors for differences across a range of areas, at both the macro (country) level and at the micro (individual) level. Social capital and institutions were once regarded as "complications" in both theoretical and empirical models, and now are included in studies on such areas as tax compliance, voting behavior and general volunteering activities. We are interested in the links between social capital, institutions, and voluntary care for the environment, and we attempt to gain a better understanding of how environmental participation is embedded in these complex notions.

Background

Previous literature has found that a better stock of social capital can influence factors such as economic development and social order (see for example, Woolcock and Narayan 2000, Knack and Keefer 1997, Grootaert and van Bastelaer 2002), and in fact, the effect of social capital on economic growth may be as strong as that of human capital or education (Whiteley 2000). The concept of social capital can be used to frame, structure, and describe a wide variety of economic and social phenomena, from the success of networks, to differing levels of development, to the output of voluntary organizations. Research on the impact of institutions has also developed over the past few decades, with papers investigating the link between institutions and international trade (e.g., Levchenko 2007), tax compliance and shadow economy (Torgler 2007, Torgler and Schneider 2007, 2009), or economic growth (North 1991, Knack and Keefer 1995, Keefer and Knack 1997), and environmental policy decisions (Neumayer 2002).

While the social capital literature and the institutional literature have developed separately, the concepts have so much in common that there is a strong argument to suggest that social capital and institutions are actually elements of the same continuum (Grootaert and van Bastelaer 2002), and Grafton and Knowles (2004: 352) even refer to institutional quality as "public social capital." The operations, formation, and influence of social capital and institutions are very similar; hence it is useful to discuss their effect on voluntary participation in the same chapter. Latham (2000) proposes that horizontal (democratic) relations such as those among citizens are relevant for understanding trust in civil society. Furthermore, vertical (hierarchical) relations such as those between citizens and people in authority (for example the police), are the types of relationships that are relevant for understanding trust in authority. Grootaert and van Bastelaer (2002) distinguish these relations as social capital (horizontal) and institutional analysis (vertical). We will come back to the interaction between social capital and institutions at the end of the chapter.

Social capital in context

It is important to establish a good understanding of social capital, as it can be seen as the "playground" or the "possibility set" in which we are going to act and play in this book. Environmental participation can be viewed as an element in civic participation (Putnam 2001) and therefore a key element of social capital. Formal and informal rules or institutions are part of this playground. They somehow define the climate of the playground (favorable or unfavorable conditions), provide the foundation of the playground, and define the formal and informal rules of how to play in the playground. Thus, to understand voluntary participation in environmental organizations, we need to understand social capital and institutions. This chapter will attempt to shed some light on the phenomenon so that readers have a better understanding of how environmental participation is embedded within this complex notion of social capital. Moreover, one should note that we are only able to scratch the surface of social capital. The topic and indeed the notion of social capital is challenging, complex, dynamic, and multidimensional. To a certain extent, it also remains quite blurry and slippery; evading precise observation, measurement and replication (in other words, circumventing the very elements that underpin the modern scientific paradigm). One of our primary challenges is that the links and the different stages within this playground are so interlocked that it is difficult to isolate which came first; that is, in many cases it is difficult to clearly determine the direction of causation.

Of course, we always have the option to just move away from this area and therefore avoid playing in such a colorful and unstructured playground. Alternatively, with some curiosity, open-mindedness, and flexibility, one can attempt to discover this playground, keeping in mind that such an exploration is full of shortcomings and caveats. Yet, at the end of it all, we hope our efforts may enhance our understanding of this playground and the people acting within. It is not only the present activities in the playground (children actively playing) but also the past (parents watching, controlling, and influencing the children's playing) that are relevant to understanding the development of social capital. We believe that there are too many important avenues of inquiry in this playground, and that they are related to a better understanding of human nature. As a consequence, we find it difficult to close our eyes and walk away. We are confident that an exploration aimed at a better understanding of this playground and its actors will provide important insights into this relatively new topic, and we hope to catch a glimpse behind the existing "veil of ignorance and uncertainty." It is an exploration of the playground with the eyes of a child driven by curiosity, fascination, fear, passion, excitement, and imperfection.

We propose that a better stock of social capital and a higher degree of institutional quality can increase participation in environmental organizations, and perhaps improve the efficacy of those groups.[2] Both social capital and institutions can be viewed as factors that condition interactions, on the one hand facilitating cooperation by reducing the transaction costs of coordinating voluntary participation, and on the other hand defining the constraints or "rules of the game," by reinforcing the formal requirements and social norms of participation for environmental protection. In addition, higher quality institutions may provide another avenue through which citizens can express their preferences, by voting, lobbying for policy changes, and holding the government accountable for its actions. However, a seemingly contradictory finding (discussed in Chapter 5) suggests that when the state is deficient, a good stock of social capital can replace the operations of formal institutions and enable collective action and cooperation to solve problems of the group (see Rose 1998). Such a result is consistent with Bowles and Gintis' (2002: F423) argument that "communities may make important contributions to governance where market contracts and government fiats fail because the necessary information to design and enforce beneficial exchanges and directives cannot effectively be used by judges, government officials, and other outsiders." Our results indicate that environmental participation seems to arise in situations when there are "frictions," or in other words, when there is a need for collective action to overcome the failures of governance. Each of these effects will have some bearing on the outcome of any attempts to organize cooperative action, and as this chapter progresses we discuss these processes in more detail. However, our results also indicate that in extreme situations where there has been a collapse of institutional structures, this has led to a formal and informal institutional vacuum. This situation occurred in the transition countries during the 1990s, hindering private attempts to organize environmental action and restore government effectiveness.

Social capital helps organize collective action and is strengthened by organizing collective action. The very existence and operation of voluntary participation in environmental organizations characterizes the main dimensions of social capital. We discuss this in further detail in the next section, but first we will examine social capital, the concept, definitions, and the dimensions. Next we will explore institutions.

What is social capital?

While the term "social capital" is now in common use, pinning down a precise definition of this concept remains problematic. As an interdisciplinary concept, social capital has encouraged social discourse among researchers, and the processes behind social capital have been studied in depth by many different disciplines. This has advanced the standing of social capital in the social sciences, providing:

> a credible point of entry for sociopolitical issues into a comprehensive multi- and interdisciplinary approach to some of the most pressing issues of our time. In social capital, historians, political scientists, anthropologists, economists, sociologists, and policy makers – and the various camps within each field – may once again begin to find a common language within to engage one another in open, constructive debate, a language that disciplinary provincialism has largely suppressed over the last one-hundred-and-fifty years.
>
> (Woolcock 1998: 188)

Yet, even though social capital is an inter-disciplinary term, and functions as an inter-disciplinary language, this (somewhat ironically) has not produced a single and widely accepted definition. However, Putnam (2001) cites one of the first and best definitions written in 1916 by L.J. Hanifan:

> Those tangible substances [that] count for most in the daily lives of people: namely good will, fellowship, sympathy, and social intercourse among the individuals and families who make up a social unit . . . The individual is helpless socially, if left to himself . . . If he comes into contact with his neighbor, and they with other neighbors, there will be an accumulation of social capital, which may immediately satisfy his social needs and which may bear a social potentiality sufficient to the substantial improvement of living

> conditions in the whole community. The community as a whole will benefit by the cooperation of all its parts, while the individual will find in his associations the advantages of the help, the sympathy, and the fellowship of his neighbors.
>
> (cited in Putnam 2001: 19)

We now investigate some of the ways that different disciplines use the social capital concept.

Political science

Political scientists have been discussing the concept of social capital since the 1960s. Almond and Verba (1963) were among the first to seriously investigate social capital, studying the relationship between culture and participation. Many years later, interest in the social basis of political and economic life has reemerged thanks to researchers such as Putnam (1993) and Fukuyama (1995), who have highlighted social capital as an important topic in the political sciences. Putnam (1993: 167) asserts the importance of social capital for the effective governance of democracy, and expresses social capital as "features of social organization, such as trust, norms, and networks that can improve the efficiency of society by facilitating coordinated actions." Fukuyama (1997: 378) defines social capital as "the existence of a certain set of informal rules or norms shared among members of a group that permits cooperation among them." In other words, it is "the ability of people to work together for common purposes in groups and organizations" (Fukuyama 1995: 10).

If we combine these perspectives, we can say that in the context of a political science explanation of social capital, environmental behaviors would be attributed to the existence of rules and norms that allow a common purpose to be achieved. We can align this conception of social capital with Grootaert and van Bastelaer's (2002) work published on the Social Capital Assessment Tool (SOCAT). The construction of this tool will be discussed later in the chapter when we examine measurement of social capital, but for now, we recognize that the input of structural dimension (networks) interacts with the cognitive dimension, and facilitates the collective action outcome.

Economics

The rapid growth of the social capital literature represents a widespread unease regarding classical economics' standard explanations for differing political and economic performances not only across nations but also across sub-national jurisdictions (Ostrom and Ahn 2003). Mainstream economists, on the other hand, hold equal reservations about the use of the term social "capital," as it can be misleading to describe the stock of trust and networks using the same term employed to describe physical capital (Arrow 2000, Solow 2000). Inkeles (2000:

246) stresses that social capital is a residual category: “It gets what is left over. But the situation is not that bad, because there is a great deal left over.”

The concept of social capital has generated a high level of interest from the field of economics:

> My own guess is that the popularity of social capital reflects a widespread belief that conventional economic approaches to behavior seem inadequate for understanding problems such as the social pathologies of the inner city. By conventional economic approach, I am referring to models of individual behavior in which the psychological and sociological influences on individuals are treated as having second order significance. The economic approach to human behavior has become immensely important throughout the social sciences; the attractiveness of social capital arguments stems, I suspect, from a growing recognition of the limitations of conventional versions of this choice-based approach.
>
> (Durlauf 2002: 272)

There are many obvious differences between social capital and other “capital” concepts; for example, unlike physical capital, social capital cannot be accumulated by one person, nor does it wear out with frequent use. On the contrary, exercising social capital increases the stock of trust and networks. From an economist’s point of view (Stiglitz 2000), social capital can be seen as knowledge, networks, and reputation, enabling communities and individuals to address the problems of moral hazard and incentives. Schiff (1992: 160) defines social capital as “the set of elements of the social structure that affects relations among people and are inputs or arguments of the production and/or utility function.” Describing social capital as inputs to a production or utility function requires that we keep in mind “how much of any individual’s scarce resources should go to building social capital” (Rupasingha *et al.* 2006: 84), as opposed to investing in physical or human capital. Portes and Sensenbrenner (1993: 1323) refer to social capital as “those expectations for action within a collectivity that affect the economic goals and goal seeking behavior of its members, even if these expectations are not oriented toward the economic sphere.” Arrow (1971: 22) also stresses that “in the absence of trust . . . opportunities for mutually beneficial cooperation would have to be foregone . . . norms of social behavior, including ethical and moral codes (may be) . . . reactions of society to compensate for market failure.”

To this end, many authors have singled out social capital as an important feature of productive social relationships (Gambetta 1988, Hardin 1993). According to Dasgupta (1988), social capital can lead to more efficient economic transactions by giving agents access to more information, enabling them to coordinate activities for mutual benefit, and, through frequent transactions with the same players, reducing the likelihood of opportunistic behavior. If we look at the conditions and contexts under which social capital is ordinarily developed, we find that it is during interactions that occur for religious, social, or cultural reasons (Grootaert and Bastelaer 2002). Environmental groups are a kind of collective organization that assist the accumulation of social capital, and that exist because there is a stock of social capital facilitating community action.

For economists, social capital is important in facilitating environmentally positive behaviors because it reduces the risk that people will behave opportunistically towards each other, and reduces the problem of asymmetric information that often prevents coordination of activities. A greater stock of social capital increases the information available about the other participants of a group with regard to their preferences, loyalties, and propensity to free-ride. With increased knowledge of each other and increased trust in the other participants, there are reduced transaction costs of organizing collective action, since there are less safeguards required to protect against free-riding, as well as a reduced cost of discovering the likelihood of other participants' defection or cooperation. Social capital aids in the organization of environmental groups and provides access to networks and resources to achieve mutual benefit, which again contributes to the generation of further social capital (multiplier effect).

Sociology

Sociologists have a long history of investigating the concept of social capital. We only briefly mention some important names here, starting with Bourdieu (1979) and Coleman (1988, 1990), who were key figures in the early days of social capital literature. Both researchers influenced the literature through their focus on individuals and small societal units. For instance, Coleman (1990: 304) points out that social capital works by "facilitating the achievement of goals that could not be achieved in its absence or could be achieved only at a higher cost." Coleman (1988) identifies three forms of social capital, namely:

> obligations and expectations, which depend on trustworthiness of the social environment, information-flow capability of the social structure, and norms accompanied by sanctions. A property shared by most forms of social capital that differentiates it from other forms of capital is its public good aspect: the actor or actors who generate social capital ordinarily capture only a small part of its benefits, a fact that leads to underinvestment in social capital.
>
> (Coleman 1988: S119)

Portes and Mooney (2002: 305) regard "the ability to secure resources by virtue of membership in social networks or larger social structures" as the most widely accepted definition of social capital in sociology.

Thus, for sociologists, social capital aids the gathering of participants and other resources in order to achieve the goal of environmental protection. This goal is reached at a lower cost than would be possible without a facilitating stock of social capital. Sociologists also maintain that social capital is a key concept, emphasizing that "social relationships form a resource that individuals can draw upon in their personal and professional lives. It provides a unique organizing principle comparable to the financial and human capital relationships of economics and a linkage to social structure" (Hofferth *et al.* 1999: 79).

This short and imperfect discussion reveals that all disciplines have in common the idea that social capital is a facilitating factor, reducing transaction costs and enabling collective action. We have indicated that the stock of social capital may be increased by participation, propinquity, and engagement. The discussion also gives us a hint that social sciences are interested in similar questions, using different theories and instruments in their investigation. Social capital is developing as a joint concept within all social sciences, and the multidisciplinary approach has the potential to foster innovation by allowing a view of the same phenomenon from different angles. Paldam (2000: 631) reminds us that even "if the operational version becomes a bit naive seen from the perspective of each social science it is important to keep communication open."

The dimensions of social capital

As discussed earlier, even though there is no definitive theory, the various conceptions of social capital do tend to converge on a few similar dimensions encompassing the interaction of social processes, networks, resources, and institutions. While some researchers describe social capital using more than three dimensions, most literature can be organized according to those defined by Grootaert and van Bastelaer (2002) in the SOCAT.[3] This categorization uses three main dimensions: membership in associations and networks (structural social capital), trust and adherence to norms (cognitive social capital), and collective action. The first two indicators (structural social capital and cognitive social capital) are regarded as input measures, while collective action is regarded as an output measure. This view is shared by Paldam (2000: 629–30), who describes three families of social capital concepts: "trust" (cognitive social capital), "cooperation" (collective action), and "networks." He points out that these conceptual families come together because "most people build trust in and networks to others and come to cooperate with them," a view that is in line with our rationale for discussing social capital measures in this book. Thus, it is possible to speak about "a culture of trust and tolerance, in which extensive networks of voluntary associations emerge" (Inglehart 1997: 188), and "the information, trust, and norms of reciprocity inhering in one's social networks" Woolcock (1998: 153).

For our purposes, we are interested in how membership in voluntary associations and networks interacts with trust and adherence to norms to influence contributions to pro-environmental collective action, our basic premise being that environmental organizations themselves can represent the structural dimension of social capital, and participation in these organizations relies on the presence of the cognitive dimension of social capital. At the same time, engagement in environmental organizations can improve the levels of trust in society. Stronger networks and greater levels of trust then lead to improved collective action outcomes as an "output," resulting in better environmental standards. We now look at each of these dimensions in a little more detail.

Cognitive social capital

This dimension of social capital is both an input to the development of social capital and an outcome of being involved in organizations (resulting in a few measurement problems, as discussed in the next section of this chapter). Cognitive social capital is measured by the SOCAT along the lines of solidarity (degree of commitment in a community to assist individuals in hardship or disaster), trust, and conflict resolution (Grootaert 2002). Trust is one of the most well-known dimensions of social capital, and is linked to altruism or philanthropic generosity, an understanding and use of the dimension which was popularized by Fukuyama (1995). Trust is an optimistic attitude or belief regarding other agents' behavior and can be perceived as the reason why people find strangers trustworthy. We can also distinguish between different types of trust. Personalized trust is a variety of trust that takes time to form, and is sometimes generated through frequent interpersonal interaction with the same individuals (Uslaner 2002). On the other hand, trust sometimes arises from a general knowledge about the people with whom one is interacting, including knowledge of their incentives and upbringing (Durlauf and Fafchamps 2004). This is referred to as generalized trust, and it is instantaneous or, at least, forms more quickly than personalized trust. Other authors refer to trust on several levels of collective organization, such as family, neighborhood, people of different ethnicity, business owners, government officials, government services providers, local governments, and other institutions (Narayan and Cassidy 2001). Levels of generalized trust and social capital can be related to the degree of homogeneity within a community. Previous literature reports on the difficulty in providing public goods to heterogeneous groups within society (La Porta *et al.* 1999; Torgler and Schneider 2007, 2009), recognizing that where there is internal conflict and ethnic or religious tensions, resources are steered towards funding conflict and attempting negotiations. The energy for collective action is directed elsewhere, which could mean that the environment is overlooked, and is less likely to be protected.

It is argued that the cognitive dimension is beneficial for economic efficiency, improving the frequency and volume of economic transactions, and that:

> inefficiency is expected to be highest in societies where the trust network is very sparse . . . Inefficiency is also large when subgroups that could benefit a lot from trading with each other are prevented from doing so by mutual isolation. This is true if even many links exists in each sub-group.
>
> (Durlauf and Fafchamps 2004:10)

We will discuss this issue in more detail in the next section, but note here that the principle of efficiency is not restricted to economic transactions – a high level of generalized trust may increase the efficiency of interactions between individuals seeking to organize themselves into collective action.

Structural social capital

The idea that trust creates efficiency by bridging isolation is linked to the formation of networks. The existence of and membership in networks forms the structural dimension of social capital. In some ways, this is the most visible dimension of social capital, as civic groups and the density of membership in voluntary groups are the least problematic elements to identify and measure. Networks require trust in order to function, hence the structural dimension is a measure of the ties among individuals, and their ability to organize groups that achieve their common goals. Sandefur and Laumann (1998: 484) pointed out that "an individual's potential stock of social capital consists of the collection and pattern of relationships in which she is involved and to which she has access, and further to the location and patterning of her associations in larger social space."

Networks may be formal or informal. Formal networks are established through groups such as clubs, student organizations, or professional associations. Informal networks are built by means of friends or family relationships. Among these informal networks, distinction is first made between families within and beyond the household, as it is anticipated that family units within one household cooperate and function in different ways to those extended networks of kin beyond the household. Informal "communities of interest" beyond family and kin include friendships and other intimate relationships as well as bonds among neighbors. These friendships or weak ties (Granovetter 1973) complement the strong ties with family and kin, creating differing levels of "bonding" or "bridging" social capital. Without these varying degrees of networks and associations, reciprocal obligations to kin (or the group level at which the strongest ties were invested) could lead to fewer, not more, interactions (Woolcock and Narayan 2000).

Formal networks of social relations concern those aspects of life most often described as civic or institutional. These include associations with formally constituted groups, as well as non-group-based activities (Stone 2001). Environmental organizations may be formal or informal. They may be large environmental organizations such as Greenpeace, with an established bureaucracy, structure, and international presence. On the other hand, they may be small neighborhood clean-up groups that are informally organized to remove weeds from the local waterway. In either case, these organizations constitute networks of members through which social capital may be accumulated, and (by building trust and networks in these groups), collective action may be organized.

Collective action dimension (output)

The dimension of civic participation or collective action is an output measure which is described as the degree of involvement with networks and institutions (Grootaert 2002). It is only possible to observe this output if a significant stock of cognitive and network social capital available to produce it exists (Grootaert 2002). Countries with consistent social networks are more likely to exhibit high levels of civic participation (Fidrmuc and Gërxhani 2005), a phenomenon that is usually captured through membership in voluntary organizations.[4] Through active participation and cooperation, individuals learn to interact with other people to achieve shared objectives and increase the levels of cognitive and network social capital in that society. These effects are achieved through participation in environmental organizations, and the process of participation reinforces these effects.

Participating members of voluntary organizations are empowered in other areas of life through their cooperation and engagement in collective action. Portes (1998: 6) defines social capital as "the ability of actors to secure benefits by virtue of membership in social networks or other social structures." Brehm and Rahn (1997: 999) reinforce this conception by defining the role of social capital as "the web of cooperative relationships between citizens that facilitates resolution of collective action problems."

This "web of cooperative relationships" enabling the actors to "secure benefits by virtue of membership in social networks" has attracted criticism as well as praise (as we describe in a later section of this chapter). On one side we have Olson (1965), who points out the "selfish" character of several organizations, such as political parties or trade unions; these are the influence groups that try to modify the redistribution system to their own benefit. Environmental groups are not immune from this charge: they may seek to satisfy their own preferences at the expense of members of a logging interest group. On the other hand, Putnam (1993) recognizes the positive character of several organizations, such as educational, religious, charitable, or environmental organizations, which act to reduce some social and environmental costs and do not impose negative externalities on the rest of the society.

The role of social capital: advantages and disadvantages

At first glance, social capital could seem like something of a silver bullet. If we increase the stock of trust, solidarity, and networks and produce collective action, then we could look forward to increased economic development, voluntary participation to provide public goods at a low cost, and a surfeit of other desirable outcomes. Of course, nothing is that simple, and in this section we discuss several positive and negative consequences of social capital stock. We are interested in understanding the role that social capital plays in the economic, social, and political development of societies. It is important to consider both the advantages and disadvantages, particularly if a policy calls for a deliberate attempt to increase social capital in order to reap the positive effects: the negative potential needs to be taken into account.

Positive effect of developing social capital

The literature has identified several ways that a good stock of social capital can improve efficiency, and Durlauf and Fafchamps (2004) distinguished three particular categories: information sharing, group identity, and explicit coordination. Thus, interactions and information transfers among people, the identification of a group, and agreement on how to organize tasks are outcomes that can improve available information, exerting an influence on people's preferences, attitudes, and behaviors. This relates to the level at which people are likely to cooperate to solve externalities or provide a public good. If the group is identified and is able to transfer information and make agreements on how to organize tasks, and has a good stock of social capital, the likelihood of solving an environmental problem is increased. Sobel (2002: 143) refers to simple positive externalities: "If there are no clubs, then there are no clubs to join. Individual action is insufficient to increase social capital, and bad outcomes persist without selfless behavior or outside intervention."

The role of social capital in economic development has been responsible for attracting a great deal of the attention to the concept. Accordingly, Durlauf and Fafchamps (2004: 11) pointed out, "much of the interest in social capital stems from the view that the absence of social capital represents one of the major impediments to economic development." Overall, there is a general consensus in the literature that a good stock of social capital is important for economic development. Putman (1993) showed that a reason for lower levels of economic development in Southern Italy was its lower social capital levels. Guiso *et al.* (2004) also studied the economic conditions in Italy, specifically exploring the role of social capital in financial development because financial contracts depend not only on the enforcement ability but also on the extent to which the counterpart is trusted. Their results indicate that social capital plays a crucial role in the level of financial development in Italy, and is particularly important where education levels are low and law enforcement is weak.

Underlying the economic development argument is the idea that social capital improves the efficiency of social exchange. It has been recognized that social capital has the ability to reduce potential inefficiencies caused by imperfect and asymmetric information. Coordination and trust are two significant issues relevant to social exchange efficiency. Interpersonal relationships and social networks can frequently help to facilitate interactions, reinforcing and supporting the role played by formal institutions. Both formal and informal processes ensure consistently reliable social and economic exchanges, leading to economic development. Social capital can lead to more efficient economic transactions by giving access to better information, enabling parties to coordinate activities for mutual benefit, and reducing opportunistic behavior, making transactions easier and more frequent (Dasgupta 1988).

A higher level of social capital has also been linked to a lower level of neighborhood violence and crime (Sampson *et al.* 1997). Moreover, social capital is necessary for the provision of public goods.[5] Many clubs or networks can produce public goods; examples of networks that seek to achieve social benefit are faith-based and non-governmental organizations. Grootaert and Van Bastelaer (2002) pointed out that social capital has a profound impact in many different areas: among other things, it affects the provision of services, in both urban and rural areas, makes the management of common resources easier, helps to improve education, can contribute to recovery from conflict, and can compensate for a deficient state. With respect to provision of the environmental public good, we argue that social capital increases social efficiency and facilitates cooperation. The public good in question (referring to Chapter 1) includes environmental services or amenity from a functioning ecosystem and management of environmental resources.

Social capital also allows the correction of several externalities. Collective action in addressing environmental problems illustrates this principle. In fact, there is a growing interest in social capital and its potential for affecting collective action in sustainable renewable natural resource institutions (Rudd 2000, Sobel *et al.* 2001, Pretty and Smith 2004). Pretty and Ward (2001) pointed out that where there is a significant stock of social capital, local groups with locally developed rules and sanctions are able to manage natural resources more efficiently than individuals working alone or in a non-cooperative way. Social capital not only reinforces and supports formal institutions and facilitates the interactions that provide public goods, but in cases where the state is weak or formal institutions are not well developed, it is advantageous to have a stock of social capital instead. At the local level, social capital can become another way of getting things done, and can develop when the state is weak, as discovered by Rose (1998) regarding the dysfunction of transitional "anti-modern" Russian institutions. Durlauf and Fafchamps (2004) claim:

> in poor countries, there are many situations in which the state could, theoretically, intervene to provide a public good, but where it is unable to do so because its tax base and its capacity to organize are limited. Collective action can serve as a substitute for the state . . . Two essential ingredients are then required: leadership and trust. A leader is required who is capable of convincing community members that they should voluntarily contribute to the public good. Trust is necessary to resolve conflicts among competing interests and to reduce fears of free-riding.
>
> (Durlauf and Fafchamps 2004:10)

So, the presence of generalized trust, networks, coordination, civic participation, and community involvement can lead to improved social exchange efficiency. In Pennar's words, social capital is "the web of social relationships that influences individual behavior and thereby affects economic growth" (Pennar 1997: 154).

Overall, the empirical studies that test for the positive influence of social capital generally return non-conclusive results, but some cases do confirm the positive influence of social capital on economic development. Miguel *et al.* (2001) found a positive relationship between the density of organization and the industrialization process in Indonesia. Knack and Keefer (1997) showed the positive impact of several methods of civic participation on economic growth. Beugelsdijk and Van Schalk (2001) pointed out that the network component (group participation) helped to explain per capita output growth. However, they did not find any significant relationship regarding trust and economic development.

Zak and Knack (2001) analyze a general equilibrium growth model in which agents facing moral hazard problems decide how much to invest in monitoring. The presence and strength of formal and informal sanctions for dishonesty are shown to have significant implications for growth due to their role in reducing the need to invest in monitoring. Similarly, Helliwell (1996) found that trust and participation in associations contribute to per capita output growth once factors such as openness are accounted for. Putnam (1995) called the generalized view of economic development into question, and showed that the decreasing rate of network and civic participation components of social capital were not correlated with the economic evolution in US states. Thus, it is possible to conclude that social capital constitutes a necessary condition for economic development, but alone it is not enough to ensure prosperity. Analogous to this conclusion is that social capital could also constitute a necessary condition for environmental protection, but alone is not enough to ensure sustainability.

Negative aspects of social capital

Negative economic and social consequences of social capital have been recognized, raising the dilemma that a stock of social capital can be simultaneously productive and counterproductive (Portes and Landolt 1996). Social capital can foster behavior that worsens rather than improves economic performance, appearing as a barrier to social inclusion and social mobility, dividing rather than uniting communities or societies and facilitating rather than reducing crime, education underachievement, and health-damaging behaviors (Aldridge *et al.* 2002).

The dimensions of social capital that we use to describe the positive effects of processes are also relevant for describing the negative effects. While networks are primarily viewed as exerting a favorable influence on economic growth, they can also lead to non-equitable situations. For example, consider the exclusion phenomena in some clubs or organizations, where several types of people are not accepted or allowed to enter. Hence, some associations have the ability to generate social capital, but at the same time they carry the potential to exclude others (Hunter 2000, Szreter 2000). The social capital literature has pointed out that the degree to which networks are open or closed has implications for the quality of the relationships they embody, and their productive output (Coleman 1988). Exclusion therefore leads to an insider–outsider distinction on a discretionary basis and may "contribute more to fostering parochial narrow-mindedness and ethnic hostility than to addressing the failures of markets and states" (Bowles 2004: 492). Hence,

> The creation of clubs may thus reinforce polarization in society between the "in"group and the "out"group. Investing in social capital by promoting clubs can thus have serious equity repercussions. This is true even if we ignore the fact that certain groups may collude to explicitly dominate or exclude others . . . A similar situation arises with networks because better connected individuals profit from their contacts.
>
> (Durlauf and Fafchamps 2004:15)

It may be that clubs or organizations work because they are good at enforcing norms: but the judgment as to whether they are good or do good things depends on what the norms are (Bowles 2004).

Additionally, the network component of social capital can facilitate the disproportionate influence of particular groups in certain situations. Such an influence is recognized in national and international negotiations (Betsill and Corell 2001). Unfortunately those "interest groups" can be working for their own benefit, without taking into account other people or social groups. This is in line with the idea of "olsonian" group mentioned previously (Olson 1965). Similarly, the chance to use network relationships to obtain individual beneficial outcomes may not be good for the society or for any other network (Sobel 2002). Results obtained by Glaeser *et al.* (2002) indicate that it is challenging to generate clear predictions in the aggregated process due to the positive and negative interpersonal externalities. Social capital as a "network" generates positive externalities while social capital as "status" (inferring the potential to reward and to punish others and capture larger rents than others) generates negative externalities. Social capital may also be connected to a standard economic investment model where individuals accumulate social capital when the private incentives are high.[6]

Determinants of social capital

Social capital does not accumulate in a vacuum. If we desire the positive aspects of social capital in the provision of public goods and increased economic development then we need to know the preconditions for existence of social capital. Unfortunately, the difficulty in measuring social capital has repercussions for the ability to measure the determinants. Glaeser *et al.* (2002: F437) point out that "while we have theory and evidence on the *effects* of social capital, we are just beginning to identify the underlying mechanisms that create social capital in the first place." In this book, we use voluntary environmental participation as a key factor to indicate social capital and we analyze the determinants of such environmental participation in the hope of shedding new light on the creation of social capital in this context.[7] Moreover, we stress that the economic and institutional development of a country may have a significant impact on social capital. The quality of formal institutions can influence accumulation of social capital. When institutions are weak or non-existent, the legal system is not able to ensure that agents respect commercial contracts and economic exchange, a common situation in developing countries.

At the same time, the development of social capital may improve the development of institutions. It may be that a higher level of trust, of informal "rules of the game," of interactions, of coordination of activities, and strong network connections may lead to the development of formal institutions, entrenching these informal processes in legislative, administrative, and operational systems. Thus, it is possible that causality relationships are not clear at all. Social capital and institutions co-evolve, each exerting an influence on the development of the other, although it may be expected that institutions usually change less quickly than social capital.

Fidrmuc and Gërxhani (2005: 5) point out that "the institutional development of a country may have an important influence on social capital." If people are able to trust one another, it is possible that they will organize themselves into associations or groups. The features of governmental and political systems matter, and:

> The relationship between democracy and social capital could appear to be symbiotic: is Democracy a product of a highly developed Social Capital or vice versa? It is difficult to answer this question. Democracy development can determine the level of generalized trust and social networks a society may have, yet its existence is no guarantee of either trust or a vibrant community.
>
> (European Commission 2005: 5)

However, it is clear that dictatorships destroy social capital, and may even generate a "negative" social capital, which can take the form of underground activities, corruption, or organized crime (Greif 1994). According to Fidrmuc and Gërxhani (2005: 6), "the gap, created by the sudden destruction of old institutions and the creation of new ones, provided a favorable environment for the persistence or even accumulation of 'negative' social capital throughout transition." Corruption and the lack of political freedom are indicators of institutional quality. These elements may have a negative influence on the levels of social capital, although if horizontal trust remains strong even as vertical trust is weak, cooperative action may still take place. We measure the effects of these indicators on the level of environmental participation in Chapter 5, and make a three-part investigation on the effect of these institutional factors in Chapter 8.

Institutional weakness includes situations in which corruption leads to inefficiency that can generate environmental exploitation. On the other hand, if people perceive that institutions and/or governments are not to be trusted, they may try to achieve environmental aims on their own. Weak and dysfunctional states may induce people to pursue their goals via the non-governmental sector, that is, through engagement in environmental organizations. Moreover, one can also argue that good governance may "crowd out" other institutions or organizations due to the complementarities between these elements of society. It may be that the presence of one institution undermines the functioning of another (Bowles 2004), or even the need of another. In Chapter 5, we analyze individual determinants of participation using institutions as an external factor that may influence the decision to engage.

Measurement of social capital

It is not necessary to be an expert in econometrics in order to foresee the problems with measurement of social capital. If it is difficult to define exactly what is meant by social capital, it is eminently problematic to find satisfactory measures. It is a challenge simply to distinguish between the inputs and outputs. This difficulty has been recognized by several previous authors, for example:

> in measurement terms, understanding social capital as a resource to action leads immediately to the need for empirical clarity about measures of social capital, and measures of its outcomes. It is necessary to recognise empirically that understanding whether or not a social process is at work is different from understanding the consequences of such a process.
>
> (Stone 2001: 4)

Some authors are quite pessimistic in the face of the problems with measuring social capital:

> The concept of measuring social interaction may be a snare and a delusion. Instead of thinking of more and less, it may be more fruitful to think of the existing social relations as a preexisting network into which new parts of the economy (for example, development projects) have to be fitted.
>
> (Arrow 2000: 4)

Many studies over the last ten years have attempted to discover the extent to which social capital can be seen as an important, albeit previously omitted, contributing factor to the different outcomes regarding voluntary participation, economic development, and other factors. One reason for the omission of social capital from previous studies was the lack of reliable and standardized methods for measuring the concept. Fortunately, in recent years, considerable progress has been made towards development of standardized tools for measuring social capital, especially through the work of the World Bank in the *Social Capital Initiative*. The output of this project has improved the understanding and knowledge regarding formation and influence of social capital, and resulted in a useful construction and explanation of the process of social capital. Different fields use different definitions of social capital, yet inspection for similarities reveals something of a consensus. This is in line with the work published in the World Bank's handbook for practitioners using the Social Capital Assessment Tool (SOCAT). The editors of the report, Grootaert and van Bastelaer (2002) also note that the similarities between the definitions, usage, and concepts of social capital are greater than the differences. Furthermore, the authors suggest that the study of social capital is now where the study of human capital was 40 years ago, and predict that as the theories and empirical tools evolve, the literature on social capital will gain greater validity (Grootaert in Grootaert and van Bastelaer 2002).[8] Putnam (2001) stresses:

> The challenge of studying the evolving social climate is analogous in some respects to the challenge facing meteorologists who measure global warming: we know what kind of evidence we would ideally want from the past, but time's arrow means that we can't go back to conduct those well-designed studies. Thus if we are to explore how our society is like or unlike our parents', we must make imperfect inferences from all the evidence that we can find.
>
> (Putnam 2001: 26)

Even without perfect tools for measurement, it is expected that a well-developed social capital literature could result in beneficial changes to environmental policies that seek to address the public good problem. Social capital is an interesting concept for environmental questions as it focuses on "what groups do rather than what people own" (Bowles and Gintis 2002: F420). We realize this is a problematic area in which to work, as discussed in the introduction, yet we perceive value in the attempt, and hope to add our contribution to the gains achieved by previous attempts. So far, the existing research has fairly convincingly identified a range of outcomes from social capital as well as several measurements of social capital. Since we will talk about the outcomes (both positive and negative) that are attributed to social capital in the next section, we will now describe some of the interesting indicators frequently used in this literature.

Indicators of social capital

Indexes used in measuring social capital have been classified into "proximal" and "distal" (Stone 2001: 5). "Proximal" indicators of social capital are related to its core components of networks, trust, and reciprocity; for example, the use of civic engagement as an indicator of social networks has been proposed. All dimensions of social capital are strongly correlated, and participation in voluntary organizations is linked to the majority of those dimensions. Putnam (2001) considered the extent of civic engagement in his seminal work on civic decline in America, basing the analysis on evidence of deteriorating membership in formal associations and groups. Other proximal indicators of social capital include actions associated with a display of confidence in others (an outcome of a norm of trust), as well as reciprocal acts or exchanges (an outcome of a norm of reciprocity) (Stone 2001).

Putnam (2001) defined several indicators of the dimensions of social capital in the United States, most of which relate to the strength of structural social capital. He measured the concept of "community" or "organizational life" through the following indicators: the percentage of individuals who served on a committee of a local organization in the last year, the percentage of individuals who served as an officer of some club or organization in the last year, the civic and social organizations per 1,000 population, the mean number of club meetings attended in the last year, and the mean number of group memberships. To measure "engagement in public affairs," he considered the turnout in presidential elections for 1988 and 1992 and the percentage of individuals who attended public meetings on town or school affairs in last year. Regarding the dimension of "community volunteerism," Putnam included the number of non-profit organizations per 1,000 population, the mean number of times worked on a community project in the last year, and the mean number of times involved in volunteer work in the last year. As measures of "informal sociability," Putnam defined the percentage of individuals who spend a lot of time visiting friends and the mean number of times an individual entertained at home last year. The majority of these measures relate to the density of organization membership, and to the concepts of both "strong" and "weak" ties in social capital. Finally, to illustrate the dimension of the "social trust" (which can be likened to the cognitive dimension of social capital), he considered the percentage of individuals who think that most people are able to be trusted and the percentage of individuals who think that most people are honest. These proximal indicators describe some fairly commonplace and universal activities, prompting Bowles and Gintis (2002) to criticize the term "social capital" and suggest that it should be substituted it with the more precise "community." Such a notion is more strongly connected to governance and institutional quality.

Similarly, Grootaert (2001) defines some representative indexes of social capital. Regarding the network dimension, he considered the number and type of associations or local institutions, the extent of membership in local associations, the extent of participatory decision making, the extent of kin homogeneity within the association, the extent of income and occupation homogeneity within the association, the extent of trust in village members and households, in government and in trade unions, the perception of the extent of community organization, the reliance on networks of support, the percentage of household income from remittances, and the percentage of household expenditure for gifts and transfers. He also considered some indicators of social integration, such as an index of social mobility, the ethnolinguistic fragmentation, the number of protest demonstrations and strikes, the homicide and suicide rates, the number of prisoners per 100,000 people, the illegitimacy rates, the percentage of single-parent homes, the divorce rate, and the youth unemployment rate. For our purposes, to indicate environmental networks we simply generate rates of membership (which may include the more passive kind of membership) and active voluntary participation in environmental organizations.

In a study that is related to our previous brief discussion on density of civic participation (Grootaert and van Bastelaer 2002), and weak and strong ties (Granovetter 1973), Bowling's (1997) work on networks and social capital included measures of several network characteristics. Examples of these measures are size (the number of people maintaining social contact), geographic dispersion (networks vary from those defined by a household, to those in a single neighborhood, and those that are more widely dispersed, observing the transport facilities which influence the frequency of contact), density or integration (the extent to which network members are in each other's networks), composition and member homogeneity (friend, neighbor, children, sibling, other relatives, and similarities between members), frequency of contact among members, strength of ties (degree of intimacy, reciprocity, expectation of durability and availability, and emotional intensity), social participation (involvement in social, political, educational, religious, and other activities), or social anchorage (years of residence in and familiarity with neighborhood, involvement in community).

On the other hand, "distal" indicators are outcomes of social capital that are not directly related to its key components. In fact, as we will discuss in the following section, sometimes the relationships between the indicators are not totally clear. According to Stone (2001: 5) some indicators such as "life expectancy, health status, suicide rates, teenage pregnancy, crime rates, participation rates in tertiary education, employment and unemployment rates, family income, marital relationship formations and dissolutions, business confidence, job growth, growth in GDP or/and balance of trade" approximate the social capital stock of a nation.

Are these measurements reliable?

Proximal and distal indicators are frequently used in social capital research, particularly in studies reliant upon secondary analyses, where data are scarce. While useful in some ways, the mixture, use, and misuse of indicators in social capital research to date, and lack of theoretical precision used in the selection of indicators, has led to considerable confusion about the concept and dimensions of social capital, as distinct from its outcomes, and what the relationship between social capital and its outcomes may be. Thus, it is necessary to establish empirical specifications of social capital that reflect the theoretical understandings of the concept. Starting with a conceptually clear definition and linking this directly to a measurement framework would improve conceptual validity and facilitate unambiguous research. This problem has been eloquently expressed:

> empirical investigations which rely upon indicators of social capital are rarely supported by direct empirical investigation of the relationship between indicators (proximal or distal outcomes) and the core components of social capital. Hence both proximal and distal outcomes may or may not be valid indicators of social capital for this reason. This raises the further tautological problem that research reliant upon an outcome of social capital as an indicator of it, will necessarily find social capital to be related to that outcome, without empirical means to explain why, or indeed whether, this is so. Social capital becomes tautologically present whenever an outcome is observed.
>
> (Stone 2001: 5)

Problems with using certain variables as both indicators of social capital and as evidence of the outcomes are related to problems with determining whether social capital is exogenous or endogenous with respect to economic development. Grootaert and van Bastelaer (2002: 66) make the observation: "All the methods and results discussed so far depend critically on the assumption that social capital is part of the household's exogenous asset endowment, that is, those assets that determine income and consumption." By implementing some instrumental variables, Grootaert and van Bastelaer (2002: 71) find that at least with respect to the data available for that analysis, "the overwhelming direction of causality is from social capital to household welfare."

Similarly, Durlauf and Fafchamps (2004: 35) pointed out that "the problem of endogeneity is obvious in many contexts . . . Many researchers have recognized that social capital is endogenous and so have employed instrumental variables to allow for consistent estimation of parameters." So, even though researchers may be faced with conceptual and econometric problems, there are also many methodological attempts to solve these problems efficiently.

Institutions

Institutions as the vertical dimension of social capital

As mentioned in the introduction, institutions provide the foundation of the "playground" and therefore the context in which decisions are made. While social capital may represent the horizontal trust and horizontal bonds between individuals, institutions may also represent a vertical dimension. Institutions can be formal or informal. Informal institutions refer to the generally established, unwritten rules of the game, whereas formal institutions are the legislative, administrative, and operational processes that ensure protection of property rights and guarantee contracts. Davis and North (1971: 6) define an institutional environment as "the set of fundamental political, social and legal ground rules that establish the basis for production, exchange and distribution." Stronger institutions may lead to increased voluntary participation due to increased trust, decreased transaction costs and ease of punishing and detecting free-riders. However, as we will discuss in our first empirical chapter, a deficient state might lead individuals to coordinate their own solutions to public good problems. It is useful to explore the impact of institutions on environmental participation or on social capital in general, as researchers have criticized the difficulty in knowing whether, for example, "people's trust may be the result not only of the social capital present in their community, but also of prompt law enforcement" (Guiso *et al.* 2004: 526). Exploring the extent to which institutions shape social capital may help to answer such questions in a better manner.

Comparing several of the definitions of institutions offered by the literature elicits some common themes: institutions are seen as constraints, as sets of rules of society and can be either formal or informal.[9] Culas (2007: 40) provides an illustrative definition: "Institutions are constraints that structure political, economic and social interaction. They consist of both informal constraints (such as sanctions, taboos, customs, traditions and codes of conduct) and formal rules (such as constitutions, law and property rights)."

These rules of society can determine whether the actors (individuals, communities, corporations, and governments) generally value and work to protect the environment or seek to exploit it. However, while most authors agree that institutions set the rules of the game, several disagree with the notion of conceptualizing institutions as constraints. The argument runs along the same lines as the discussion on social capital. Ostrom (2000), Vatn (2005), and Searle (2005) maintain that institutions do not constrain, but rather empower by increasing the human capacity for action through such fundamental elements of modern society as private property, governments, marriages, stock markets, and universities (Searle 2005). In establishing these foundations, they create new power relationships, enabling and providing opportunities to solve collective action problems (Vatn 2005, Searle 2005). By facilitating capacity for action and providing opportunities to solve collective action problems, institutions increase the ability of individuals to organize community action to solve externalities and to provide public goods.

Intrinsic motivation and/or obligation toward the environment can influence institutional protection of the environment while shaping informal institutions and social norms on an individual level.

Institutions set the rules of the game for conduct in everyday life; they exhibit inertia in taking a long time to evolve or change; and they empower and enable human capacity for action. Formal and informal institutions, for example, ensure cars remain on the correct side of the road through the power of traffic rules, ensure criminals are imprisoned, impel taxpayers to comply with regulations, and guarantee that money is recognized as a unit of exchange when we wish to buy something. These situations do not exist by their own physical merit; they require agreement from all participants.[10] Thus, institutions "serve to coordinate beliefs and select equilibria" (Sobel 2002: 147).

Yet, despite the extent of institutional analysis, so far there is no definitive theory of institutions.[11] The lack of unified theory on institutions means that even though we are convinced of the importance of institutions in everyday life, for development, economic growth, providing public goods in general and environmental quality in particular, the problem mirrors the difficulty with social capital, in that "we know very little about how to create such polities" (North 1994: 366). Researchers have offered suggestions on how to strengthen institutions through increased government concern and capacity building (Levy *et al.* 1992). Unfortunately, the gaps in understanding the mechanisms through which institutions operate continue to confound the search for policy solutions. However, just as a lack of precise tools for measurement of social capital and human capital does not preclude the analysis of various situations using these concepts; neither does the absence of a coherent theory of institutions prevent the use of this element in empirical and theoretical literature. The real consequence of this lack of unified theory is the effect on the conclusions that are drawn from research, as there are no direct ways in which institutions can be measured or included in an empirical analysis. Keefer and Knack (1997) point out that this is partly due to the lack of objective valuations combined with the lack of understanding regarding the "relative contribution of different institutions" (Keefer and Knack 1997: 592). Researchers must therefore either find proxies to represent institutional quality, or rely on measurements of institutional sub-factors. In Chapter 8 we implement measures of institutional sub-factors to gain a global picture of institutional influence on environmental participation and outcomes.

The effect of institutional quality

The empirical analysis in Chapter 8 investigates the effect of institutional quality on environmental participation and outcomes at the macro level. The idea is that quality institutions facilitate participation and better collective action outcomes in a similar way to social capital: that is, by reducing transaction costs, increasing trust, and reinforcing the efficacy of the network dimension and the cognitive dimension. It is generally agreed that a functioning institutional framework will include high-quality legal, economic, political, and social institutions.

As with social capital, previous work on measuring institutional quality has used indirect measurements in empirical analysis. One example can be found in the study by Grootaert (2001). With respect to civic and political society, he included (among others) an index of civil liberties, the percentage of population facing political discrimination, an index of intensity of political and economic discrimination, the percentage of population involved in separatist movements, several indexes of political rights and freedom, several indicators of democracy, corruption and government inefficiency, the strength of democratic institutions, the degree of decentralization of government, voter turnout, political assassinations, and constitutional government changes.

Types of institutional quality

Democracy

Democracy is related to the voice and accountability measure used in the empirical work in Chapter 8. High quality political institutions and a "good" government (La Porta *et al.* 1999) are crucial in empowering citizens and in providing public goods. If citizens have a voice in democratic political representation and freedom of speech, there are more avenues through which they can influence policies. As citizens are empowered to take action there is a greater motivation to be involved in issues of public and personal concern. Politicians are held accountable through the stronger voice of the public, ensuring the collective will is enacted by authorities. Neumayer (2002) points to the theoretical motivations for presuming democracy to have a positive impact on the environment: it can be expected that a democratic country will have greater freedom of press, freedom of speech, freedom of association, and freedom of voting whereas an undemocratic country will restrict the citizens' access to information, restrict their voice in matters of public interest, and restrict their ability to organize themselves around particular interests (for example, protection and conservation of the environment and addressing the problem of negative externalities).

Previous literature on the influence of institutions in environmental issues has indicated the relevance of including an analysis on democracy. Neumayer (2002) constructs and tests the hypothesis that the environmental commitment of democracies will be stronger than non-democracies by using proxies for environmental commitment such as signing and ratification of multilateral agreements, membership in intergovernmental organizations, and the existence of a national council on sustainable development. Using four different measures of democracy, he finds strong evidence for participation of democracies in environmental agreements and in protecting a greater percentage of their land. However, democracies can cause greater damage to the environment: by encouraging private property rights, democracies allow business and private individuals to exploit natural resources. Even though not all democracies are developed countries, it is generally the case that all developed countries are democracies. The process of development places increased pressure on the environment, leading to pollution and ecological destruction (Desai 1998). Nevertheless, the evidence remains that democracies are also more likely to take action to repair that damage, because if voters and citizens are concerned with environmental problems "they are more likely to require policymakers to exhibit stronger environmental commitment" (Neumayer 2002:140). Further, he suggests that democracy could encourage peace by organizing resources and preventing the sorts of scarcities that can lead to violence.

Corruption

Corruption is a serious impediment to institutional quality, leading to lack of trust and damaging reciprocity on every level. It may be minimized formally through legal and political processes and informally through social sanctions. The *International Country Risk Guide* (ICRG) Codebook refers to insidious corruption which pervades all areas of business and society, and is far more damaging than the blatant corruption (for example, bribes that are expected to facilitate administration). Insidious corruption involves the capture of political and economic power for the elites and for those on the inside of the circle of influence, destroying morale, reciprocity, and the motivation to take collective action in providing any public good, including environmental protection. Corruption leads to inefficiency as business deals and favors go to the market participants with the most influential contacts. This inefficiency and lack of accountability can lead to environmental exploitation. To measure the strength of legal, political, and cultural institutions regarding corruption, we employ control of corruption from Kaufmann *et al.* (2006) in Chapter 8.

Pellegrini and Gerlagh (2006) find that corruption is even more significant than democracy in explaining environmental outcomes. The existing literature on corruption and environmental policy supports the conclusion that "institutional settings affect the way policy makers respond to environmental concerns" (Pellegrini and Gerlagh 2006: 11). Further, they argue that as the developing countries suffer from what they term as "institutional disarray" this will make it difficult for them to achieve the same stringency of environmental policy as is achieved by the developed countries. As increased corruption often means decreased growth, they suggest a double dividend is possible: if developing countries work to reduce corruption they could also increase their growth. The authors use OLS on a cross-sectional sample of 62 countries and employ an index of environmental regulatory regime as the dependent variable. The results indicate that corruption and income alone have most of the explanatory power, and democracy is not significant. Overall they determine that institutional settings will strongly influence environmental policy stringency. Democracy on its own will not be sufficient: institutional quality and reduction of corruption is far more important.

Special interest groups can be another symptom of corruption or undue influence on policy makers. Formation of environmental policy is likely to be "representative of many other forms of government decision making," hence Fredriksson and Svensson (2003: 1384, 1401) examine how special-interest groups will influence this process. The authors claim that interaction "between corruption and political instability is important in determination of other forms of economic policy." Investigating the interaction between corruption and political instability and how these interactions influence formation of environmental policy, the authors first use a modeling approach to discover the effect of producer lobbies on government policy by offering bribes. The model predicts that the degree of corruption is the primary factor exerting influence over the stringency of environmental policy, and producers will find it less attractive to offer the government a bribe if there is a high degree of instability making it less likely that the government will remain in power. The authors come to the interesting conclusion that when a country is very corrupt but fairly stable it performs worse with regard to environmental policy. Regimes of this type would likely be autocratic types and face "little to no political opposition" (Fredricksson and Svensson 2003: 1396). In this case, bribery will yield a significant payoff. They test the results of the model by estimating the relationship empirically, using 63 developed and undeveloped countries, and proxy corruption with the International Country Risk Guide (ICRG) variable and political instability. Their empirical results confirm that interactions between corruption and political instability influence other forms of policy.

A functioning legal system will ensure protection of property rights and provide more opportunities for redress along with clear punishment of criminality of any sort – including crimes against the environment. Legal action and compensation are available to those who have suffered losses from environmental damage, and legal action can even be taken by the state on behalf of the environment. In Chapter 8, we use some measurements to account for the strength of the legal institutions.

Institutions are valuable in reducing production costs insofar as they reduce transaction costs, improving allocative efficiency and "feasibility of engaging in economic activities" (North cited in Culas 2007: 430). Culas (2007) then suggests it is the failure of developing economies to guarantee secure property and contractual rights that discourages investment and specialization. North holds this absence of property rights accountable for the stagnation and underdevelopment of those economies. Case studies suggest that macroeconomic policies by these countries could be improved to turn around the tendency for environmental damage. However, Esty and Porter (2005) indicate that in spite of these investigations establishing the link between institutions and environmental outcomes; no clear empirical relationship has been established regarding just how a country's regulations and underlying economic and legal system can impact on environmental outcomes. The resulting lack of clear foundations leaves policy to form on the basis of crude analysis, heated rhetoric and imprecise concepts such as sustainable development.

Accountability (and transparency)

Voting and accountability create a sense of civic duty and higher willingness to contribute to public goods such as environmental quality. It is also utility in itself. Citizens value the right to participate, because it produces a kind of procedural utility as their opportunity set increases. Taking an example from the tax compliance literature, participation leads to an outcome (acceptance of the amnesty or not) that is preferred when compared to the situation where no such voting possibility exists. From an institutional perspective, the relationship between tax morale and tax compliance can be understood as a "psychological contract". If taxpayers can vote on the way taxes will be spent, they may feel more inclined to pay their taxes. The more taxpayers are able to participate in the political decision making process by popular rights, the more this contract is based on trust, which will, in turn, foster cooperation. Rule obedience and cooperation is therefore enhanced by rules which evolve through an active involvement of citizens, positively affecting their sense of obligation (for a general overview see Torgler 2007). This process can be related to the cognitive dimension of social capital: the same tendency to trust formal institutions fosters cooperation with those authorities. The literature uses the notion of "procedural fairness," supporting the relevance of legitimacy and allegiance to authority in compliance decisions (e.g., Tyler 1997). This is similar to the decisions made in environmental conservation. Previous studies have also shown that democracy and accountability is positively correlated with a higher willingness to cooperate. For example, Pommerehne and Weck-Hannemann (1996) and Torgler and Schneider (2007) utilize Swiss data and find that tax evasion and the shadow economy is lower in cantons with a higher degree of direct political control. Torgler (2005) shows that a higher level of direct democracy in a jurisdiction leads to an increased willingness to pay taxes. Furthermore, Alm and Torgler (2006) analyze tax morale in the United States and in Europe. They find that countries with a higher level of democracy have a higher willingness to pay taxes. Finally, accountability leads to a lower level of public debt (Schaltegger and Torgler 2007) and a higher level of compliance in a laboratory experimental setting (Torgler *et al.* 2003, Torgler and Schaltegger 2005).

If these active citizens value the environment, they have more power in a democracy to demand that it is protected. By using the *Quality of Governance Index* from 2000 (Kaufmann *et al.* 2006) based on indicators of voice and accountability and government effectiveness,[12] we gain a partial insight into the strength of these kinds of political institutions. The ability of governments to coordinate actions in providing public goods (including environmental outcomes), to regulate for industry or environmental protection, and the quality and integrity of those regulations all contribute to the overarching strength of political institutions. These characteristics of institutional quality are vital in ensuring environmental public goods are provided and are measured through government effectiveness and regulatory quality. The existence of a stable and relatively independent bureaucracy will determine longevity and continuity of policies regardless of which political party is in power. Political stability affects the lobbying power of interest groups as well as the potential for corruption; political stability will determine the ability of a government to stay in power and carry out its policies. If the environment becomes an "election issue" in a democracy, gains can be made in protection of habitats and funding for rehabilitation of degraded areas. On the other hand, the government may only be concerned with short-term exploitation to harness maximum rents for both itself and its networks. The measure of political stability captures this aspect of political institutions. These measures are elements that constitute the broader context of institutional strength, and can be differentiated from the measures of "perceived corruption" that are used in Chapter 5. The broader structures of institutions are facilitating factors that enable engagement to take place; therefore, they will demonstrate a positive relationship with voluntary participation in environmental groups.

Summary

In this chapter we have stressed that it is important to get a good understanding of social capital as it can be seen as the "playground" for our interactions in the book. Voluntary environmental participation is an important element in civic participation and therefore a key element of social capital. At the same time, the existence of a good stock of social capital can facilitate and create favourable conditions for engaging in the activities of environmental organizations. Similarly, formal and informal rules or institutions are part of this playground. They provide a foundation, define the limitations, and reinforce the formal and informal rules regarding how to play. Institutions build the playground area and define how users of the playground can play in order to have fun. Transferring this metaphor into the broader environment, one can argue that institutions provide a method through which people can organize themselves in order to "face fundamental problems of coordinating their activities to survive within a given environment" (Turner 1999: 97). This influence acts through several dimensions of social capital, each reinforcing the other. Better quality institutions will increase the likelihood of cooperation and coordination of activities. Through decreasing the transaction costs of interactions, improving the efficiency and quantity of interactions; through identification with a group; through reciprocity and trust in others, voluntary participation in environmental organizations can be improved. Collective action outcomes are improved, public goods can be provided for the group, and externalities can be addressed. It is through these informal and formal processes that we can find the facilitating factors to empower community action and to address environmental problems.

Several dimensions of social capital have been analyzed in this chapter, paying special attention to the network component, as it is related to the subject of the book (namely participation in environmental organizations). If one thing is clear, it is that we desire the positive effects of social capital and institutions, but do not have a unified theory for the development or precise tools for measurement of these variables. Not only does this make it difficult to analyze outcomes, it is difficult to determine exactly the process through which social capital and institutions will influence participation in voluntary organizations. Thus, it is no surprise that more evidence is required to understand the underlying mechanisms that create social capital. Focusing on a particular dimension, such as voluntary participation in environmental organizations, may help to shed some new light into this discussion.

Moreover, it is highly relevant to focus on the nature of individual participation by working with a micro data set as a first step. Working at the individual level helps to take into account the heterogeneity among individuals. The importance of this factor is highlighted by Durlauf's (2002) criticism of Putnam's (2001) work for not paying attention to the nature of individual decision-making. If we assume that social capital is endogenous we need to explain the determinants of social capital, or in our case, the determinants of voluntary participation in environmental organizations. Exploring the determinants at both the micro and at the macro level may help to generate policy implications and recommendations on how to increase voluntary participation in environmental organizations.

Thus, we can see that there is value in continuing to concentrate on the self-reported willingness and commitment to contribute to environmental organizations. Yet we must keep in mind that a good stock of social capital and quality institutions will act as the foundation that facilitates the individual's decision to cooperate.

Notes

1 However, there is an argument that the size of the group or the level at which the members invest their identities can influence the provision of "public goods." The size of the group can affect the amount of information that is available about each person, which then affects the willingness of group members to contribute to a public good. We discuss this problem of incomplete information in more detail later in the chapter. Furthermore, public goods are rarely "pure" insofar as they are not available to the entire world. Public goods are largely provided by groups and for groups, because there is always some level at which "others" are excluded from consuming the good.

2 A possibility we consider in Chapter 8.

3 Liu and Besser (2003) distinguished four dimensions of social capital: informal social ties, formal social ties, trust, and norms of collective action. Narayan and Cassidy (2001) identified a range of dimensions, such as group characteristics, generalized norms, togetherness, everyday sociability, neighborhood connections, volunteerism, and trust.

4 Membership can be active or passive. It can either be through paying membership fees or through actually participating. See Chapter 3 for a review of which type of membership is most effective.

5 The goods produced by social capital can also occur at different levels of the social structure (Paxton 1999). In this respect, there is no consensus in the literature. Social capital itself can be seen as a private good or a public good depending on the level (Aldridge *et al.* 2002). Onyx and Bullen (2000) pointed out that social capital appears to be both a private and a public good. Coleman (1988) argued that social capital is a public good, however Fukuyama posited that it is in fact a private good (Fukuyama 2002). According to Dasgupta (1999: 325) "social capital is a private good that is nonetheless pervaded by externalities, both positive and negative". Yet another perspective sees social capital as a club good, as it is excludable but non-rival in consumption

6 For example, Glaeser *et al.* (2002) apply a standard model of individual investment. Such model implies that investment in social capital should increase with patience and with the relevance of positive externalities in the return to social capital investment whereas it decreases with higher expected mobility, the opportunity cost of time, the rate of depreciation and the degree of community-specificity of social capital.
7 However, Grootaert (2002) cautions against using results obtained during attempts at measuring social capital for the purposes of attempting to identify the causes, as the creation of social capital is the result of many complex processes.
8 We note that even though accumulation of human capital is not directly or quantitatively measured, it is still common to use certain input measures as proxies (such as years of schooling and years of work experience). Human capital is also considered a valid variable in theoretical work analyzing production functions. Furthermore, as Grootaert and van Bastelaer (2002) point out, despite not having direct measurements of the human capital concept, there exists a well developed and accepted literature on human capital that has resulted in many beneficial changes to educational policy.
9 See Levy *et al.* (1992), Searle (2005), Vatn (2005) and Culas (2007).
10 See Searle (2005) for an exposition on institutional facts and collective agreements.
11 This lack has been blamed on classical economics. Bowles (1998) criticizes the deliberate oversight and argues that even though ignoring the influence of institutions makes the formation of economic theory far easier, it also decreases the explanatory power of any such theory because it fails to ensure policy relevance and ethical coherence. Searle (2005) highlights the differences between the science of economics and the reality of disciplines like physics and chemistry, pointing out that economics actually "presupposes institutions" by assuming that market actors only pursue self-interest in a "gentlemanly manner" (Granovetter 1985). Economic theory and the associated reality are more reliant on human beliefs and attitudes (which are dynamic processes rather than static axioms), thus we do not appear to have "immutable laws" of economics in the same way as physics and chemistry (Searle 2005).
12 We will explain those indexes properly in Chapter 8.

References

Aldridge, S., Halpern, D. and Fitzpatrick, S. (2002) "Social capital: a discussion paper," London: Performance and Innovation Unit.

Alm, J. and B. Torgler (2006) "Culture differences and tax morale in the United States and Europe," *Journal of Economic Psychology*, 27: 224–46.

Almond, G.A. and Verba, S. (1963) *The Civic Culture: Political attitudes and democracy in five nations*, Princeton, NJ: Princeton University Press.

Arrow, K. (1971) "Political and economic evaluation of social effects and externalities," in M.D. Intriligator (ed.), *Frontiers of Quantitative Economics*, Amsterdam: North Holland.

—— (2000) "Observations on social capital," in P. Dasgupta and I. Serageldin (eds), *Social Capital: A multifaceted perspective*, Washington, DC: World Bank.

Betsill, M.M. and Corell, E. (2001) "NGO influence in international environmental negotiations: a framework for analysis," *Global Environmental Politics*, 1: 65–85.

Beugelsdijk, S. and Van Schalk, T. (2001) "Social capital and regional economic growth", mimeo, Tilburg University.

Bourdieu, P. (1979) "Les trois états du capital culturel," *Actes de la Recherche en Sciences Sociales*, 30: 3–6.

Bowles, S. (1998) "Endogenous preferences: the cultural consequences of markets and economic institutions," *Journal of Economic Literature*, 36: 75–111.

—— (2004) *Microeconomics: Behavior, institutions, and evolution*, New York: Princeton University Press.

—— and Gintis, H. (2002) "Social capital and community governance," *Economic Journal*, 112: F419–36.

Bowling, A. (1997) *Measuring Health: A review of quality of life measurement scales*, Buckingham: Open University Press.

Brehm, J. and Rahn, W. (1997) "Individual-level evidence for the causes and consequences of social capital," *American Journal of Political Science*, 41: 999–1023.

Coleman, J.S. (1988) "Social capital in the creation of human capital," *American Journal of Sociology*, 94: 95–121.

—— (1990) *Foundations of Social Theory*, Cambridge, MA: Belknap Press of Harvard University Press.

Culas, R. (2007) "Deforestation and the environmental Kuznets curve: an institutional perspective," *Ecological Economics*, 61: 429–37.

Dasgupta, P. (1988) "Trust as a commodity," in D. Gambetta (ed.), *Trust: Making and breaking cooperative relations*, Oxford: Basil Blackwell.

—— (1999) "Economic progress and the idea of social capital," in P. Dasgupta and I. Serageldin (eds), *Social Capital: A multifaceted perspective*, Washington, DC: World Bank.

Davis, L. and North, D. (1971) *Institutional Change and American Economic Growth*, Cambridge: Cambridge University Press.

Desai, U. (1998) *Ecological Policy and Politics in Developing Countries: Economic growth, democracy, and environment*, New York: State University of New York Press

Durlauf, S.N. (2002) "Bowling alone: a review essay," *Journal of Economic Behavior and Organization*, 47: 259–73.

—— and Fafchamps, M. (2004) "Social capital," NBER Working Paper 10485.

Esty, D.C. and Porter, M.E. (2005) "National environmental performance: an empirical analysis of policy results and determinants," *Environment and Development Economics*, 10: 391–434.

European Commission (2005) *Social Capital: Special Eurobarometer*, Brussels: European Commission.

Fidrmuc, J. and Gërxhani, K. (2005) "Formation of social capital in Central and Eastern Europe: understanding the gap vis-à-vis developed countries," CEPR Discussion Paper 5068.

Fredriksson, G. and Svensson, J. (2003) "Political instability, corruption and policy formation: the case of environmental policy," *Journal of Public Economics*, 87: 1383–1405.

Frost, R. (1915) *North of Boston*. New York: Henry Holt and Company: 1–3.

Fukuyama, F. (1995) "Social capital and the global economy," *Foreign Affairs*, 74: 89–103.

—— (1997) "Social Capital and the Modern Capitalist Economy: Creating a high trust workplace," *Stern Business Magazine*, 4.

—— (2002) "Social capital and development: the coming agenda," *SAIS Review*, 22: 23–37.

Gambetta, D. (1988) *Trust, Making and Breaking Cooperative Relations*, Oxford: Blackwell.

Glaeser, E. L., Laibson, D., Sacerdote, B. (2002) "An economic approach to social capital," *Economic Journal*, 112: F437–58.

Grafton, R.Q. and Knowles, S. (2004) "Social capital and national environmental performance: a cross-sectional analysis," *The Journal of Environment Development*, 13: 336–70.

Granovetter, M. (1973) "The strength of weak ties," *American Journal of Sociology*, 78: 1360–80.

—— (1985) "Economic action and social structure: the problem of embeddedness," *American Journal of Sociology*, 91: 481–510.

Greif, A. (1994) "Cultural beliefs and the organization of society: a historical and theoretical reflection on collectivist and individualist societies," *Journal of Political Economy*, 102: 912–50.

Grootaert, C. (2001) "Social capital: the missing link?" in P. Dekker and E. Uslaner (eds), *Social Capital and Participation in Everyday Life*, London: Routledge.

—— (2002) "Quantitative analysis of social capital data," in C. Grootaert and T. van Bastelaer (eds), *Understanding and Measuring Social Capital: A multidisciplinary tool for practitioners*, Washington, DC: World Bank.

——and van Bastelaer, T. (2002) "Social capital: from definition to measurement," in C. Grootaert and T. van Bastelaer (eds), *Understanding and Measuring Social Capital: A multidisciplinary tool for practitioners*, Washington, DC: World Bank.

Guiso, L., Sapienza, P., and Zingales, L. (2004) "The role of social capital in financial development," *American Economic Review*, 94: 526–56.

Hardin, R. (1993) "The street-level epistemology of trust," *Politics and Society*, 21: 505–31.

Helliwell, J.F. (1996) "Do borders matter for social capital? Economic growth and civic culture in U.S. states and Canadian provinces," NBER Working Paper 5863.

Hofferth, S.L., Boisjoly, J., and Duncan, G.J. (1999) "The development of social capital," *Rationality and Society*, 11: 79–110.

Hunter, B. (2000) *Social Exclusion, Social Capital and Indigenous Australians: Measuring the social costs of unemployment*, Canberra: Centre for Aboriginal Economic Policy Research, ANU.

Inglehart, R. (1997) *Modernization and Post-modernization: Cultural, economic and political change in 43 Societies*, Princeton: Princeton University Press.

Inkeles, A. (2000) "Measuring social capital and its consequences," *Policy Sciences*, 33: 245–68.

Kaufmann, D., Kraay, A. and Mastruzzi, M. (2006) *Governance Matters V: Aggregate and individual governance indicators for 1996–2005*, Washington, DC: World Bank, September.

Keefer, P. and Knack, S. (1997) "Why don't poor countries catch up? A cross-national test of an institutional explanation," *Economic Inquiry*, 35: 590–602.

Knack, S. and Keefer, P. (1995) "Institutions and economic performance: cross-country tests using alternative institutional measures," *Economics and Politics*, 7: 207–27.

——and —— (1997) "Does social capital have an economic impact? A cross-country investigation," *Quarterly Journal of Economics*, 112: 1252–88.

La Porta, R., Lopez-de-Silanes, F., Shleifer, A., and Vishny, R. (1999) "The quality of government," *Journal of Law, Economics and Organization*, 15: 222–79.

Latham, M. (2000) "If only men were angels: social capital and the Third Way," in I. Winter (ed.), *Social Capital and Public Policy in Australia*, Melbourne: Australian Institute of Family Studies.

Levchenko, A.A. (2007) "Institutional quality and international trade," *Review of Economic Studies*, 74: 791–819.

Levy, M., Haas, P., and Keohane, R. (1992) "Institutions for the earth: promoting international environmental protection," *Environment* 34: 12–36.

Liu, A.Q. and Besser, T. (2003) "Social capital and participation in community improvement activities by elderly residents in small towns and rural communities," *Rural Sociology*, 68: 343–65.

Miguel, E., Gertler, P., and Levine, D. (2001) "Did industralization destroy social capital in Indonesia?," mimeo, University of California, Berkeley.

Narayan, D. and Cassidy, M.F. (2001) "A dimensional approach to measuring social capital: development and validation of a social capital inventory," *Current Sociology*, 49: 59–102.

Neumayer, E. (2002) "Do democracies exhibit stronger international environmental commitment? A cross-country analysis," *Journal of Peace Research*, 39: 139–64.

North, D. (1991) "Institutions," *Journal of Economic Perspectives*, 5: 97–112.

—— (1994) "Economic performance through time," *American Economic Review*, 84: 359–68.

Olson, M. (1965) *The Logic of Collective Action: Public goods and the theory of groups*, Cambridge, MA: Harvard University Press.

Onyx, J. and Bullen, P. (2000) "Sources of social capital," in I. Winter (ed.), *Social Capital and Public Policy in Australia*, Melbourne: National Library of Australia.

Ostrom, E. (2000) "Collective action and the evolution of social norms," *The Journal of Economic Perspectives*, 14: 137–58.

—— and Ahn, T.K. (2003) *Foundation of Social Capital*, Critical Studies in Economic Institutions, Cheltenham, Glos.: Edward Elgar.

Paldam, M. (2000) "Social capital: one or many? Definition and measurement," *Journal of Economic Surveys*, 14: 629–53.

Paxton, P. (1999) "Is social capital declining in the United States? A multiple indicator assessment," *The American Journal of Sociology*, 105: 88–127.

Pellegrini, L. and Gerlagh, R. (2006) "Corruption, democracy and environmental policy: an empirical contribution to the debate," *The Journal of Environment Development*, 15: 332–54.

Pennar, K. (1997) "The tie that leads to prosperity: the economic value of social bonds is only beginning to be measured," *Business Weekly*: 153–55.

Pommerehne, W.W. and Weck-Hannemann, H. (1996) "Tax rates, tax administration and income tax evasion in Switzerland," *Public Choice*, 88: 161–70.

Portes, A. (1998) "Social capital: its origins and applications in modern sociology," *Annual Review of Sociology*, 24: 1–25.

—— and Landolt, P. (1996) "The downside of social capital," *The American Prospect*, 26: 18–23.

—— and Mooney, M. (2002) "Social capital and community development," in M.F. Guillén, R. Collins, P. England and M. Meyer (eds), *The New Economic Sociology: Development in an emerging field*, New York: Russell Sage Foundation.

—— and Sensenbrenner, J. (1993) "Embeddedness and immigration: notes on the social determinants of economic action," *American Journal of Sociology*, 98: 1320–50.

Pretty, J. and Smith, D.J. (2004) "Social capital in biodiversity conservation and management," *Conservation Biology*, 18: 631–38.

—— and Ward, H. (2001) "Social capital and the environment," *World Development*, 29: 209–27.

Putnam, R.D. (1993) "The prosperous community: social capital and public life," *The American Prospect*, 4: 11–18.

1995) "Bowling alone: America"s declining social capital," *Journal of Democracy*, 6: 65–78.

—— (2001) *Bowling Alone: The collapse and revival of American community*, New York: Simon and Schuster.

Rose, R. (1998) "Getting things done in an anti-modern society: social capital networks in Russia," Social Capital Initiative Working Paper No. 6, Washington, DC: World Bank.

Rudd, M.A. (2000) "Live long and prosper: collective action, social capital and social vision," *Ecological Economics*, 34: 131–44.

Rupasingha, A., Goetz, S.J. and Freshwater, D. (2006) "The production of social capital in US counties," *The Journal of Socio-Economics*, 35: 83–101.

Sampson, R., Raudenbush, S. and Earls, F. (1997) "Neighborhoods and violent crime: a multilevel study of collective efficacy," *Science*, 277: 918–24.

Sandefur, R.L. and Laumann, E.O. (1998) "A paradigm for social capital," *Rationality and Society*, 10: 481–501.

Schaltegger, C.A. and Torgler, B. (2007) "Government accountability and fiscal discipline: a panel analysis using Swiss data," *Journal of Public Economics*, 91: 117–40.

Schiff, M. (1992) "Social capital, labour mobility, and welfare: the impact of uniting states," *Rationality and Society*, 4: 157–75.

Searle, J.R. (2005) "What is an institution?" *Journal of Institutional Economics*, 1: 1–22.

Sobel, J. (2002) "Can we trust social capital?" *Journal of Economic Literature*, XL: 139–54.

——, Curtis, A., and Lockie, S. (2001) "The role of Landcare group networks in rural Australia: exploring the contribution of social capital," *Journal of Rural Studies*, 17: 265–76.

Solow, R. (2000) "Notes on social capital," in P. Dasgupta and I. Serageldin (eds), *Social Capital: A multifaceted perspective*, Washington, DC: World Bank.

Stiglitz, J. (2000) *Economics of the Public Sector*, New York: W.W. Norton and Company.

Stone, W. (2001) "Measuring social capital: towards a theoretically informed measurement framework for researching social capital in family and community life," Research paper 24, Melbourne: Australian Institute of Family Studies.

Szreter, S. (2000) "Social capital, the economy, and education in historical perspective," in T. Schuller (ed.), *Social Capital: Critical perspectives*, Oxford: Oxford University Press.

Torgler, B. (2005) "Tax morale and direct democracy," *European Journal of Political Economy*, 21: 525–31.

—— (2007) *Tax Compliance and Tax Morale: A theoretical and empirical analysis*, Cheltenham, Glos.: Edward Elgar.

—— and Schneider, F. (2007) "Shadow economy, tax morale, governance and institutional quality: a panel analysis," IZA Discussion Paper 2563; CESifo Working Paper Series 1923.

—— and —— (2009) "The impact of tax morale and institutional quality on the shadow economy," *Journal of Economic Psychology*, 30: 228–45.

——and C.A. Schaltegger (2005) "Tax amnesties and political participation," *Public Finance Review*, 33: 403–31.

——, —— and Schaffner, M. (2003) "Is forgiveness divine? A cross-culture comparison of tax amnesties," *Swiss Journal of Economics and Statistics*, 139: 375–96.

Turner, J.H. (1999) "The formation of social capital," in P. Dasgupta and I. Serageldin (eds), *Social Capital: A multifaceted perspective*, Washington, DC: World Bank.

Tyler, T.R. (1997) "Procedural fairness and compliance with the law," *Swiss Journal of Economics and Statistics*, 133: 219–40.

Uslaner, E. M. (2002) *The Moral Foundation of Trust*, Cambridge: Cambridge University Press.

Vatn, A. (2005) *Institutions and the Environment*,Cheltenham: Edward Elgar Publishing.
Whiteley, P. (2000) "Economic growth and social capital," *Political Studies*, 48: 443–66.
Woolcock, M. (1998) "Social capital and economic development: towards a synthesis and policy framework," *Theory and Society*, 27: 151–208.
—— and Narayan, D. (2000) "Social capital: implications for development theory, research, and policy," *World Bank Research Observer*, 15: 225–50.
Zak, P. and Knack, S. (2001) "Trust and growth," *Economic Journal*, 111: 295–321.

3 Participation in environmental organizations

What matters?

> I am of the opinion that my life belongs to the whole community and as long as I live, it is my privilege to do for it whatever I can. I want to be thoroughly used up when I die, for the harder I work the more I live.
>
> (George Bernard Shaw 1903: 352)

Introduction

While the stock of social capital and quality of institutions provide the context for participation in environmental organizations, there are other factors to consider. In this chapter we investigate and report on the existing literature to inform our own empirical analysis in the chapters to follow. We ask what is meant by pro-environmental behaviors, identify participation in environmental organizations as one of those behaviors, and discuss factors affecting the decision whether to participate or not. We also take a closer look at the costs and benefits of voluntary participation, noting that the notion of costs and benefits is not restricted to material or monetary considerations. We recognize that neither costs nor benefits will be borne equally by every sector of the population. Hence, it is important to determine which socio-demographic and socio-economic factors influence the decision to volunteer in an environmental organization.

In order to discover what matters in the decision to engage in voluntary participation it is possible to simply administer a survey. However, one of the problems with relying on self-reported attitudes towards an issue is the potential for respondents to provide misleading information, either to ease their own guilt about their behavior, or out of a desire to please the interviewer. Thus, we examine existing literature to discover the reported encouragements or impediments to participation, and to get some idea of the costs and benefits of participation. We look at literature that has not only used survey data but has also used information on actual participation. The advantage of focusing on participation in environmental organizations is that individuals' behavior can be compared to studies that have empirically investigated individual environmental attitudes and behaviors. Thus, we may determine whether intentions match or result in actions. Moreover, it allows us to build the bridge between the social capital literature that focuses on volunteering and the existing literature on pro-environmental actions.

Participation in environmental organizations as a pro-environmental behavior

What is the meaning of the term "pro-environmental behavior"? Kollmuss and Agyeman (2002) define it as an individual's actions that consciously seek to minimize the negative impact of human activities on the environment. Jensen (2002) refers to those personal actions that are directly related to environmental improvements.

Some daily activities at home and work are private actions that contribute to the preservation of nature. Examples of such steps are minimizing resource and energy consumption, reducing and recycling waste, not littering, buying organically produced food, or electing to use public transport. In previous studies, some pro-environmental actions have been analyzed in a multi-country context, either using a global viewpoint (Schultz and Zelezny 1998, OECD 2008) or considering a more concrete behavior. These studies compared country participation in actions such as waste recycling (Guagnano *et al.* 1995, Guerin *et al.* 2001, Berglund 2006), collaboration on green programs (Clark *et al.* 2003), the choice of recreational activities (Jackson 1987, Ajzen and Driver 1992, Luzar *et al.* 1995), organic food consumption (Jolly 1991) or the use of public transport (Johansson-Stenman 2002, de Abreu e Silva *et al.* 2006).

According to Clark *et al.* (2003: 238), from an economic perspective, this kind of behavior "exemplifies an individual's voluntary effort to provide an environmental public good." The discussion in Chapter 1 briefly introduced some of the reasons why individuals would take actions that result in collective benefits, and explained that while the traditional outlook predicts a free-rider effect in the private provision of public goods (Olson 1965), in practice, the observed levels of provision are higher than the theoretical predictions (Andreoni 1988, Piliavin and Charng 1990).[1]

Participation in environmental organizations is a type of pro-environmental behavior and is crucial to the development of environmental policies that target more widespread behavioral changes. The good news is that

> much of the initial impetus towards change for protecting environmental quality came from concerned individuals who have often come together and formed voluntary non-profit associations to collectively address environmental concerns. Their persistent lobbying and advocating for environmental protection has changed public sentiment, thereby convincing government and businesses to pay attention to their demands. Some of these voluntary associations have mobilised into large formal not-for-profit organisations and were sustained by donations and memberships, whilst others remained small and informal, and yet others disbanded. Nevertheless, many environmental non-profit organisations continue to play an important role in advocating a better environmental quality.
>
> (Handy 2001: 648)

This describes an individual pro-environmental behavior that is reinforced by the framework of collective action.

A moderate degree of participation in environment-friendly organizations is positively correlated with other pro-environmental behaviors and attitudes, such as paying higher taxes to preserve the environment, recycling, resource conservation or responsible consumerism (Olli *et al.* 2001, Torgler and García-Valiñas 2007, OECD 2008). The willingness to engage in such pro-environmental behaviors is vital to the efficacy and success of policy requiring behavioral change. Modeling these actions sets an example and encourages increased participation by others in the community. As we pointed out in the previous chapter, these behaviors exemplify some of the dimensions of social capital, such as networks and collective action.

Different levels of participation in pro-environmental behavior

There are different degrees of participation in environmental organizations. Individuals may be members of environmental organizations, but only "participate" by paying the periodic membership fees or by being a general member. The differentiation between passive participation and active participation where the member also takes part in the activities of the organization is therefore quite valuable.[2]

Accordingly, when Martinez and McMullin (2004) conducted their study about the factors that affect decisions to volunteer in the Appalachian Trail Conference, they categorized an active member as a person who donated time to the environmental organization and a non-active member as one who only pays membership fees. The different levels of participation (active or passive) have different implications for the development of social capital, hence it is reasonably important to distinguish between the two. Grafton and Knowles (2004: 364) raise this point when criticizing the use of simple membership numbers in estimating civic engagement, as different levels of participation will have different effects on developing social capital, distinguishing between the "bonding" and "bridging" social capital (discussed in Chapter 2).

It is possible to be even more accurate in qualitative terms. Fidrmuc and Gërxhani (2005: 9), in trying to explain the stock of social capital in 27 European countries pointed out that "one builds up social capital through interacting with fellow members and participating in common activities, not by paying membership dues and holding a membership card." When Olli *et al.* (2001) investigated the impact of social context on pro-environmental behaviors in Norway, they categorized a person as an active member if they met at least two of the following criteria: (1) participation at least once a month; (2) voluntary work of at least three hours duration a month; (3) meeting with other members of the organization on a regular basis.[3]

Obviously, the more intensive the participation, the stronger the network and civic participation components of social capital, arguably reinforcing global environmental polices (Pretty and Smith 2004). In analyzing the frequency of environmental volunteerism in Australia, Randle and Dolnicar (2006) used a five-point scale from 0 (= never) to 4 (= always). They define "environmental volunteers" as those respondents who indicated that they volunteer sometimes (2), often (3), or always (4). This scale captures not only the incidence of active participation, but also the intensity. Active collaboration is undoubtedly a more interesting method of participation in environmental organizations, because its contribution to social capital formation can be more significant.

In light of the importance of this type of cooperative behavior, we initially turn our focus to the factors that influence such behavior, as only a few studies have analyzed the determinants of participation in environmental organizations (Mohai 1992, Thompson and Barton 1994, Martinez and McMullin 2004). Furthermore, given that empirical studies on this topic are scarce, we see the value of including the next section. We provide an overview of studies that have analyzed pro-environmental behaviors or have discussed factors that encourage active participation in voluntary organizations in general (Bekkers 2005), or in environmental organizations in particular.

Factors that influence participation: a review

In describing the factors that influence active participation in environment-friendly organizations, we recognize that this issue can be analyzed from several points of view. A number of factors, such as altruism, social norms, internalized norms, and intrinsic motivations, are linked to cooperative behaviors (Frey and Stutzer 2006). Experts from different fields, such as sociology, psychology, and economics have studied this topic, each contributing to improved explanations of the phenomenon. In this section, it is our intention to utilize this multidisciplinary approach as we explore the possible explanations of volunteerism and active membership in environmental Non-Governmental Organizations (NGOs). We provide a summary of the main studies which have analyzed this topic in the Appendix to this chapter. As Martinez and McMullin (2004) suggest, it is necessary to define the main reasons that people engage in active participation, in order to identify effective methods for recruitment and for motivating continuous participation. It is equally necessary to avoid formulating misguided policy that will crowd out community behaviors and collective action.

What is behind non-participation?

While the focus of the book is on environmental participation, and this section is primarily about explaining the reasons why people do participate, it is arguably just as important to understand the reasons why they do not. Possible explanations are that people have neither the motivation nor the capacity to become involved in environmental organizations. In addition, free-riding behaviors can reduce the level and intensity of active participation in this kind of organization.

Lack of capacity

It is not difficult to find arguments implicating the lack of capacity or the absence of motivations as culprits for non-participation in general. Martinez and McMullin (2004), following the hypothesis proposed by Verba *et al.* (1995), pointed out that:

> access to resources and capacity to take part, in conjunction with motivation to take part, are necessary for members to become active. It also suggests that requests for participation act as catalyst for participation among those with the resources and desire to become active.
>
> (Martinez and McMullin 2004: 113)

Thus, not only do individuals need to possess intrinsic motivation and personal values for the environment, but they also require the resources to take action. Resources could be financial, physical, time, intellectual, or social. Furthermore, if no request (catalyst) to participate is forthcoming, engagement might not occur.

Free-riding

The "free-rider" effect is another possible explanation for why people do not actively participate in voluntary organizations in general.[4] This argument suggests that if an individual perceives that they can benefit from any successful outcome of collective action, whether or not they contributed to obtain it, then they can (and will) decide not to contribute at all. Such a perception will result in the individual "free-riding" on the efforts of the others. Of course, in general, there are interactions between other people's behavior and own behavior, leading to a spiral of tit-for-tat retaliation and free-riding that erodes the possibility of cooperation in future.

The free-rider argument is easier to defend in those scenarios where individuals can observe or at least can gather information about how many people are actively participating in the environmental organization, and the effectiveness of those members in achieving the aims of the organization. In small or local environmental organizations, there will be a higher probability of finding well-informed members; that is, each member will be aware of the extent to which the other members are contributing, and will be aware of the success of the organization in achieving its purpose. As a consequence of the former condition, there will be less of a free-rider effect, and as a consequence of the latter condition, there could be a greater free-rider effect. However, in environmental organizations at the national or even international level, the large number of members can generate the free-rider effect. The higher the number of participants, the higher the probability that work will be carried out by other people. Hence, the effect is not totally clear. It is not possible to predict a priori the relationship between the kind (size) of environmental organization and the intensity of that free-rider effect.

The extent to which an individual is able to influence an outcome will affect their feeling of efficacy, which is another dimension in the discussion of the free-rider effect. When collective action is analyzed, is necessary to

> incorporate the logic of free riding by acknowledging that the contribution of a single individual only raises the probability of successfully providing a public good by small amount. From this perspective, how individuals perceive their own personal influence on collective outcomes is the critical value.
>
> (Lubell *et al.* 2006: 150)

Furthermore, the authors point out that free-rider behavior could be more frequent in large groups or in organizations with many participants rather than in small organizations. In this respect, "when an individual has little chance of influencing collective outcomes, it is rational to free ride on the efforts of others" (Lubell *et al.* 2006: 150). Thus, the free-rider effect is a significant additional argument as to why people might fail to actively participate in environmental groups.

Of course, it is possible that the opposite reaction also occurs. Some people think that cooperative behavior is only rational in terms of solutions to the social dilemma problem if enough other people are willing to cooperate as well. Cooperation can motivate further cooperation, and may encourage more intensive or more frequent cooperation. If there is a good reason to trust that others will cooperate, maybe some individuals would also be more willing to cooperate (De Vries and Wilke 1992).

What is behind participation?

Let us begin describing the motivations that lead individuals to participate in environmental organizations. In this section we are going to discuss both theoretical and empirical factors that influence such pro-environmental behavior. The individual decision about whether to participate or not, as well as the level of participation, depends on the motivations and on the costs and benefits linked to their participation. In this respect, socio-demographic issues are generally taken into account in order to demonstrate that cost-benefit dilemma.

Motivations: intrinsic and extrinsic

One of the most important factors that will determine engagement in environmental organizations is linked to the individual's motivations to participate. In their empirical analysis of volunteer motivations, Cappellari and Turati (2004) explain the difference between intrinsic and extrinsic motivations. Intrinsic motivation refers to the moral and ethical features that define people's preferences (Frey 1992, 1997). Individual ethics are comprised of values such as solidarity, altruism, equality, autonomy, or democracy. Other collectives' welfare affects their own benefits, so utility functions are connected. Interdependent utilities are used to model social network effects, which are related to the idea that agents share links with each other, and that these links potentially have important economic consequences. In general, interdependent preferences are related to social networks, since they specify (for each pair of agents) how one's utility function depends on the other's characteristics. Accordingly,

> traditional economics has been based on methodological individualism. Until quite recently, with some rare exceptions, it has not been appreciated that this method can be, or perhaps I should say, should be, extended in describing social decisions to include dependence of individuals' utility on the utility or actions of others.
>
> (Akerlof 1997: 1005)

On the other hand, the extrinsic motivation theory suggests that monetary compensations are necessary to modify individuals' behavior. The degree to which this type of motivation is able to explain participation in environmental organizations is related to the importance of economic issues in an individual's life. In basic terms, the financial costs of participation are taken into account and are weighed up against the benefits. Aside from monetary considerations, there are other external factors that can motivate ecological activism. For example, the institutional context, the kind of organization, the individuals' perception of environmental damage or threat, or the efficacy of their participation are some features which have been considered as possible reasons to take part in environmental organizations.

Lubell (2002) reinterpreted the problem using a cost-benefit analysis in which the costs and benefits are not necessarily financial. He pointed out that the expected value of environmental activism depends on the collective benefits, the selective benefits and costs.[5] In this model, the individuals' intrinsic and extrinsic characteristics determine the individual benefits and costs. If the balance between benefits and costs is positive, the probability of participation will be higher. For each individual, the proportion of intrinsic/extrinsic reasons will be different, so the benefits and costs will also be weighted differently. In addition, Lubell *et al.* pointed out that:

> people will participate in a collective endeavour when the expected value of participation is greater than the expected value of not participating. People judge the expected value by assessing the total value of the public good, the probability their participation will affect collective outcomes, and the selective benefits and costs of participation.
>
> (Lubell *et al.* 2006: 149)

Moreover, contextual influences are additional factors that condition the perception of both benefits and costs, so it is necessary to consider these in the explanation of individuals' participation decisions. Using a model based on costs and benefits is an interesting approach, which can be used in order to make a detailed presentation of the main factors which influence pro-environmental behaviors.

The costs of participation

This is quite a controversial topic and very difficult to accurately resolve. Some of the more usual costs considered are the energy and time costs, but it is also possible to find additional penalties, such as the disappointment of failing to achieve goals, being associated with radicalism or extremism or being arrested. Those costs are usually linked to high levels of environmental involvement and political activism. However, we have focused our attention on the most common "costs." According to Lubell (2002):

> the ability to pay the selective costs of environmental activism is related to the availability of the money, time, and civic skills necessary for effective

> participation (Verba *et al.* 1995). In turn, the availability of money, time and civic skills is linked to many demographic variables that are traditionally considered in research on environmental behavior.
>
> (Lubell 2002: 437)

Thus, socio-demographic and socio-economic variables are usually included in empirical studies as control variables, but also to characterize the costs of ecological activists participating actively in environmental organization.

Previous studies have shown the importance of socio-demographic and socio-economic factors when investigating the preferences for environment protection (Whitehead 1991, Cameron and Englin 1997, Blomquist and Whitehead 1998, Engel and Pötschke 1998, Witzke and Urfei 2001, Dupont 2004, Israel and Levinson 2004, Hidano *et al.* 2005, Torgler and García-Valiñas 2007). The socio-demographic and socio-economic factors influencing preferences will also affect the perception and construction of participation costs, thereby affecting the decisions about whether to participate. Thus, it is relevant to consider what kinds of socio-demographic and socio-economic factors might exert this kind of influence, and to review the findings of previous literature.

Socio-demographic and socio-economic determinants of environmental participation

The literature has empirically identified several typical features of a participant in environmental organizations. At first glance it seems in general that young, urban, better educated, and upper-class females present higher environmental concern (Jones and Dunlap 1992, Fransson and Gärling 1999, Carrus *et al.* 2005, Torgler and García-Valiñas 2007). However, as we will see, if we focus on our specific pro-environmental behavior and findings in the volunteerism literature, the outcome is slightly different. Several studies have found that volunteers are usually middle-aged men, with middle to high income, highly educated and employed full-time (Curtis and Van Nouhuys 1999, Cappellari and Turati 2004, Martinez and McMullin 2004).

Additionally, if we take into consideration the different degrees of involvement in environmental organizations, the differences that have been found between active members and non-active members with regard to socio-demographic characteristics are not very significant (Olli *et al.* 2001, Martinez and McMullin 2004). However, some small differences have been recognized in other studies on other kinds of voluntary organizations.

So, let us first look at socio-demographic characteristics. Despite implementation of these factors in the majority of empirical studies, it seems that these variables have not had a significant role in explaining environmentally friendly behaviors. Manzo and Weinstein (1987) showed that several socio-economic characteristics such as age, gender, or social/labor status were not predictors of volunteerism and involvement, but instead helped to estimate the probability of an individual joining such an organization. Sometimes, several of those variables are not significant at all (Hernandez and Hidalgo 2000, Carrus *et al.* 2005), and Olli *et al.* (2001) found that socio-demographic factors explained around 10 percent of pro-environmental acts. Nevertheless, it is important to include these factors because they serve an important role as control variables related to the cost of participation. In fact, Martinez and McMullin (2004) describe family issues or financial and employment commitments as competing commitments, at odds with participation in an environmental organization. The extent of competition for the attention and time of the individual has its effect on the decision to volunteer.

These variables certainly help us to characterize the socio-economic profile of people who are usually active participants in environmental organizations. Identification of these characteristics can be especially useful in the context of public policy and in guiding the design of information campaigns or other kinds of environmental policy to encourage active participation in environmental organizations. We now analyze some commonly identified socio-demographic and socio-economic characteristics and their effects on environmental participation.

Age

The main hypothesis is that young people might have more energy to contribute to environmental groups. In addition, young people have stronger preferences for environmental quality, as demonstrated in the empirical literature by Howell and Laska (1992), who found that younger people are more concerned about environmental problems than are older people, and by Nord *et al.* (1998) who demonstrated a strong and negative relationship between age and environmental concern.

However, in terms of environmental behaviors, the relationship is not at all clear. In fact, depending on the pro-environmental behavior, age patterns can be very different (Serret and Ferrara 2008). For instance, previous studies have found that individuals over the age of 50 are more likely to volunteer than younger people, because they have more free time (Wymer 1998), yet it is also possible that physical barriers to volunteering will increase with age. Active participation would at times require considerable effort, so there is a higher probability that older people will experience physical limitations and health problems.

A positive and significant correlation between age and the probability of working in several voluntary organizations was demonstrated by Cappellari and Turati (2004). Further evidence for age and environmental participation comes from Martinez and McMullin (2004), who showed that both active and non-active members of environmental organizations tended to be between the ages of 36 to 55. However, Curtis and Van Nouhuys (1999) found that in general, participants in community Landcare groups in Australia (there are over 4,000 groups, involving over 120,000 volunteer members) were young people. Many of these young people are working to conserve biodiversity and to generate sustainable use of farming lands. Lubell (2002) found a negative and strong relationship between age and environmental activism. Thus, while the findings of the empirical literature are clear on the link between age and pro-environmental preferences, it is not as clear on the link between age and environmental behaviors.

Gender

Both experimental and empirical studies have shown gender differences in activities such as charitable giving and tax morale, as well as in norms against corruption, areas which are closely related to social capital and bargaining or household decision making (Brown-Kruse and Hummels 1993, Nowell and Tinkler 1994, Andreoni and Vesterlund 2001, Torgler 2006, Torgler and Valev 2009). It is often argued that traditional gender socialization, cultural norms, women's roles as caregivers and nurturers, and encouragements to be cooperative and to feel compassion lead to a higher concern for the maintenance of life and environment. The "traditional" domain of working at home induces a greater likelihood to engage privately in behaviors aimed at preservation of the environment.[6] Thus, women have a tendency to be more concerned with the environment than men. Olli *et al.* (2001: 200) found that women "exhibit more environmental friendly behavior than men . . . , not restricted to areas directly connected to household tasks."

There is an argument that gender differences arise due to motherhood and child protection, a view contradicted by Zelezny *et al.* (2000), who find strong evidence that environmentalism does not begin in adulthood. Women demonstrate more concern for the environment than men *at every age*, and volunteer more than men (Bekkers 2005), although political volunteers are more likely to be male (Bussell and Forbes 2003). The competition between work and volunteering recognized by Martinez and McMullin (2004) is reinforced by the findings of Costa and Kahn (2003), who concluded that the reduction of United States social capital produced outside the home, via activities such as volunteering, was strongly linked to higher female labor force participation.

However, literature reviews in the 1980s report that the relationship between environmental attitudes or preferences and gender is meager and inconsistent (Van Liere and Dunlap 1980, Hines *et al.* 1986–87, Mohai 1992). The meta-review by Zelezny *et al.* (2000) covers the years between 1988 and 1998 and reports that out of 13 studies, nine found that women are significantly more active in pro-environmental behaviors than men, three found no statistically significant difference between males and females, and one study reports a greater participation of men. Davidson and Freudenburg (1996), Bord and O'Connor (1997), and Hunter *et al.* (2004) found higher values for women, while Kealy *et al.* (1990), Swallow *et al.* (1994) and Cameron and Englin (1997) found the opposite result. Finally, Brown and Taylor (2000) did not find any gender difference. The validity of the relationship between gender and voluntary participation is further called into question by the argument that the studies relying on self-reports might be biased if women give more socially desirable responses in surveys. However, Zelezny and Yelverton (2000) report that social desirability is not related to gender. A recent study in several OECD countries (Dalen and Halvorsen 2009) analyzed gender differences in relation to several households' environmental behaviors. The findings show that except in the case of car driving, no significant differences between genders can be identified. Additionally, they found that any differences are reflected in the roles and sharing of domestic tasks.

In addition, the empirical results are not conclusive regarding the participation in environmental organizations. Lubell (2002) did not find a significant relationship between gender and environmental activism. Olli *et al.* (2001) found that, among activists, gender differences were not significant. Martinez and McMullin (2004) corroborated this result, showing that the percentage of people who voluntarily collaborate in an organization to protect natural resources did not differ significantly on the basis of gender. Finally, Westerman *et al.* (2005) found that some characteristics such as collaboration, solidarity, and conflict resolution all increase in natural resource management groups where women participate.

Marital status

Marital status is a further control variable considered in studies on pro-environmental behavior and attitude. It could be argued that married people are more concerned about environmental degradation than others, especially compared to singles, because they are more constrained by their social network and often strongly involved in the community (Tittle 1980). However, Fidrmuc and Gërxhani (2005) found that married people are less likely to participate in organizations that pursue social aims than they are to participate in organizations that work for individual objectives (interest groups).

Moreover, married people might be more concerned with environmental problems than singles as the "parent effect" makes them seek their children's future welfare (Dupont 2004). As Lubell *et al.* (2006: 152) pointed out, since "children are generally more susceptible to the negative effects of air pollution; citizens are more likely to receive material benefits from air policy activism if they belong to households with children." However, caring for children requires a considerable time investment, so it would be possible to find the opposite relationship. Parents of big families spend a lot of time organizing family life, which reduces the time available to work in environmental organizations. This argument does not mean that families with children do not present pro-environmental behaviors, since they could still be mindful of the environment, especially with respect to daily activities. However, they may be less likely to engage in activities that require time-consuming commitments.

Ethnicity

Previous research has found that ethnicity is related to environmental activism, although there is no consensus in the literature about the effect of this variable (Mohai 1990). On one hand, the environmental justice literature has found that ethnic minorities are more likely to cooperate in environmental activism, however, minorities could also be less environmentally active due to higher costs of collective participation. Minority groups may suffer institutional discrimination, and have greater difficulties in accessing political and cultural resources (Musick *et al.* 2000). Lubell *et al.* (2006: 156) found that Hispanics, African, Americans, and Asian Americans were significantly more "likely than whites to participate in air quality activism." They concluded that those minority groups have higher perceptions of risk from air pollution, so they are more actively cooperating in environmental groups. In view of the mixed results, there is not enough evidence in the literature to conclude that minorities are more participative in pro-environmental organizations.

Education: formal and informal

Formal education is recognized as a significant factor in explaining voluntary participation overall, and is directly related to environmental behaviors and attitudes. General knowledge and even specific abilities related to environmental sciences are acquired through the educational system. In fact, the last wave of the OECD Programme for International Student Assessment (PISA) focused on sciences (2006), and demonstrated the importance that schools have in the transmission of environmental science knowledge.[7] Around 50 percent of secondary school students recognized that they have acquired environmental knowledge during their formal education.

Several studies have discovered a positive correlation between education and participation in voluntary organizations (Curtis and Van Nouhuys 1999, Wilson and Musick 1999, Bekkers 2005). According to Fidrmuc and Gërxhani (2005),

> the positive relationship between education and the stock of social capital may indicate that social and human capital are complementary: individuals who acquire a high stock of one also invest in the other. In addition, education may reduce the cost of investing in social capital by improving one's communication skills, or by generating positive externalities.
>
> (Fidrmuc and Gërxhani 2005: 15)

Individuals with a higher level of education may be more socially aware. The costs of environmental activism might be lower for better-educated people because they have more civic skills (Lubell 2002). Furthermore, they may be allocated better jobs when they enter the voluntary sector (Wilson and Musick 1999). The extent to which citizens are well-informed could also affect the propensity towards being involved in pro-environmental actions. This point is related to the earlier discussion around the reasons why people participate in environmental organizations: it may depend on their feelings of efficacy. It is important that the participants have detailed knowledge about current and future environmental problems and the impact they might have in working to address these issues. In this sense, education has been identified as one of the most consistent predictors of volunteerism (Reed and Selbee 2000) and, furthermore, Fidrmuc and Gërxhani

(2005) found that people with secondary or university studies are more likely to actively participate in voluntary organizations than those with primary education.

As mentioned previously, the empirical literature consistently reports a positive relationship between pro-environmental behavior and attitudes and the educational level (Van Liere and Dunlap 1980, Hines *et al.* 1986–87, Nord *et al.* 1998, Guerin *et al.* 2001, Lubell 2002, Torgler and García-Valiñas 2007). Martinez and McMullin (2004) showed that around 90 percent of the members of a US environmental organization have a higher education level than high school.

Yet it is not only formal education that influences whether an individual participates in an environmental organization. Several previous studies have stressed the relevance of information or informal education in this respect (Whitehead 1991, Blomquist and Whitehead 1998, Lubell 2002, Hidano *et al.* 2005). We pay particular attention to this variable in the empirical analysis presented in the following chapters, most particularly in Chapter 5, where we employ a measurement of political interest as a proxy for informal education. Further, in the previously mentioned PISA study, a significant percentage of secondary school students reported that they had acquired environmental knowledge not only at school but also through the media, by watching television or even reading newspapers. This finding is indicative of the importance of non-formal education channels in generating environmental awareness.

A noteworthy implication of both formal and informal education is demonstrated in the findings of a meta-analysis by Hines *et al.* (1986–87), who established a positive correlation between knowledge and responsible and pro-environmental behaviors. The deeper the knowledge, the higher the probability that an individual is involved in actions to protect the environment (Kollumuss and Agyeman 2002). Further implications arise from the study by Govindasamy and Italia (1999), who found that people with knowledge about environment-friendly techniques in agriculture were more likely to pay a premium for organic food. Additionally, it has been shown that information campaigns regarding the benefits of pro-environmental behaviors and the negative consequences of irresponsible behaviors are definitely effective in achieving better attitudes and behaviors (Serret and Ferrara 2008).

One explanation is that well-informed citizens who know about environmental problems might have stronger pro-environmental attitudes, because they are better aware of the possible damage (Danielson *et al.* 1995, Olli *et al.* 2001). As Lubell pointed out (2002: 437), "environmentally knowledgeable citizens will also face lower costs of environmental activism, because they are better able to target their activities." In fact, it has been recognized that

> environmental non-profits spend a considerable part of their resources disseminating information to the public and exhorting people both to donate and to become more environmentally conscious. They now reach out to minorities, senior citizens, children, and the religious community in an effort to build mainstream environmentalism . . . There would be a heavy reliance on moral suasion via educational programs and the dissemination of information

> as this strategy would also serve another purpose: to elicit donations and recruit new members.
>
> (Handy 2001: 650, 661)[8]

Of course, while the question of measuring formal education is a straightforward quantitative matter, the question of how to determine the level of environmental knowledge or the level of informal education is entirely another matter. Two different methods have been proposed. The first one is more direct, and it is more convenient when collecting information for the analysis of specific environmental problems. It consists of simply asking people several questions about the environmental problem. To this end, Lubell *et al.* (2006) implemented an index of environmental knowledge using the proportion of correct answers to some questions related to air pollution in Texas. The second method is more indirect, but it has been used in areas of broader study. One example is the work by Torgler and García-Valiñas (2007), in which an alternative variable is used to proxy the level of people's environmental knowledge. The authors analyzed the interest that individuals showed in political issues, assuming that attitude would be correlated with environmental knowledge. In both cases, a positive and significant effect was found.

Economic situation

The economic situation of an individual is another significant variable for our analysis, as income is clearly linked with the opportunity costs of participation. Fidrmuc and Gërxhani (2005: 15) pointed out that "social capital may require not only time but also monetary outlays." A negative effect on volunteering has been found for people who hold economic values in high regard.[9] A relevant study by Martinez and McMullin (2004) discovered a negative relationship between income and the active participation in an environmental association. However, while some economic models of volunteering assume that people with a high value of time face higher opportunity costs and should be less likely to volunteer, some previous studies have shown that a more privileged social status is often correlated with higher levels of voluntarism and civic participation (for an overview see Hwang *et al.* 2005).

It has been found that high and middle-income people are more involved in pro-environmental actions (Guerin *et al.* 2001, Clark *et al.* 2003). It can be argued that environmental quality is not only a public good, but also a normal good, and hence, demand may increase with income (Franzen 2003). Once material well-being is sustained for several years, new generations may place a higher value on other qualities of life, such as equality or clean environment (Olli *et al.* 2001).

Additionally, the flexible budget of those on higher incomes may enable better support of the costs of environmental activism (Lubell 2002, Lubell *et al.* 2006). In this respect, the perceived income restriction may depend on the financial satisfaction of an individual and not per se on the level of income. Financial dissatisfaction might negatively influence the willingness to pay more taxes in order to protect the environment. Such dissatisfaction can create a sense of distress, especially when taxes have to be paid and there is a discrepancy between the actual and the aspired financial situation. Thus, taxes might be perceived as a strong restriction, which increases the incentives not to contribute. In cases where the income variable is integrated in the equation, we can analyze the "stress" component of financial dissatisfaction (Torgler and García-Valiñas 2007).

Employment status

Employment status is another significant variable for which the direction of the effect is not at all clear. It is possible that job flexibility could be an important issue. People without stringent working hours have more freedom to allocate their time between labor and participation in environmental organizations. For those who face long hours at work it may be more difficult to arrange the time away in order to take part in voluntary activities. This is related to the earlier discussion on "competing commitments" (although the earlier discussion was in the context of family commitments). At the same time, this variable is linked in some sense with income, and as a consequence with opportunity cost (Menchik and Weisbrod 1987). Although it has been found that higher and middle-income earners are more likely to volunteer, they may face higher opportunity costs of giving their time for free.

Regarding volunteering, Smith (1999) found differences in the employment status among young volunteers. Fidrmuc and Gërxhani (2005) found that the unemployed, retirees, and house-persons presented lower levels of overall civic participation. As they pointed out, the negative effect of some labor categories (unemployed, retired, or a house-person) on the stock of social capital is reflecting their exclusion from the labor market. Additionally, they observed that the self-employed and white-collar workers seemed to participate more intensively in "Putnamesque" (environmental organizations) rather than "Olsonian groups."[10] Veisten *et al.* (2004) showed that unemployed people occasionally present lower preferences for environmental protection policies. However, sometimes the latter relationship is neither clear nor significant (Engel and Pötschke 1998, Witzke and Urfei 2001). Martinez and McMullin (2004) found that around 60 percent of members in environmental organizations are employed full-time.

City/town size

The size of a city or town and the degree of urbanization may influence the level of participation in environmental organizations. However the evidence is also mixed in this case. Previous literature has investigated the city/town size (Carlsson and Johansson-Stenman 2000, Israel and Levinson 2004), the rural/urban character of the place where a household is located (Danielson *et al.* 1995, Veisten *et al.* 2004)[11] and proximity to the damaged area (Bulte *et al.* 2005). At least for town size and degree of urbanization, evidence for the relationship is not clear. On one hand, small towns are more "rural," which may lead to higher environmental preferences. On the other hand, rural people may have "a more utilitarian approach to nature because their survival depends more directly on it, whereas urban residents' non utilitarian approach to nature may be strengthened by the pollution and environment degradation they face in the cities" (Olli *et al.* 2001: 185). Additionally, both medium and large cities are generally more active in implementing environmental policies, representing higher preferences for environment protection.

However, there is no guarantee that urban citizens will try to fight against pollution. Olli *et al.* (2001) analyzed the impact of having grown up on a farm, and of the character of the town or city of residence on several pro-environmental behaviors. They concluded that current urban residents are less fond of practicing environment-friendly behavior. However, having grown up on a farm is not significant in explaining active participation in environmental organizations (Randle and Dolnicar 2006).

Proximity to the problem

Previous work on the link between proximity to an environmental problem and environmental participation has discovered a positive relationship. For example, it has been shown that people who suffer water supply restrictions during drought periods continue to moderate their consumption in those periods where no restrictions are applied (Roibas *et al.* 2007). This aspect is clearly linked to the knowledge of environmental problems insofar as the closer one is to the environmental disaster, the more likely that details of the problem will be known. Martinez and McMullin (2004) found that the distance to activities of the organization (or even other physical limitations) conditioned the active participation in environmental organizations.[12]

Additionally, if people are living close to the damaged area, they could perceive it as a real threat. Lepore and Evans (1996: 350) define stressors as those "conditions that the average person perceive as actually or potentially threatening, damaging, harmful or depriving." Pollution in domestic and work context or natural disasters are good examples. Homburg and Stolberg (2006) found that those so-called stressors have a significant impact on several pro-environmental acts.[13] The significance of an environmental problem and its economic importance are additional factors to consider. Lubell (2002) obtained a positive and significant sign between the severity of an environmental problem and the degree of ecological activism.

Internal or intrinsic factors of environmental participation

As mentioned previously, several studies on participation in voluntary associations or incidence of environmental concerns have shown the importance of political and psychological characteristics and attitudes. These have been labeled as "internal or intrinsic factors" (Kollmuss and Agyeman 2002, Cappellari and Turati 2004). Bekkers (2005), for example, found that people more interested in politics participate more actively in voluntary associations. Extraversion, solidarity, and empathic concern for other people are other factors that matter (Cappellari and Turati 2004, Bekkers 2005).

Political attitudes

We now turn to socio-political values and attitudes. The political party of choice (Engel and Pötchske 1998, Witzke and Urfei 2001) and their ideology are both important considerations. For example, voters who choose "green" parties are more likely to work towards environmental protection. However, we should not forget that voters' choices are often not exclusively linked to political programs and policies. Citizens sometimes vote for a party not because of their ideological issues but in order to punish the current government.

It has been observed that those who vote for the left demonstrate a higher sensitivity for environmental problems (Witzke and Urfei 2001). This finding can be explained by the higher preferences for economic growth shown by the voters of right-wing parties. In addition, it has been found that egalitarianism presents a strong correlation with environmental values (Grendstad and Selle 1999) and then with pro-environmental behaviors. Moreover, according to Olli *et al.* (2001: 186), a radical political attitude could lead people "to be more willing to support an agenda seeking social and environmental change." Lubell (2002) found that more conservative citizens showed lower levels of environmental activism.

Identification with state or region

Another interesting and relatively novel variable to consider is the tendency to identify with either the state or the region, which may encourage cooperation among individuals and result in an increased desire to preserve a country's or region's environmental conditions.[14] Tyler (2000) argues that in general, pride influences people's behavior in groups, organizations and societies. It gives a basis for encouraging cooperative behavior. Torgler and García-Valiñas (2007) showed that national pride was correlated with higher preferences towards environmental protection. A contrary finding by Bonaiuto *et al.* (2002) observed that when local residents face a social dilemma regarding a protected area, and policy is then imposed by extra-local government that goes against local wishes, the relationship between regional identity and support for protected area is negative.

However, this finding pertains to a very specific context. If there is no unpopular extra-local policy being imposed on the local area, then the opposite relationship can be observed. In this respect, Carrus *et al.* (2005) identified a positive relationship between regional identity and the support for protected areas in Italy. Randle and Dolnicar (2006) found that environmental volunteers have a higher sense of regional identity than do non-volunteers.

A related concept is the level at which individuals invest their perception of belonging: do they identify with their nation or with their region? It is difficult to make a clear prediction on this question. Individuals' attitudes can depend on the importance of the different types of environmental problems (global, national, regional, etc.). Individuals who see themselves as citizens of the world as a whole may have relatively high environmental values, since in many cases, environmental pollution produces externalities at the global level.

A study by Reed and Selbee (2000) showed that volunteers hold a worldview predisposing them towards a concern for provision of common goods. Torgler and García-Valiñas (2007) found that people who felt they belong to the "world as a whole" showed the strongest preference for environmental protection. On the other hand, individuals strongly attached to the local area are less likely to act as free-riders and have stronger preferences to reduce environmental damages at the local level.

Environmental values

Environmental values are another significant variable. The higher the values are, the higher the level of participation in environmental protection. According to Lubell (2002: 437), "citizens with strong environmental values are more likely to receive psychological benefits from expressing their preferences through environmental activism or enjoy the social benefits of participating with like-minded citizens." In the extreme, we find theories of ecocentrism, which mean that environmental interests have priority over human interests (Eckersley 1992). Some statements such as "all ecological systems however small and significant have a right to exist" or "each human being must increase his or her self-awareness so that she or he may feel at one with all living creatures" are representative of that theory. In this respect, Grendstad and Wollebaek (1998) obtained a positive but moderate relationship between ecocentrism attitudes and pro-environmental behavior.

Olli *et al.* (2001) found a positive relationship in only a couple of pro-environmental acts, such as responsible consumerism. In general, pro-environmental attitudes emerge as an important predictor of active participation in environmental groups and vice versa. Randle and Dolnicar (2006) showed that volunteers for environmental organizations are more likely to behave in an environmentally responsible way at home and on vacation. Serret and Ferrara (2008) pointed out the positive and significant impact of environmental attitudes on several households' pro-environmental behaviors, such as recycling, water and energy savings, or car use.

However, it is more usual to measure environmental attitudes and concern by using a set of questions. Lubell (2002) found a positive relationship between environmental activism and a set of three questions about environmental attitudes.[15] In this respect, one of the most well known scales is the NEP (New Environmental Paradigm). It was proposed initially by Dunlap and Van Liere (1978), and was considered (both in its original structure and slightly modified) in several studies as a consistent explanatory factor of pro-environmental behaviors. Olli *et al.* (2001) showed a positive link between NEP[16] in almost all the environmental behaviors analyzed. In their study, ecological attitudes explained about 25 percent of active environmental behaviors. Similarly, Randle and Dolnicar (2006) found that environmental volunteers present more environmentally friendly attitudes than do non-volunteers. Pato and Tamayo (2006) showed the positive impact of environmental attitudes on ecological activism.

Altruism

In addition, altruism is a very important value which has been analyzed in several empirical studies. This could be regarded as the opposite behavior to free-riding. Wymer (1998) found that people who actively participate in non-governmental organizations report more pro-social attitudes. According to Katz and Rosenberg (2005: 432), "altruistic individuals (defined as caring and community minded) often express their altruistic tendencies by participating in institutional and non-institutional volunteering." To examine this relationship, Randle and Dolnicar (2006) used a scale to measure the level of altruism,[17] and found that volunteers showed moderate levels of altruism, but levels were higher than that of non-volunteers.

There are several determinants of collective interest connected to altruism. Some experts have emphasized the importance of efficacy, and the process through which this feeling is reinforced. When an individual takes an active role in a voluntary organization the successful experiences of the past will contribute to their feelings of efficacy. In general, past experience is considered as a powerful predictor of current behaviors and future intentions. Perhaps not surprisingly, past environmental activism is linked to greater intentions to engage in environmental activism in the future (Terry *et al.* 1999).

Efficacy

It is important for individuals to perceive that their personal environmental acts and the actions of their institutions can and will lead to a successful end. Mohai (1985) distinguished between "internal" and "external political efficacy," or, in Lubell's (2002) words, "personal" and "government efficacy." He found that efficacy of participation is more heavily weighted in the decision to volunteer than other variables, and this is true for both active and non-active members. The expectation of attaining a particular goal is instrumental in more active participation in environmental organizations.

Thus, internal or personal efficacy is linked to beliefs about own individual competence in influencing the political system to achieve environmental aims.[18] It is expected that higher levels of this kind of efficacy may lead people to participate more actively in environmental organizations. In this respect, experiences are quite significant, a hypothesis reinforced by several empirical studies (Mohai 1985, Lubell 2002, Martinez and McMullin 2004).

External political or government efficacy refers to individual perceptions about the level of public institutions' responsibility and the response to citizens' environmental demands.[19] According to Lubell *et al.* (2006: 158), "citizen perceptions of the likely success of collective-action are driven in part by their trust in the policy elites who are crucial shapers of policy outcomes." Woolcock (1998: 187) points out that the "structure of the state, the nature and extent of its involvement in civic and corporate life, and the organization of society together constitute the key factors determining whether a country succeeds or fails in development."

However, the relationship is not clear. In fact, Lubell (2002), found that perceived government efficacy is not relevant in explaining such pro-environmental behaviors. On the one hand, Lubell (2002: 436) pointed out, it is expected that "citizens who believe that government actors are responsive and have an important influence on the environment are more likely to participate in environmental activism." In developed countries, there are many valid channels for citizens' actions and for the expression of preferences. The democratic structure allows individuals to influence the government to a certain extent. Furthermore, the government has a higher incentive to take citizens' preferences into account when making policy decisions.

On the other hand, if people perceive that institutions and/or government are not able to be trusted, they may try to achieve environmental aims on their own. Weak and dysfunctional states induce people to pursue their goals via the non-governmental sector, one example of which would be through environmental organizations. Smith (1985) concludes that environmental organizations appear when there is the possibility of influencing the provision of public goods, an idea that could be related to the level of external *and* internal efficacy. According to Handy (2001),

> governments provide many essential environmental goods and services in society. However, there also exists a fairly large and unsatisfied demand for environmental quality that is not met by the government . . . [20] Governments can be pressured and lobbied by ENGOs (Environmental Non-Governmental Organizations) for change in three distinct ways: to change or modify existing legislation and regulations; monitor and critique government agencies responsible for enforcing environmental legislation or providing environmental services as mandated; and attempt to change the public attitudes on environmental issues through education. In the latter case, a successful change in public sentiments may further pressure government, as politicians are sensitive to voter demands.
>
> (Handy 2001: 649–51)

As Paldam (2000) pointed out, corruption is the best available index of negative social capital. If people realize that corruption precludes the achievement of environmental protection, then it is possible that they will seek out participation in environmental organizations to pursue that aim. However, there might be limitations to such an engagement. We will show that in situations where there has been a rapid collapse of the institutional (formal and informal) and government structure (institutional and social capital vacuum) environmental participation will be lower.

Perceptions of the level of governmental corruption might be an indirect way of measuring corruption (Tanzi 2002), but they are strongly correlated with the actual degree of corruption, measured by means of several corruption indexes such as the ICRG (International Country Risk Guide) or the Gallup International (Torgler and García-Valiñas 2007).

Contextual or external factors in the decision to participate

The context in which people make their decisions to participate will affect the extent of voluntary participation that is offered to environmental organizations. Of course, there are many external factors that could affect the decision, but two of the important influences are the characteristics of the organization itself and the institutional regime in which the organization and the participant find themselves. In particular, institutional quality has been discussed at length in Chapter 2, however we repeat and extend a small part of that argument here.

Characteristics of environmental organizations

The characteristics of the environmental organization are an external factor to take into account (Babchuck and Booth 1969, Manzo and Weinstein 1987, Martinez and McMullin 2004). The organization structure, the membership rules and the organization's maturity are aspects that determine the proportion of active members in the organization (Manzo and Weinstein 1987).[21]

Generally speaking, in voluntary groups, the management style and the number of members are key factors in determining the effectiveness of the organization.[22] Donald (1997) found that the active members of an environmental group to restore the Don River Watershed in Toronto (Canada) were not substantially different from the inactive group upon first joining, but that differences between the groups developed after joining. This finding supports the idea that organizational factors play a role in determining the level of engagement from the members.

Institutional quality

In Chapter 2 we discussed the idea that social capital and institutions may decrease the transaction costs of becoming involved in voluntary organizations. Fidrmuc and Gërxhani (2005), considered several variables of institutional quality and development in their analysis of the determinants of social capital. They implemented several indexes, including the Transparency International (TI) perceived-corruption index, the average of indexes of political freedom and civil liberties reported by the Freedom House, and the economic freedom index compiled by the Frasier Institute. They found that institutional quality exerts a significant influence over active participation in several organizations. Additionally, after controlling for economic features (which partially reflect the quality of institutions) no large differences between candidate European Union (EU) countries and EU members were observed, and the former showed even higher active participation levels.

The benefits of participation

The benefits of participation in environmental organizations may either be consciously sought out by those who contribute, they may be incidental to the activity, or may not even be perceived directly by the activist. Participation that is based on psychological preferences (as outlined in the previous section) will certainly lead to a private benefit of satisfying one's own partiality and living according to ones values. Personal and social goals may be satisfied at the same time (Lubell 2002). First of all, private or selective benefits can be obtained through actively participating in environmental groups if the participants also use natural resources for recreational activities. Other individual benefits of participation could include the opportunity to contribute to change, to allow people to have their opinions heard, to feel good protecting the environment, to grow as an individual, or even to make friends. These private benefits are largely related to the satisfaction of the psychological values discussed in the previous section, including intrinsic values, serving political preferences, improving and strengthening the identification with the state, internal environmental values, and improving internal and personal efficacy.

Private benefits

There is some evidence in the empirical literature that socio-political and environmental attitudes and values are linked to the private benefits of environmental participation. Kaiser *et al.* (1999) and Olli *et al.* (2001) found that those attitudes explain around 40 percent of pro-environmental behaviors. We are going to explain some of these values in detail, mainly those on which psychology experts have concentrated. As Carrus *et al.* (2005) pointed out, in recent years the social psychological basis of environmental concern and behavior has been recognized, trying to specify models linked to classical psychological concepts, such as values or beliefs.

Networking

Individual benefits could also include the opportunity to meet and network with other people. In western societies there is

> the widespread concern about the presumed decline in social and political engagement in Western society, which is claimed to affect volunteering too. Civic commitment to the common good is supposed to be eroding, due to various interconnected trends associated with modernization: rationalization, at the expense of traditional religious values and moral obligations; the ascent of individualism, manifesting itself in values of autonomy, self-realization,

> and personal freedom; and the concomitant rise of the "calculative citizen," which hampers pro-social behavior in general and volunteering in particular.
> (Dekker and Van den Broek 1998: 16)

Martinez and McMullin (2004) found that knowing or meeting other people with similar interests or who were involved in the same activities was an important reason to participate actively in environmental organizations. Solidarity incentives are interpersonal rewards such as fellowship, friendship, prestige, and similar positive outcomes from personal relationships (Rouse and Clawson 1992). Curtis amd Van Nouhys (1999) found that environmental participants were motivated by task orientation, a desire for learning and for social interaction. However, personal growth, which implies improved experience for future employment and opportunities to grow as a person, was not a very relevant factor, but was less significant for non-active members (Martinez and McMullin 2004).

Summary

In this chapter, we have explored those factors that have a significant influence on participation in environmental organizations. Key studies consulted for this discussion are summarized in the Appendix to this chapter. We have distinguished two levels of participation based on differing degrees of involvement. Contributions may be passive, by either signing up as a member or simply paying dues, or they may also be through active engagement in pursuing the goals of the organization. This involves sacrificing time in order to preserve and protect the environment, and although both kinds of participation will contribute in some way to the development of social capital, the latter certainly provides a stronger reinforcement.

In identifying the significant variables in voluntary participation, we have constructed the discussion around the costs and benefits of volunteering. Participation in environmental groups and the intensity of engagement depends on the costs and benefits (financial and otherwise) that such a contribution generates. We also recognize that some socio-demographic and socio-economic features, such as age, gender, marital status, income, or education can condition the availability of resources (money and time) for protecting the environment. Additionally, we have compared the socio-demographic characteristics that define people who actively participate with the characteristics of people who engage in other environmental behaviors. We have also analyzed active and non-active participation. The higher the intensity of participation or involvement, the higher will be the contribution to social capital formation.

Regarding the benefits of participation, several issues such as perceived efficacy and previous experiences are important features to take into account, as these factors influence both current activities and future intentions. In this respect, institutional quality is an important factor in explaining the success of environmental programs. Moreover, we have observed that some attitudes and values are significant in generating individual benefits. Altruism, ideology, or free-riding attitudes have been examined from the perspective of prior empirical literature. The idea of efficacy (internal or governmental) is quite significant in explaining why people participate in environmental organizations. If individuals perceive that their efforts have not achieved their initial goals, then the probability of participating actively is reduced considerably. Certainly, both internal and external factors matter in explaining the degree of participation in environmental organizations.

Finally, it is crucial that we describe and explore each of the factors considered in this chapter, as this will guide the variable choice in empirical exercises. The majority of previous studies focused on small areas or particular topics. In the following chapters, we analyze voluntary participation in environmental organizations using a broad data set covering many countries. Hence, we are going to consider several factors described in this section, in order to identify the micro and macro variables that are most relevant to our understanding of this topic.

Appendix

Refer to the Table on pp. 80–3.

Table A3.1 Participation in environmental organizations and environmental activism: a summary

Author/s	*Research question*	*Dependent variable*	*Independent variables*	*Data base*	*Key results*
Manzo and Weinstein (1987)	Exploring the factors that produce a significant behavioral commitment to environmental protection	Activist/non activist	Socio-demographic features (age, gender, marital status, length of membership, rural/urban area, owns present home, employed), early experiences, harm suffered, reasons for joining (outings, environmental concern, social relationships) politics, perceived efficacy, values, participation in other organizations	Survey: 93 members of the New Jersey Chapter of the Sierra Club (USA)	Active and non-active members do not differ in socio-demographic features. Most respondents in both groups mentioned environmental concerns as the initial reason for joining the Club. Perceived efficacy is significant in explaining activism.
Curtis and Van Nouhuys (1999)	Identifying environmental volunteers profile and the reasons to join Landcare groups	Intensity of Landcare participation	Socio-economic variables (age, education, level of knowledge), farmers' characteristics (property size, aware land degradation issues, extent of farm work) and attitudes (stewardship, ethic attitudinal scale, concern for impact of economic and environmental issues)	1993 survey: 352 landholders in Victoria (Australia)	2005 survey: 180 Landcare groups in Victoria (Australia) Landcare respondents are more likely to be middle-aged and better educated, members of greater numbers of voluntary community groups and more concerned about the economic impacts of land degradation.
Olli *et al.* (2001)	Searching correlations among environmental behaviors	Index of several friendly environmental behaviors	Socio-demographic factors (age, gender, education, income, employed at public sector, urban residence, proximity to farm), political	1995 Survey: 5,686 individuals (2,000 from general population and 3,686 members of	Social participation in environmental networks have a strong impact on the remaining pro-environmental behaviors.

			attitudes, environmental attitudes and knowledge, intensity of participation in environmental organizations, environmental behaviors	environmental organizations) in Norway	
Ryan *et al.* (2001)	Researching the relationship between volunteer commitment and motivation, as well as the effect that volunteering has on participants' behavior and attitudes toward the environment	Commitment, frequency and duration of volunteering. Continuous participation	Experience, kind of activity, motivations (helping the environment, learning, project organization, social relationships, reflection, individual items)	Survey: 148 long-term volunteers in three ecological stewardship programs in Michigan (USA)	Helping the environment and learning were important initial motivations. Other motivations, including social factors and project organization, were found to be significant predictors of volunteer commitment.
Lubell (2002)	Testing if environmental activism is a function of citizen beliefs and cost/ benefits of participation	Activism behavior (membership of ENGO, signing a petition, demonstrations) and activism intentions (willingness to pay higher prices and taxes, accept cuts in standard of living)	Collective interest variables (environmental threat, economic importance, personal efficacy, government efficacy, citizen efficacy), selective benefits (environmental values, party identification), selective costs (age, gender, income education, minority, environmental knowledge, social capital)	1993 Survey: 1,606 US citizens	1999 Survey: 657 residents in Peconic Bay watershed (Long Island, USA) Socio-demographic factors matter, because they are related to activism costs. The model fits well in explaining activism behavior, but it is not so robust in explaining activism attitudes.

continued

Table A3.1 Continued

Author/s	*Research question*	*Dependent variable*	*Independent variables*	*Data base*	*Key results*
Martinez and McMullin (2004)	Identifying factors with influence on the decision to participate in ENGOs	Active/non active members	Organizational characteristics (membership length, total NGO memberships, hours donated to other NGOs in 1 year), membership type, socio-demographic variables (age, gender, income, employed, education), motivations (efficacy, competing commitments, social networks, lifestyle changes, personal growth)	1997 survey: 868 members (476 non-active/ 392 active) of the Appalachian Trail Conference (USA)	Active and non-active members have similar demographic characteristics. Efficacy is perceived as a great motivation for both groups. Competing commitments have more importance for non-active members.
Fidrmuc and Gërxhani (2005)	Analyzing the determinants of social capital in European countries (members and candidates)	Index of civic participation measured by means of the active participation in nongovernmental organizations (including organizations for the protection of nature, animals and the environment)	Socio-demographic factors (age, age squared, gender, marital status, education, income, labor status) town size, rural/urban, macro variables of institutional quality (GDP pc, Gini coefficient, corruption, economic freedom), candidate country	2000, 2003 Eurobarometer survey: between 17,010 and 19,019 observations	The capital at individual level is affected by very similar factors in member and candidate EU countries. The low average stock of capital in central and eastern European countries can be attributed to the lower level of economic development and the low quality of institutions.
Randle and Dolnicar (2006)	Finding differences between environmental	Frequency of environmental volunteering	Altruism level, environmental attitudes, environmental behavior at home and on	Survey: 1,000 individuals (160 environmental	No significant differences were found in the socio-demographic profile of

	volunteers and other groups' volunteers	(0= "never"; 4= "always")	vacation, likelihood of adopting recycled and desalinated water, socio-demographic variables (age, gender, income, occupation, marital status, religion, frequency of travel, nationalism, rural/urban location, second language speakers)	volunteers, 840 other volunteers or non-volunteers) in Australia	environmental volunteers. These are more pro-environmental attitudes and a higher regional identity.
McFarlane and Hunt (2006)	Researching the causal influences of activism directed at the forest sector	Activism index built from nine self-reported behaviors to express views and opinions on forest management in Ontario.	Socio-demographic variables (age, gender, education), knowledge about forest-related facts, membership of an environmental organization, dependence of a household member on a natural resource sector	2001 survey: 1,557 respondents (general population) in Ontario (Canada)	Results provide support for an elaborated model of environmental activism that includes an individual's characteristics interacting with macro-factors such as the social, economic, and cultural context in which activism occurs.
Measham and Barnett (2007)	Analyzing motivations of environmental volunteers	Different modes of environmental volunteering (activism, education, monitoring, restoration, sustainable living)	Motivations (helping a cause, social interaction, improving skills, learning about environment, general desire to care for the environment, desire to care for a particular place)	2006 survey: 32 participants from metropolitan Sydney and the Beast Coast (Victoria)	In urban and peri-urban areas, self-education is relatively less important as a motivation for environmental volunteering compared to other sectors. However, community education seems to be a major focus of environmental volunteer groups.

Notes

1 In this respect, it is necessary to distinguish the concept of "environmental activism" from the idea of environmental participation. Activism can involve more diverse behaviors than environmental participation. Lubell (2002) measured the degree of environmental activism behavior by posing the three following questions: (a) Are you a member of any group whose main aim is to preserve or protect the environment? (b) In the past 5 years, have you signed a petition about an environmental issue? (c) In the past 5 years, have you taken part in a protest or demonstration about an environmental issue? Additionally, the same author approximates the degree of "environmental activism intentions" using an average of the scores for items in the brackets: How willing would you be to [pay much higher prices/pay much higher taxes/accept cuts in your standard of living] to protect the environment? Individuals can answer a scale from 1 (= not at all willing) to 5 (= very willing).

2 Olli *et al.* (2001: 191) pointed out arguments to reject criticism and defend the criteria they proposed: "On one hand, the three criteria may be too weak because they only ensure that individuals are part of a social network. On the other hand, employing stronger criteria for social context would make it difficult to separate participation from environmental behaviors because they could become related by definition."

3 The free-rider effect is a fundamental concept in economic literature. Free-riding is usually considered to be an economic "problem" only when it leads to the non-production or under-production of a public good (and thus to Pareto inefficiency), or when it leads to the excessive use of a common property resource.

4 The model proposed by Lubell (2002) can be summarized in the following expression:

$$EV = [(p_g+p_i)*V]-C+B$$

Environmental activism (EV) depends on the probability that the group will be successful (p_g), the marginal influence of the individual's contribution on the probability of success (p_i), the value of the collective good (V), the costs linked to participate (C) and the benefits generated by the participation (B). The first part of the equation (the variables in brackets) represents the collective interest variables (Finkel and Muller 1998).

5 For an overview see Hunter *et al.* (2004).

6 PISA tries to evaluate several aspects of the knowledge and abilities of students who are close to finishing obligatory secondary school. PISA tests are carried out every three years, and in each wave there is a specific area: Reading (in 2000), Mathematics (in 2003) and Sciences (in 2006). The programme is conducting a second phase of evaluations in 2009 (Reading), 2012 (Mathematics) and 2015 (Sciences). The main area in each wave takes up approximately 66 percent of the study, with the two remaining areas accounting for 17 percent each. This permits a broad and detailed view of students' education every nine years, with an approximation of their evolution every three years. The wave carried out in 2006 focused on Sciences, and included some specific questions about environmental sciences.

7 Handy (2001), in a survey of 60 Environmental Non Governmental Organizations in Canada showed that all of them used educational and informational programs to raise environmental concern. Of them, 38 percent were involved in education programs aimed at business, 30 percent at governments, 97 percent at the general public.

8 Cappellari and Turati (2004) found that people who change their job for a higher salary are less likely to volunteer (extrinsic features).

9 Differences between both groups are explained in Chapter 1.

10 In this respect, Witzke and Urfei (2001) included the variable "households in the building" as a proxy of the rural/urban character of the town/city.

11 Choi (2003) found that health status was a significant factor in explaining older people's voluntarism.

12 The authors tried to approximate the threat and harm from pollution that people perceived by the use of several items. The questions used to measure threat are: (1) I am not worried about the health consequences of pollution; (2) I feel that my health is threatened by pollution in everyday life; (3) The thought of this pollution makes me uneasy. Regarding the harm, the items included are: (1) So far, pollution in everyday life has not harmed me; (2) My health has become worse by the pollution in everyday life; (3) I have lost hope, because pollution has just got worse and worse. In both cases, item 1 was negatively formulated. Lubell (2002) used the average of the responses of two questions related to several environmental problems (in brackets), in order to measure the environmental threat: (a) In general, do you think [air pollution by cars/nuclear power/air pollution by industry/pesticides/water pollution] is (1 = not dangerous for environment . . . 5 = extremely dangerous)? and (b) Do you think [air pollution by cars/nuclear power/air pollution by industry/pesticides/water pollution] is (1 = not dangerous for you and your family . . . 5 = extremely dangerous)?

13 A study by Carrus *et al.* (2005) included several items in order to approximate individuals' regional identity. They looked at two dimensions of regional identity: regional pride and regional empowerment. First of all, they measured people's regional pride by means of the following items: (1) I'm proud to be of my region; (2) I feel myself Italian rather than of my region; (3) It's the right thing to keep alive the culture of our region;(4) It's the right thing that we adopt some traditions of other regions; (5) The quality of life in my region is better than in other places; (6) It's a wrong thing to teach the language of my region in the schools; (7) My region has got something special compared with any other place; (8) The traditional culture of my region is too backward. Second, they approximated regional empowerment by asking the following questions: (1) It's a right thing that my region is autonomous; (2) My region is more looked after by the national government rather than by the regional government; (3) For the people of my region, independence is a primary goal; (4) My region would not be able to go without Italy; (5) It's better to rule us by ourselves than being ruled by Rome; (6) Being an autonomous region does not bring us any advantage; (7) The institutions of my region can pursue our interests better than the national ones; (8) Independence would bring us only troubles. In both dimensions, to obtain homogeneity, some of items are recoded in a reverse way (2,4, 6 and 8).

14 He considered the average of the three following questions: (1) We worry too much about the future of the environment and not enough about prices and jobs today; (2) People worry too much about human progress harming the environment; and (3) To protect the environment, America needs economic growth. Individuals can answer in a scale from 1 (= strongly agree) to 5 (= strongly disagree).

15 They modified the original NEP, obtaining a 15 item scale, according to Dunlap *et al.* (2000). The items are the following: (1) We are approaching the limit of the number of people the earth can support; (2) The earth has plenty of natural resources if we just learn to develop them; (3) The earth is like a spaceship with only limited room and resources; (4) Humans have the right to modify the natural environment to suit their needs; (5) Plants and animals have as much right as humans to exist; (6) Humans were meant to rule over the rest of nature; (7) When humans interfere with nature it often produces disastrous consequences; (8) The balance of nature is strong enough to cope with the impacts of modern industrial nations; (9) The balance of nature is very delicate and easily upset; (10) Human ingenuity will ensure that we do not make the earth unlivable; (11) Despite our special abilities, humans are still subject to the laws of nature; (12) Humans will eventually learn enough about how nature works to be able to control it; (13) Humans are severely abusing the environment; (14) The so-called ecological crisis facing humankind has been greatly exaggerated; (15) If things continue on their present course, we will soon experience a major ecological catastrophe. In order to obtain homogeneity, some of the previous questions are recoded in reverse (2, 4, 6, 8, 10, 12, and 14).

16 The authors formulated the scale based on the study by Clark *et al.* (2003), who included the following items to approximate the degree of altruism in the participation of a green electricity program: (1) I worry about conserving energy only when it helps to lower my utility bills; (2) Contributions to community organizations can greatly improve the lives of others; (3) The individual alone is responsible for his or her satisfaction in life; (4) It is my duty to help other people when they are unable to help themselves; (5) Many of society's problems result from selfish behavior; (6) Households like mine should not be blamed for environmental problems caused by energy production and use; (7) My responsibility is to provide only for my family and myself; (8) Use of renewable energy is the best way to combat global warming; and (9) My personal actions can greatly improve the well-being of people I don't know.

17 Lubell (2002) tried to measure the individuals' personal efficacy asking them the following question: It is just too difficult for someone like me to do much about the environment. Individuals can answer in a scale from 1 (= strongly agree) to 5 (= strongly disagree). Martinez and McMullin (2004) went into further detail on this issue, showing that some individual factors are significant in explaining participation in environmental organizations. These factors include: the ability to help in protecting the environment, the ability to ensure the existence of natural resources for future generations and their own satisfaction in the idea of being able to contribute to management of natural resources.

18 Additionally, in the same study, Lubell (2002) approximated governmental efficacy by means of this item: Most public officials (people in public office) are not really interested in the problems of the average man. Individuals can answer in a scale from 0 (= agree) to 1 (= disagree).

19 One of the reasons that governments might not meet this demand for environmental goods is that governments can be subject to influence from interest groups, lobby groups, and vested interests. Governments are not always leaders in change (particularly if it will negatively affect vocal interest groups). The government process of enacting regulation can also tend to be reactive rather than proactive with regard to community feeling. There are long lags between proposing and enacting legislation. One example of how governments can be slow to react or understand community feeling is described by Professor Ian Lowe: he reminds us that in 1989 the Stasi were still steaming open envelopes and tapping phones, even as the citizens of East Germany were breaking down the Berlin Wall (Lowe 2009).

20 Westermann *et al.* (2005) distinguish three stages of environmental groups' maturity using seven criteria: (1) Group objectives in relation to natural resources management which reflect whether the group is reactive (focused on eco-efficiency by reducing cost and environmental harm), regenerative (adopting regenerative technologies and some principles of sustainability), or innovative (adopting new technologies to fit the old systems, innovating to develop entirely new systems of management); (2) the group's views on change (avoiding change, adjusting to change, or creating new opportunities); (3) whether the group monitors and evaluates its own progress; (4) the degree of reliance on external facilitators to solve problems; (5) collective or individual planning and testing; (6) the importance of external aid for the formation of the group; and (7) the likelihood of the group breaking up.

21 We previously mentioned the number of members in the environmental organization, because is clearly linked to free-riding behaviors.

References

de Abreu e Silva, J., Golob, T.F., and Goulias, K.G.(2006) "The effects of land use characteristics on residence location and travel behavior of urban adult workers," paper presented at the 85th Transportation Research Board Annual Meeting, Washington, DC.

Ajzen, I. and Driver, B.L. (1992) "Application of the theory of planned behavior to leisure choice," *Journal of Leisure Research*, 24: 207–13.

Akerlof, G. (1997) "Social distance and social decisions," *Econometrica*, 65: 1005–27.

Andreoni, J. (1988) "Privately provided public goods in a large economy: the limits of altruism," *Journal of Public Economics*, 35: 57–73.

—— and Vesterlund, L. (2001) "Which is the fair sex? Gender differences in altruism," *Quarterly Journal of Economics*, 116: 293–312.

Babchuck, N. and Booth, A. (1969) "Voluntary association membership: a longitudinal analysis," *American Sociological Review*, 34: 31–45.

Bekkers, R. (2005) "Participation in voluntary associations: relations with resources, personality, and political values," *Political Psychology*, 26: 439–54.

Berglund, C. (2006) "The assessment of households' recycling costs: the role of personal motives," *Ecological Economics*, 56: 560–69.

Blomquist, G.C. and Whitehead, J.C. (1998) "Resource quality information and validity of willingness to pay in contingent valuation," *Resource and Energy Economics*, 20: 179–96.

Bonaiuto, G.C., Carrus, G., Martorella, H., and Bonnes, M. (2002) "Local identity process and environmental attitudes in land use changes: the case of natural protected areas," *Economic Psychology*, 23: 631–53.

Bord, R. J. and O' Connor, R. E. (1997) "The gender gap in environmental attitudes: the case of perceived vulnerability to risk," *Social Science Quarterly*, 78: 830–40.

Brown, K. and Taylor, L. (2000) "Do as you say, say as you do: evidence on gender differences in actual and stated contributions to public goods," *Journal of Economic Behavior and Organization*, 43: 127–39.

Brown-Kruse, J. and Hummels, D. (1993) "Gender effects in laboratory public goods contribution: do individuals put their money where their mouth is?" *Journal of Economic Behavior and Organization*, 22: 255–67.

Bulte, E., Gerking, S., List, J.A. and De Zeeuw, A., (2005) "The effect of varying the causes of environmental problems on stated WTP values: evidence from a field study," *Journal of Environmental Economics and Management*, 49: 330–42.

Bussel, H. and Forbes, D. (2003) "Understanding the volunteer market: the what, where, who and why of volunteering," *International Journal of Nonprofit and Voluntary Sector Marketing*, 7: 244–57.

Cameron, T.A. and Englin, J. (1997) "Respondent experience and contingent valuation of environmental goods," *Journal of Environmental Economics and Management*, 33: 296–313.

Cappellari, L. and Turati, G. (2004) "Volunteer labour supply: the role of workers' motivations," *Annals of Public and Cooperative Economics*, 75: 619–43.

Carlsson, F. and Johansson-Stenman, O. (2000) "Willingness to pay for improved air quality in Sweden," *Applied Economics*, 32: 661–69.

Carrus, G., Bonaiuto, M. and Bonnes, M. (2005) "Environmental concern, regional identity and support for protected areas in Italy," *Environment and Behavior*, 37: 237–57.

Choi, L.H. (2003) "Factors affecting volunteerism among older adults," *Journal of Applied Gerontology*, 222: 179–96.

Clark, C.F., Kotchen, M.J., and Moore, M.R. (2003) "Internal and external influences on pro-environmental behavior: participation in a green electricity program," *Journal of Environmental Psychology*, 23: 237–46.

Costa, D. and Kahn, M. (2003) "Understanding the decline in American social capital: 1953–98," *Kyklos*, 561: 17–46.

Curtis, A. and Van Nouhuys, M. (1999) "Landcare participation in Australia: the volunteer perspective," *Sustainable Development*, 7: 98–111.

Dalen, H.M. and Halvorsen, B. (2009) "Household behavior and environmental policy: gender differences in environmentally related behavior," Final Report presented at the OECD Conference on "Household Behavior and Environmental Policy," Paris: OECD.

Danielson, L., Hoban, T.J., Van Houtven, G., and Whitehead, J.C. (1995) "Measuring the benefits of local public goods: environmental quality in Gaston County, North Carolina," *Applied Economics*, 27: 1253–60.

Davidson, D.J. and Freudenburg, W.R. (1996) "Gender and environmental risk concerns: a review and analysis of available research," *Environment and Behavior*, 28: 302–29.

De Vries, S. and Wilke, H. (1992), "Constrained egoism and resource management under uncertainty," in W. Liebrand, D.M. Messick and H.A.M. Wilke, *Social Dilemmas: Theoretical Issues and Research Findings*, Oxford: Pergamon.

Dekker, P. and Van den Broek, A. (1998) "Civil society in comparative perspective: involvement in voluntary associations in North America and Western Europe," *Voluntas: International Journal of Voluntary and Nonprofit Organizations*, 9: 11–38.

Donald, B.J. (1997) "Fostering volunteerism in an environmental stewardship group: a report on the task force to bring back the Don, Toronto, Canada," *Journal of Environmental Planning and Management*, 404: 483–505.

Dunlap, R.E. and Van Liere, K.D. (1978) "The 'New Environmental Paradigm': a proposed measuring instrument and preliminary results," *Journal of Environmental Education*, 9: 10–19.

——, Mertig, A.G. and Jones, R.E. (2000) "Measuring endorsement of the New Ecological Paradigm: a revised NEP scale," *Journal of Social Issues*, 56: 425–42.

Dupont, D.P. (2004) "Do children matter? An examination of gender differences in environmental valuation," *Ecological Economics*, 49: 273–86.

Eckersley, R. (1992) *Environmentalism and Political Theory: Towards an ecocentric approach*, London: UCL Press.

Engel, U. and Pötschke, M. (1998) "Willingness to pay for the environment: social structure, value orientations and environmental behavior in a multilevel perspective," *Innovation*, 11: 315–32.

Fidrmuc, J. and Gërxhani, K. (2005) "Formation of social capital in Central and Eastern Europe: understanding the gap vis-à-vis developed countries," CEPR Discussion Paper 5068.

Finkel, S. E. and Muller, E. N. (1998) "Rational choice and the dynamics of collective political action: evaluating alternative models with panel data," *American Political Science Review*, 92: 37–49.

Fransson, N. and Gärling, T. (1999) "Environmental concern: conceptual definitions, measurement methods and research findings," *Journal of Environmental Psychology*, 19: 369–82.

Franzen, A. (2003) "Environmental attitudes in international comparison: an analysis of the ISSP surveys 1993 and 2000," *Social Science Quarterly*, 84: 297–308.

Frey, B.S. (1992) "Tertium datur: pricing, regulating and intrinsic motivation," *Kyklos*, 45: 161–84.

—— (1997) *Not Just for Money: An economic theory of personal motivation*, Cheltenham, Glos.: Edward Elgar.

—— and Stutzer, A. (2006) "Environmental moral and motivation," Working Paper 288, Institute for Empirical Research in Economics, University of Zurich.

Grafton, R.Q. and Knowles, S. (2004) "Social capital and National Environmental Performance: a cross-sectional analysis," *The Journal of Environment Development*, 13: 336–70.

Grendstad, G. and Selle, P. (1999) "The formation and transformation of preferences: cultural theory and post-materialism compared," in M. Thompson, G. Grendstad, and P. Selle (eds), *Cultural Theory as Political Science*, London: Routledge.

—— and Wollebaek, D. (1998) "Greener still? An empirical examination of Eckersley's ecocentric approach," *Environment and Behavior*, 30: 653–75.

Govindasamy, R. and Italia, J. (1999) "Predicting willingness-to-pay for a premium for organically grown fresh produce," *Journal of Food Distribution Research*, 30: 44–53.

Guagnano, G.A., Stern, P.C., and Dietz, T. (1995) "Influences on attitude-behavior relationships: a natural experiment with curbside recycling," *Environment and Behavior*, 27: 699–718.

Guerin, D., Crete, J., and Mercier, J. (2001) "A multilevel analysis of the determinants of recycling behavior in the European countries," *Social Science Research*, 30: 195–218.

Handy, F. (2001) "Advocacy by environmental nonprofit organizations: an optimal strategy for addressing environmental problems?," *International Journal of Social Economics*, 288: 648–66.

Hernandez, B. and Hidalgo, M.C. (2000) "Actitudes y creencias hacia el medio ambiente," in J.I. Aragonés and M. Amérigo (eds), *Psicología Ambiental*, Madrid: Pirámide.

Hidano, N., Kato, T., and Aritomi, M. (2005) "Benefits of participating in contingent valuation mail surveys and their effects on respondent behavior: a panel analysis," *Ecological Economics*, 52: 63–80.

Hines, J., Hungerford, H., and Tomera, A. (1986–87) "Analysis and synthesis of research on responsible environmental behavior," *Journal of Environmental Education*, 18: 1–8.

Homburg, A. and Stolberg, A. (2006) "Explaining pro-environmental behavior with a cognitive theory of stress," *Journal of Environmental Psychology*, 26: 1–14.

Howell, S.E. and Laska, L.B. (1992) "The changing face of the environmental coalition: a research note," *Environment and Behavior*, 24: 134–44.

Hunter, L.M., Hatch, A., and Johnson, A. (2004) "Cross-national gender variation in environmental behaviors," *Social Science Quarterly*, 85: 677–94.

Hwang, M., Grabb, E., and Curtis, J. (2005) "Why get involved? Reasons for voluntary-association activity among Americans and Canadians," *Nonprofit and Voluntary Sector Quarterly*, 34: 387–403.

Israel, D. and Levinson, A. (2004) "Willingness to pay for environmental quality: testable empirical implications of the growth and environmental literature," *Contributions to Economic Analysis and Policy*, 3: art. 2.

Jackson, E.L. (1987) "Outdoor recreation participation views on resource development and preservation," *Leisure Sciences*, 9: 235–50.

Jensen, B.B. (2002) "Knowledge, action and pro-environmental behavior," *Environmental Educational Research*, 8: 325–34.

Johansson-Stenman, O. (2002) "Estimating individual driving distance by car and public transport use in Sweden," *Applied Economics*, 34: 959–67.

Jolly, D.A. (1991) "Determinants of organic horticultural products consumption based on a sample of California consumers," *Acta Horticulturae*, 295: 141–48.

Jones, R.E. and Dunlap, R.E. (1992) "The social bases of environmental concern: have they changed over time?" *Rural Sociology*, 57: 28–47.

Kaiser, F.G., Wolfing, S., and Fuhrer, U. (1999) "Environmental attitude and ecological behavior," *Journal of Environmental Psychology*, 19: 1–19.

Katz, E. and Rosenberg, J. (2005) "An economic interpretation of volunteering," *European Journal of Political Economy*, 21: 429–43.

Kealy, M., Montgomery, M., and Dovidio, J. (1990) "Reliability and predictive validity of contingent values: does the nature of the good matter?" *Journal of Environmental Economics and Management*, 19: 244–63

Kollmuss, A. and Agyeman, J. (2002) "Mind the gap: why do people act environmentally and what are the barriers to pro-environmental behavior?," *Environmental Educational Research*, 8: 239–60.

Lepore, S. and Evans, G. (1996) "Coping with multiple stressors in the environment," in M. Zeidner and N.S. Endler (eds), *Handbook of Coping: Theory, research, applications*, New York: Wiley.

Lowe, I. (2009) "Does the "Zurich consensus' provide grounds for cautious optimism?" transcript of guest lecture given at National Taipei University, March 23, 2009. <http://pa.ntpu.edu.tw/phrd/file.php?A_ID = 000806>.

Lubell, M. (2002) "Environmental activism as collective action," *Environment and Behavior*, 34: 431–54.

——, Vedlitz, A., Zahran, S., and Alston, L.T. (2006) "Collective action, environmental activism and air quality policy," *Political Research Quarterly*, 591: 149–60.

Luzar, E.J., Diagne, A., Gan, C., and Henning, B.R. (1995) "Evaluating nature based tourism using the new environmental paradigm," *Journal of Agricultural Applied Economics*, 272: 544–55.

Manzo, L.C. and Weinstein, N.D. (1987) "Behavioral commitment to environmental protection: a study of active and non-active members of the Sierra Club," *Environment and Behavior*, 19: 673–94.

Martinez, T.A. and McMullin, S.L. (2004) "Factors affecting decisions to volunteer in nongovernmental organizations," *Environment and Behavior*, 36: 112–26.

Menchik, P.L. and Weisbrod, B.A. (1987) "Volunteer labour supply," *Journal of Public Economics*, 32: 159–83.

Mohai, P. (1985) "Public concern, and elite involvement in environmental conservation issues," *Social Science Quarterly*, 66: 820–38.

—— (1990) "Black environmentalism," *Social Science Quarterly*, 714: 744–65.

—— (1992) "Men, women, and the environment: an examination of the gender gap in environmental concern and activism," *Society and Natural Resources*, 5: 1–19.

Musick, M.A., Wilson, J., and Bynum, W.R. Jr. (2000) "Race and formal volunteering: the differential effects of class and religion," *Social Forces*, 784: 1539–70.

Nord, M., Luloff, A.E., and Bridger, J.C. (1998) "The association of forest recreation with environmentalism," *Environment and Behavior*, 30: 235–46.

Nowell, C. and Tinkler, S. (1994) "The influence of gender on the provision of a public good," *Journal of Economic Behavior and Organization*, 25: 25–36.

OECD (2008) *Households' Behavior and the Environment: Reviewing the evidence*, Paris: OECD.

Olson, M. (1965) *The Logic of Collective Action: Public goods and the theory of groups*, Cambridge, MA: Harvard University Press.

Olli, E., Grendstad, G., and Wollebaek, D. (2001) "Correlates of environmental behaviors: bringing back social context," *Environment and Behavior*, 33: 181–208.

Paldam, M. (2000) "Social capital: one or many? Definition and measurement," *Journal of Economic Surveys*, 14: 629–53.

Pato, C. and Tamayo, A. (2006) "Valores, creencias ambientales y comportamiento ecológico de activismo," *Medio Ambiente y Comportamiento Humano*, 7: 51–66.

Piliavin, J.A. and Charng, H.-W. (1990) "Altruism: a review of recent theory and research," *Annual Review of Sociology*, 16: 27–65.

Pretty, J. and Smith, D. J. (2004) "Social capital in biodiversity conservation and management," *Conservation Biology*, 18: 631–38.

Randle, M. and Dolnicar, S. (2006) "Environmental volunteers: are they driven by altruism and a strong feeling or regional identity?," Working Paper 88, Faculty of Commerce, University of Wollongong.

Reed, P.B. and Selbee, L.K. (2000) "Distinguishing characteristics of active volunteers in Canada," *Nonprofit and Voluntary Sector Quarterly*, 294: 571–92.

Roibas, D., García-Valiñas, M.A. and Wall, A. (2007) "Measuring welfare losses from interruption and pricing as responses to water shortages: an application to the case of Seville," *Environmental and Resource Economics*, 38: 231–43.

Rouse, S.B. and Clawson, B. (1992) "Motives and incentives of older adult volunteers," *Journal of Extension*, 30: 1–6.

Schultz, P.W. and Zelezny, L.C. (1998) "Values and pro-environmental behavior: a five-country survey," *Journal of Cross-Cultural Psychology*, 29(4): 540–58.

Serret, Y. and Ferrara, I. (2008) "Conclusions and policy implications: special issue (number 2) on Household Behavior and the Environment," OECD General Papers.

Shaw, G.B. (1903) *Man and Superman*, New York: Epistle Dedicatory.

Smith, D.J. (1999) "Poor marketing or the decline of altruism? Young people and volunteering in the United Kingdom," *International Journal of Nonprofit and Voluntary Sector Marketing*, 4: 372–77.

Smith, V.K. (1985) "A theoretical analysis of the green lobby," *American Political Science Review*, 79: 132–47.

Swallow, S., Weaver, T., Opaluch, J., and Michelman, T. (1994) "Heterogeneous preferences and aggregation in environmental policy analysis: a landfill siting case," *American Journal of Agricultural Economics*, 76: 334–431.

Tanzi, V. (2002) "Corruption around the world: causes, consequences, scope, and cures," in G.T. Abed and S. Gupta (eds), *Governance, Corruption and Economic Performance*, Washington: International Monetary Fund.

Terry, D.J., Hogg, M.A., and White, K.M. (1999) "The theory of planned behavior: self-identity, social identity and group norms," *The British Journal of Social Psychology*, 38: 225–44.

Tittle, C. (1980) *Sanctions and Social Deviance: The question of deterrence*, New York: Praeger.

Thompson, S.C.G. and Barton, M.A. (1994) "Ecocentric and anthropocentric attitudes toward the environment," *Journal of Environmental Psychology*, 14: 149–57.

Torgler, B. (2006) "The importance of faith: tax morale and religiosity," *Journal of Economic Behavior and Organization*, 61: 81–109.

—— and García-Valiñas, M.A. (2007) "The determinants of individuals' attitudes towards preventing environmental damage," *Ecological Economics*, 63: 536–52.

—— and Valev, N.T. (2009) "Gender and public attitudes towards corruption and tax evasion," *Contemporary Economic Policy*, forthcoming.

Tyler, T.R. (2000) "Why do people cooperate in groups?," in M. Van Vught, M. Snyder, M.T.R. Tyler, and A. Biel (eds), *Cooperation in Modern Society: Promoting the welfare of communities, states and organizations*, London: Routledge.

Van Liere, K. and Dunlap, R. (1980) "A review of studies that measured environmental attitudes and behaviors," *Environment and Behavior*, 11: 22–38.

Veisten, K., Hoen, H.F., Navrud, S., and Strand, J. (2004) "Scope insensitivity in contingent valuation of complex environmental amenities," *Journal of Environmental Management*, 73: 317–31.

Verba, S., Schlozman, K.L. and Brady, H.E. (1995) *Voice and Equality: Civic volunteerism in American politics*, Cambridge, MA: Harvard University Press.

Westerman, O., Ashby, J., and Pretty, J. (2005) "Gender and social capital: the importance of gender differences for the maturity and effectiveness of natural resource management groups," *World Development*, 33: 1783–99.

Whitehead, J.C. (1991) "Environmental interest group behavior and self-selection bias in contingent valuation mail surveys," *Growth and Change*, 22: 10–21.

Wilson, J. and Musick, M.A. (1999) "Attachment to volunteering," *Sociological Forum*, 14: 243–72.

Witzke, H.P. and Urfei, G. (2001) "Willingness to pay for environmental protection in Germany: coping with the regional dimension," *Regional Studies*, 35: 207–14.

Woolcock, M. (1998) "Social capital and economic development: toward a theoretical synthesis and policy framework," *Theory and Society*, 27: 151–208.

Wymer, W.W. (1998) "Youth development volunteers: their motives, how they differ from other volunteers and correlates of involvement intensity," *International Journal of Nonprofit and Voluntary Sector Marketing*, 3: 321–36.

Zelezny, L.C. and Yelverton, J.A. (2000) "Feminine identity, collectivism, and environmental attitudes and behaviors," paper presented at the meeting of the Western Psychological Association, Portland.

——, Chua, P.P. and Aldrich, C. (2000) "Elaborating on gender differences in environmentalism," *Journal of Social Issues*, 56: 443–57.

4 Participation in environmental organizations

An explorative approach

> Voluntaristic environmental activities have been rather neglected by economists but play a considerable role in everyday behaviors.
>
> (Frey 1997: 60)

Introduction

In this chapter we provide a descriptive analysis of the available data that can be used to explore participation and membership in environmental organizations, giving readers a good idea of the sort of data we are going to work with in the empirical section. The last section of the chapter explores some simple correlations and comprises the foundation of the macro chapter. We think it best to warn readers: you will be confronted with a large set of tables due to the explorative nature of the chapter. However, it is possible to for a reader with limited time (and patience) to selectively focus on the tables of interest without losing the central theme of this chapter. This is particularly the case for the first part of the chapter. Now, we are aware that some readers may perceive this chapter as relatively "dry material," and we cannot disagree with such an estimation. Nevertheless, we believe that this chapter is quite valuable and informative. Readers with an interest in the relationships behind the regression equations presented in future chapters will be interested in the descriptive statistics, and readers with less technical knowledge will gain a good overview of what can be expected in the following chapters.

Dataset

The data used in the present study are taken from the World Values Survey (WVS) and European Values Survey (EVS), worldwide investigations of socio-cultural and political change, based on representative national samples. The research was carried out in several waves, beginning in 1981–83. In this book we have used information taken from the waves 1990–91, 1995–96 and 1999–2000. Data from these surveys are made publicly available for use by researchers interested in how views, values, and attitudes change with time. The interesting feature from our point of view is the ability to use a behavioral variable instead of an attitudinal one to investigate environmental involvement or environmental preferences. Moreover, we decided to use the WVS and EVS data as it covers a broad variety of countries and variables, allowing detailed investigation of the causes and consequences of environmental participation.

The WVS/EVS methodological approach is explained in detail elsewhere; for example, in the Inglehart *et al.* (2000) source book, which provides information on response rates, the stages of sampling procedures, the translation of the questionnaire, and field work, along with measures of coding reliability, reliability, and data checks. All country surveys were carried out by experienced professional survey organizations, and were performed through face-to-face interviews among samples of adult citizens aged 18 years[1] and older. The survey is coordinated centrally, providing the guidelines to guarantee the use of standardized information in the surveys and the national representativeness of the data. To avoid framing biases, the questions were asked in the prescribed order. The response rate varies from one country to another; but is in general relatively high (e.g., 60 percent). The total file provided by the World Values Survey also covers the European Values Survey (EVS). This explains why in some cases we may even have two surveys for one country within the same wave. In general, the EVS and WVS questions are almost identical.

In many instances we are going to explore single questions that focus on membership participation and unpaid voluntary work. This raises the issue of whether it is more appropriate to use an index instead of a single question to proxy the level of participation. We believe that a single question has an advantage, as it can avoid problems that arise from the complexity of an index, especially regarding the measurement procedure or a low correlation between the items. The use of a single question item is relatively common: we observe that many studies on environmental attitudes typically measure environmental values using a single item.[2] In addition, several studies on volunteering also use single questions (Cappellari and Turati 2004, Bekkers 2005). Naturally, we recognize that there are some good reasons to use a multi-item index instead of a single question. For example, a single-item measure may have difficulty in adequately capturing the interrelated facets of participation and volunteering, and may also be adversely affected by random errors in measurement. A further advantage of a multi-item index is that errors should tend to average out, therefore producing a more reliable measure. Compared to a single-item measure, a multi-item index is likely to provide a more reliable score by pooling information that the items have in common; a multi-item tool also increases validity by providing a more representative sample of information about the underlying concept, and it increases precision by decreasing score variability. However, due the fact that we are exploring a "behavioral variable" rather than an "attitudinal variable," a single-item variable might be less problematic in this regard.

In our case we are going to work with two variables, namely whether a person belongs to a voluntary environmental organization and whether a person has carried out unpaid voluntary work. Putnam (2000: 156) has expressed criticism regarding the use of membership rates and number of voluntary associations as indicators of civic engagement. He stresses that active participation has collapsed within a few decades despite the increase in education that should foster civic engagement. He sees membership as "an honorific rhetorical device for fund-raising" and the positive trend is "not a deeper civic consciousness, but direct mail." Greenpeace became the largest environmental organization in the US through an extremely aggressive direct-mail program, for example, and it is unclear whether some organizations such as Greenpeace really involve their members directly in activities. Giving a check helps to lower the costs of participation, yet this action transforms members into consumers. Nevertheless, while such a criticism may affect our first variable it may not necessarily affect the second one.

Furthermore, this criticism may also indicate that one should be careful in interpreting official statistics. Even Putnam (2000: 158) admits the advantages of surveys in this regard. He refers to the situation in which individuals giving to the Environmental Defense Fund have stressed that "I don't really think of myself as a member; the money I send is just a contribution." Thus, one may posit that such individuals would not have declared themselves as belonging to an environmental organization during a survey such as the WVS. Moreover, the question we use from the WVS is very broad, and does not ask directly about membership payments. Although, we note that this certainly reduces the possibility of validity checks, which can also be regarded as a disadvantage (see Neumayer 2002).

We should also note that we will in fact use the same approach (single-item variable) in Chapter 6 when we explore the justifiability of littering as a dependent variable. Notwithstanding the previous criticisms of implementing a single-item variable, such an approach for an attitudinal variable is consistent with the research by many economists in recent years focusing on such topics as happiness and the willingness to comply (Frey and Stutzer 2002, Clark *et al.* 2008, Torgler 2007) although one should be aware that social psychologists might be more critical of such an approach.

Membership and active participation

In this section we want to get the big picture by looking at the participation issue from a very broad and general point of view. Hence, we are going to explore the incidence of membership in environmental organizations, without differentiating between people who only pay their fees and those who make an additional active contribution in the environmental organization. Associations formed for the purpose of environmental protection have become one of the most trusted institutional forms when it comes to the task of solving environmental problems. At the beginning of the century, the Eurobarometer (European Opinion Research Group 2002) showed that almost 50 percent of Europeans hold a high level of trust in these organizations. In fact, the degree of trust in environmental organizations is higher than the degree of trust in their national governments or the institutions of the European Union.[3]

A general view: membership

We first explore the following question:

> Please look carefully at the following list of voluntary organizations and activities and say which, if any, you belong to.
>
> Conservation, environment groups
> 0 Not mentioned
> 1 Belong

This question was only asked in the second wave of the WVS (early 1990s). Table 4.1 presents the results, sorted in descending order: the country with the highest level of participation is at the top of the table and the country with the lowest is at the bottom. It is clear that the highest participation rate is observable in the Netherlands, followed by Denmark, Sweden, Switzerland, and the United States. The lowest values are observable for Argentina, Romania, China, and Japan.

The table indicates that European countries exhibit the highest membership rates out of all countries. In particular, northern European countries are more involved in environmental organizations than the rest of the world. Interestingly, people in the Netherlands are almost twice as likely to belong to an environmental organization as the next most active citizens in Denmark. On the other hand, some southern European countries such as Portugal and Spain present very low values. Can we blame their attitude on the latitude? Or is it something more prosaic? In a recent survey in EU15 (European Opinion Research Group 2002), people from southern European countries rate themselves as "not very well informed" about environmental problems. The percentage of people who declare themselves to have good knowledge of environmental issues in Spain is around 34 percent, and in Portugal is about 36 percent. In comparison, the citizens of Denmark seem to be very well-informed, reporting one of the highest percentages (58 percent) of knowledge about environmental problems. As we mentioned in the previous chapter, information and education are important factors which have a notable influence in pro-environmental behaviors and attitudes.

In a next step we explore the values from a slightly different angle:

> Please look carefully at the following list of voluntary organizations and activities and say which, if any, you belong to.
>
> Conservation, environment, animal rights groups
> 0 Not mentioned
> 1 Belong

While the previous question only referred to conservation and environmental participation, this question also covers involvement in animal rights groups and has been asked in more than one year. The data indicates that the overall country averages are highly correlated with the previous question ($r = 0.90$). To construct

Table 4.1 Participation rate in environmental organizations

Country	*Participation rate %*
Netherlands	23.3
Denmark	12.5
Sweden	10.6
Switzerland	10.5
United States	8.5
Belgium	7.7
Canada	7.5
Czech Republic	6.7
Great Britain	5.9
Slovakia	5.8
Finland	5.4
Iceland	4.8
Latvia	4.3
Germany	4.2
Norway	4.1
Bulgaria	3.8
Italy	2.9
Brazil	2.8
Mexico	2.8
Austria	2.7
Estonia	2.7
France	2.3
Ireland	2.3
Northern Ireland	2.3
Lithuania	2.1
Republic of Korea	2.0
Russian Federation	1.7
Slovenia	1.7
Chile	1.6
Poland	1.5
Hungary	1.4
Malta	1.4
Portugal	1.4
Spain	1.4
Japan	1.1
China	1.0
Romania	1.0
Argentina	0.2

a better idea of the development over time, we report values from different years in Table 4.2. For simplicity, we report the values in alphabetical order. The Netherlands again has the highest membership rate (43.5 percent in 1999). However, Bangladesh (20.3) is now second to the Netherlands and the United Republic of Tanzania (20.1) is third. These countries are followed by the United States and Denmark. The lowest values are observed for Turkey (0.2), Morocco (0.5), Portugal (0.5), Latvia (0.7), Lithuania (0.7), and Russia (0.7). This ranking is similar to that of the previous question. In particular, former Soviet Union countries return very low rates of participation. Most of the data is derived from the fourth wave. However, as can be seen in Table 4.2, some countries have two period values. Interestingly, we observe quite dramatic changes over time; for example, the Netherlands' level of participation is almost four times higher in the late 1990s compared to the early 1980s. The values for Belgium, Sweden, and the USA tripled within 20 years and Canada's and Italy's values doubled within the same period. Similarly, Denmark's reported participation rate is almost three times higher in the later survey. A positive effect is also observable for France. On the other hand, several countries have decreased their participation rates: Great Britain (strongest, three times lower), Germany (West), and Northern Ireland. Relatively stable values are reported by Iceland, Malta, and Ireland, while Spain reports up and downs within the 20 year period.

To obtain a ranking consistent with that used in Table 4.1 we report in Table 4.3 the overall total values within the entire time period. The Netherlands is again number one, followed by countries such as the United Republic of Tanzania, Venezuela, Greece, Luxembourg, Albania, Uganda, and Austria. The results for the western countries are strongly driven by substantially lower values in the 1980s. At the lower end we observe Turkey, Portugal, Morocco, Ukraine, Russian Federation, Lithuania, Latvia, and Belarus. The former Soviet Union countries again report relatively low values.

Active participation

The previous two questions referred to belonging to an environmental organization. We now focus the analysis and investigate whether individuals were doing unpaid voluntary work. Simply "belonging" to a voluntary organization provides only limited information as to whether or not individuals have contributed actively to such an organization (e.g., by actually getting out and working for them). Thus, we are going to explore the following two questions:

> And for which, if any, are you currently doing unpaid voluntary work?
>
> > Conservation, environmental groups.
> > 0 Not mentioned
> > 1 Belong
>
> Conservation, environmental, animal rights groups.
>
> > 0 0 Not mentioned
> > 1 Belong

A correlation matrix at the macro level covering all the countries available is presented in Table 4.4. It is interesting to observe that there is a significant correlation between unpaid work in the area of conservation, the environment, and animal rights and belonging to these groups. Similarly, there is a correlation between the unpaid work and membership when focusing only on conservation and environment. However, there is no significant correlation when comparing

Table 4.2 Broader participation rate

Country (year)	*Belong %*	*Country (year)*	*Belong %*
Albania (2002)	10.4	Morocco (2001)	0.5
Algeria (2002)	4.4	Netherlands (1981)	11.3
Argentina (1999)	2.2	Netherlands (1999)	43.5
Austria (1999)	9.1	Norway (1982)	4.4
Bangladesh (2002)	20.3	Peru (2001)	3.1
Belgium (1981)	3.2	Philippines (2001)	8.0
Belgium (1999)	11.4	Poland (1999)	1.2
Bosnia and Herzegovina (2001)	1.9	Portugal (1999)	0.5
Bulgaria (1999)	1.3	Puerto Rico (2001)	3.8
Belarus (2000)	0.9	Romania (1999)	1.0
Canada (1982)	4.7	Russian Federation (1999)	0.7
Canada (2000)	9.1	Singapore (2002)	1.0
Chile (2000)	3.0	Slovakia (1999)	2.6
China (2001)	1.2	Vietnam (2001)	7.6
Croatia (1999)	2.1	Slovenia (1999)	3.3
Czech Republic (1999)	6.6	South Africa (2001)	4.1
Denmark (1981)	5.6	Zimbabwe (2001)	2.4
Denmark (1999)	13.1	Spain (1981)	1.3
Estonia (1999)	1.7	Spain (1999)	2.5
Finland (2000)	4.5	Spain (2000)	1.7
France (1981)	1.4	Sweden (1982)	3.4
France (1999)	2.2	Sweden (1999)	11.3
Greece (1999)	11	Turkey (2001)	0.2
Hungary (1999)	1.7	Uganda (2001)	10.1
Iceland (1984)	4.7	Ukraine (1999)	0.6
Iceland (1999)	4.6	Macedonia. Republic of (2001)	4.9
India (2001)	7.0	Great Britain (1981)	4.7
Ireland (1981)	2.8	Great Britain (1999)	1.5
Ireland (1999)	2.6	Tanzania, United Republic Of (2001)	20.1
Italy (1981)	1.8		
Italy (1999)	3.8	United States (1982)	5.4
Japan (2000)	3.2	United States (1999)	15.6
Republic of Korea (2001)	6.2	Venezuela (2000)	11.9
Kyrgyzstan (2003)	2.6	Germany, West (1981)	3.5
Latvia (1999)	0.7	Germany, West (1999)	2.8
Lithuania (1999)	0.7	Germany, East (1999)	2.1
Luxembourg (1999)	10.6	Northern Ireland (1981)	2.7
Malta (1983)	2.1	Northern Ireland (1999)	1.2
Malta (1999)	2.0	Serbia (2001)	0.8
Mexico (2000)	4.5	Montenegro (2001)	4.4

group participation with and without animal rights involvement. Thus, there seems to be some sort of subject pool change once animal rights issues are also considered. It may be that active participation in animal protection requires more specific knowledge and abilities (biology, veterinary, etc.) to take care of the animals. For example, almost all people could help to clean a protected natural area, but not everyone would be able to cure an injured or ill animal.

Table 4.3 Overall ranking

Country (year)	*Belong %*	*Country (year)*	*Belong %*
Netherlands	25.8	Peru	3.1
Bangladesh	20.3	Chile	3.0
Tanzania. United Republic of	20.1	Italy	3.0
Venezuela	11.9	Ireland	2.7
Greece	11.0	Kyrgyzstan	2.6
Luxembourg	10.6	Slovakia	2.6
Albania	10.4	Germany	2.5
Uganda	10.1	Serbia and Montenegro	2.5
Austria	9.1	Zimbabwe	2.4
Denmark	9.1	Argentina	2.2
United States	8.9	Croatia	2.1
Belgium	8.3	Malta	2.1
Philippines	8.0	Bosnia and Herzegovina	1.9
Vietnam	7.6	France	1.9
Sweden	7.4	Estonia	1.7
Canada	7.3	Hungary	1.7
India	7.0	Spain	1.7
Czech Republic	6.6	Northern Ireland	1.6
Republic of Korea	6.2	Bulgaria	1.3
Macedonia. Republic of	4.9	China	1.2
Iceland	4.7	Poland	1.2
Republic of Moldova	4.6	Romania	1.0
Finland	4.5	Singapore	1.0
Mexico	4.5	Belarus	0.9
Algeria	4.4	Latvia	0.7
Norway	4.4	Lithuania	0.7
South Africa	4.1	Russian Federation	0.7
Puerto Rico	3.8	Ukraine	0.6
Germany, West	3.5	Morocco	0.5
Slovenia	3.3	Portugal	0.5
Japan	3.2	Turkey	0.2
Great Britain	3.2		

Let us now focus on the tables that explore the involvement in such organizations through voluntary unpaid work. Rates of participation are always lower than the rates of membership, quite probably because the costs related to volunteerism make it more difficult and uncomfortable to actively participate in environmental organizations. There is a difference between membership that just "talks the talk" and membership that actually "walks the walk." First, in Table 4.5, (as in Table 4.1), we report the percentages of involvement in conservation and environmental groups. Interestingly, Latvia reports the strongest participation rate, with 4.9 percent of individuals engaged in environmental organization. In previous tables Latvia had returned the highest involvement among FSU countries, however in this case, Latvia moved from number 13 to number 1 overall. We also observe in Table 4.5 that countries such as the United States, Canada, Finland, Slovakia, and the Netherlands have high participation rates. Bulgaria is in the top group, and

Table 4.4 Correlation matrix

	Unpaid work in conservation, the environment, ecology, animal rights	*Unpaid work in conservation, the environment, ecology*	*Belong to conservation, the environment, ecology, animal rights*	*Belong to conservation, the environment, ecology*
Unpaid work in conservation, the environment, ecology, animal rights	1			
Unpaid work in conservation, the environment, ecology	0.121 (0.484)	1		
Belong to conservation, the environment, ecology, animal rights	0.469*** (0.000)	0.253 (0.137)	1	
Belong to conservation, the environment, ecology	–0.047 (0.786)	0.405** (0.013)	0.895*** (0.000)	1

Note: Significance levels: ** at the 5% and *** at the 1% levels.

also had relatively high values in Table 4.1 (3.8 percent). Once again, we recognize previous countries such as Portugal, Romania, Malta, and Chile in the bottom group. However, it comes as a surprise that Norway and Denmark report low values, particularly as Denmark was ranked number 2 in Table 4.1. Nevertheless, the overall tendency is similar and statistically significant as reported in Table 4.4.

Table 4.6 reports results in line with Table 4.2, using all the available survey results for the extended question that also refers to participation in animal rights groups, but with the additional investigation of tendencies over time. We observe a strong involvement in unpaid work for China (27.7 percent), United Republic of Tanzania (21.1), Bangladesh (19.4), Greece (9.5) and the Philippines (8.8). Previously active countries such as the Netherlands, Belgium, and Denmark report relatively low values. However, it should be noted that Bangladesh, Tanzania, Greece and the Philippines also returned relatively high values in Table 4.2. At the lower end we again find many Former Soviet Union and Central Eastern European countries such as Ukraine (0.3), Serbia (0.3), Russian Federation (0.4), Lithuania (0.4), Latvia (0.5), and Poland (0.5). In addition Turkey (0.2) and Portugal (0.4) also report relatively low values. In 1981, Denmark originally showed a very low rate of participation (0.2). However, within 18 years, the rate substantially improved to 2.2 percent by the time the later survey was conducted.

Table 4.5 Unpaid work in conservation and environmental groups

Country (year)	*Participation rate %*
Latvia (1990)	4.9
United States (1990)	3.6
Canada (1990)	3.5
Bulgaria (1990)	3.4
Finland (1990)	3.2
Slovakia (1991)	3.0
Netherlands (1990)	2.8
Czech Republic (1991)	2.8
Belgium (1990)	2.6
Sweden (1990)	2.5
Republic of Korea (1990)	2.4
Mexico (1990)	2.4
Iceland (1990)	2.0
Estonia (1990)	2.0
China (1990)	2.0
Germany East (1990)	1.9
Lithuania (1990)	1.8
Great Britain (1990)	1.8
Poland (1990)	1.6
France (1990)	1.5
Slovenia (1992)	1.4
Russian Federation (1990)	1.4
Italy (1990)	1.4
Germany, West (1990)	1.4
Brazil (1991)	1.4
Austria (1990)	1.4
Hungary (1991)	1.3
Japan (1990)	1.2
Spain (1990)	1.0
Northern Ireland (1990)	1.0
Romania (1993)	0.9
Denmark (1990)	0.9
Chile (1990)	0.9
Norway (1990)	0.8
Malta (1991)	0.8
Portugal (1990)	0.7
Ireland (1990)	0.6

This brings us to the investigation of potential time effects. The initial results indicate a general improvement over time for many western countries. The United States and Great Britain report the strongest improvement (from 1.6 to 8.5 percent for the US and 1 to 7.8 for Great Britain). This result paints a different picture of participation in Great Britain to that of Table 4.2. In Belgium, Malta, and Italy the participation also doubled. Similarly, the Netherlands' involvement increased from 1.1 to 2.3 percent (although, this is still relatively low in relation to previous results). For Canada, we observe a strong increase from 1.8 to 4.4 percent. The

Table 4.6 Unpaid work in conservation, environmental, and animal rights groups

Country (year)	*Belong %*	*Country (year)*	*Belong %*
Albania (2002)	7.0	Mexico (2000)	3.0
Algeria (2002)	6.0	Republic of Moldova (2002)	4.2
Argentina (1999)	1.4	Netherlands (1981)	1.1
Austria (1999)	2.1	Netherlands (1999)	2.3
Bangladesh (2002)	**19.4**	Norway (1982)	1.0
Belgium (1981)	1.9	Peru (2001)	2.2
Belgium (1999)	3.5	**Philippines (2001)**	**8.8**
Bosnia and Herzegovina (2001)	1.5	Poland (1999)	0.5
		Portugal (1999)	***0.4***
Bulgaria (1999)	1.2	Puerto Rico (2001)	2.5
Belarus (2000)	2.2	Romania (1999)	0.6
Canada (1982)	1.8	***Russian Federation (1999)***	***0.4***
Canada (2000)	4.4	Singapore (2002)	1.2
Chile (2000)	2.0	Slovakia (1999)	2
China (2001)	**27.7**	Vietnam (2001)	7.9
Croatia (1999)	1.5	Slovenia (1999)	2.9
Czech Republic (1999)	3.2	South Africa (2001)	1.5
Denmark (1981)	***0.2***	Zimbabwe (2001)	1.2
Denmark (1999)	2.2	Spain (1981)	1.4
Estonia (1999)	1.1	Spain (1999)	1.0
Finland (2000)	2.0	Spain (2000)	1.2
France (1981)	0.9	Sweden (1982)	4.2
France (1999)	0.9	Sweden (1999)	3.8
Greece (1999)	**9.5**	***Turkey (2001)***	***0.2***
Hungary (1999)	1.8	Uganda (2001)	8.0
Iceland (1984)	1.7	***Ukraine (1999)***	***0.3***
Iceland (1999)	1.3	Macedonia, Republic of (2001)	3.1
India (2001)	5.3	Great Britain (1981)	1.0
Ireland (1981)	1.4	Great Britain (1999)	7.8
Ireland (1999)	0.9	**Tanzania, United Republic Of (2001)**	**21.1**
Italy (1981)	0.9		
Italy (1999)	1.8	United States (1982)	1.6
Japan (2000)	1.2	United States (1999)	8.5
Republic of Korea (2001)	4.5	Germany, West (1981)	1.0
Kyrgyzstan (2003)	1.2	Germany, West (1999)	1.0
Latvia (1999)	***0.5***	Germany, East (1999)	1.1
Lithuania (1999)	***0.4***	Northern Ireland (1981)	1.2
Luxembourg (1999)	4.3	Northern Ireland (1999)	0.6
Malta (1983)	0.9	***Serbia (2001)***	***0.3***
Malta (1999)	1.8	Montenegro (2001)	2.5

level of activities in France remains stable. Only the results for Iceland, Spain, and Northern Ireland indicate a decrease over time.

Table 4.7 illustrates the ranking situation. At the top we have China, the United Republic of Tanzania, Bangladesh, Greece, the Philippines and Uganda. Western countries are notable by their absence from this top group. On the other hand, the bottom of the ranking is driven by Eastern European countries such Turkey, Ukraine, Russian Federation, Lithuania, Poland, Latvia, and Romania.

Table 4.7 Ranking unpaid work in conservation, environmental, and animal rights groups

Country	*Belong %*	*Country*	*Belong %*
China	27.7	Bosnia and Herzegovina	1.5
Tanzania, United Republic of	21.1	Croatia	1.5
Bangladesh	19.4	Iceland	1.5
Greece	9.5	Malta	1.5
Philippines	8.8	South Africa	1.5
Uganda	8.0	Argentina	1.4
Vietnam	7.9	Italy	1.4
Albania	7.0	Serbia and Montenegro	1.3
Algeria	6.0	Spain	1.3
India	5.3	Bulgaria	1.2
Republic of Korea	4.5	Denmark	1.2
Luxembourg	4.3	Ireland	1.2
Republic of Moldova	4.2	Japan	1.2
Great Britain	4.1	Kyrgyzstan	1.2
Sweden	4.0	Singapore	1.2
United States	3.9	Zimbabwe	1.2
Canada	3.4	Estonia	1.1
Czech Republic	3.2	Germany	1.1
Macedonia, Republic of	3.1	Germany, West	1.0
Mexico	3.0	Norway	1.0
Belgium	2.9	France	0.9
Slovenia	2.9	Northern Ireland	0.7
Puerto Rico	2.5	Romania	0.6
Belarus	2.2	Latvia	0.5
Peru	2.2	Poland	0.5
Austria	2.1	Lithuania	0.4
Chile	2.0	Portugal	0.4
Finland	2.0	Russian Federation	0.4
Slovakia	2.0	Ukraine	0.3
Hungary	1.8	Turkey	0.2
Netherlands	1.7		

Describing relationships

Let us now explore some of the relationships among participation and several explanatory variables. First of all, we are going to focus on socio-demographic features, and then we investigate the links between environmental participation and other kind of volunteering behaviors, environmental attitudes and outcomes.

Socio-demographic differences

In the next couple of tables we are going to explore whether we observe socio-demographic differences in participation trends, using the results based on gender, age, and marital status. Socio-demographic factors hold a prominent place in the literature. As described in Chapter 3, several previous studies have shown the importance of these factors when investigating the preferences for environment protection. Focusing on socio-demographic factors also helps to explore societies' heterogeneity with factors that are also clearly exogenous.

Gender

We first check whether we observe gender differences in rates of participation. We mentioned previously (in Chapter 3) that the literature has found some differences between the attitudes held by men and women and subsequently has found different behaviors towards environmental protection. Some evidence suggests that women are usually more concerned with environmental problems, but it is not totally clear that they are more engaged with environmental organizations than men. Tables 4.8 to 4.11 differentiate between female and male participation rates. Tables 4.8 and 4.9 focus on membership participation; Tables 4.10 and 4.11 on unpaid work. We observe in Table 4.8 that men's participation is higher (average of 4.84 compared to 3.94; statistically significant with a t-value of –5.87). Similarly, Table 4.9 shows also higher values for men (t = 5.48) than for women (t = 4.40). Also here the difference is statistically significant (t = 2.68). These results are also confirmed when focusing in Table 4.10 (t = 3.77) and 4.11 on unpaid work (t = 3.64).

One could argue that these results contradict some previous findings which showed that women are more concerned with environmental issues. It is also at odds with the opportunity-cost argument, which assumes that, on average, women

Table 4.8 Gender and membership in conservation and environment groups

Country (year)	*Female %*	*Male %*	*Country (year)*	*Female %*	*Male %*
Austria (1990)	2.3	3.2	Malta (1991)	0.6	2.4
Belgium (1990)	6.5	8.9	Mexico (1990)	2.4	3.1
Brazil (1991)	2.5	3.2	Netherlands (1990)	23.2	23.3
Bulgaria (1990)	3.3	4.3	Norway (1990)	3.3	4.9
Canada (1990)	6.2	8.8	Poland (1990)	0.8	2.4
Chile (1990)	1.4	1.8	Portugal (1990)	1.0	1.9
China (1990)	0.8	1.2	Romania (1993)	0.5	1.5
Czech Republic (1991)	5.3	8.1	Russian Federation (1990)	1.4	2.0
Denmark (1990)	12.1	13.0	Slovakia (1991)	5.4	6.3
Estonia (1990)	1.8	3.7	Slovenia (1992)	1.3	2.3
Finland (1990)	4.9	5.9	Spain (1990)	0.9	2.0
France (1990)	1.1	3.6	Spain (1990)	0.8	1.9
Hungary (1991)	1.0	1.9	Sweden (1990)	10.0	10.4
Iceland (1990)	5.2	4.5	Switzerland (1989)	10.4	10.6
Ireland (1990)	2.7	1.9	Great Britain (1990)	6.1	5.6
Italy (1990)	2.3	3.6	United States (1990)	7.6	9.4
Japan (1990)	1.1	1.0	Germany, West (1990)	4.0	5.1
Republic of Korea (1990)	2.3	1.7	Germany, East (1990)	3.2	4.2
Latvia (1990)	4.3	4.4	Northern Ireland (1990)	2.8	1.6
Lithuania (1990)	1.1	3.2			

Table 4.9 Gender and membership in conservation, environment, and animal rights groups

Country (year)	*Female* %	*Male* %	*Country (year)*	*Female* %	*Male* %
Albania (2002)	10.1	10.7	Republic of Moldova (2002)	5.3	3.9
Algeria (2002)	3.8	4.9	Morocco (2001)	0.6	0.5
Argentina (1999)	1.5	3.1	Netherlands (1981)	10.4	12.2
Austria (1999)	9.7	8.4	Netherlands (1999)	47.2	39.8
Bangladesh (2002)	15.6	24.1	Norway (1982)	3.8	4.9
Belgium (1981)	2.3	4.2	Peru (2001)	2.3	3.8
Belgium (1999)	11.4	11.4	Philippines (2001)	6.6	9.5
Bosnia and Herzegovina (2001)	1.6	2.3	Poland (1999)	0.5	2.0
			Portugal (1999)	0.2	0.8
Bulgaria (1999)	1.7	0.8	Puerto Rico (2001)	4.1	3.1
Belarus (2000)	0.5	1.3	Romania (1999)	0.2	2.0
Canada (1982)	4.1	5.2	Russian Federation (1999)	0.8	0.6
Canada (2000)	7.5	10.7	Singapore (2002)	1.7	0.2
Chile (2000)	2.6	3.4	Slovakia (1999)	1.9	3.4
China (2001)	0.8	1.6	Viet Nam (2001)	6.1	9.1
Croatia (1999)	0.7	3.7	Slovenia (1999)	1.3	5.7
Czech Republic (1999)	6.1	7.2	South Africa (2001)	3.6	4.4
Denmark (1981)	4.8	6.3	Zimbabwe (2001)	1.3	3.7
Denmark (1999)	16.2	9.9	Spain (1981)	0.6	2.1
Estonia (1999)	1.5	2.0	Spain (1999)	2.6	2.4
Finland (2000)	5.1	3.8	Spain (2000)	1.6	1.8
France (1981)	0.9	1.9	Sweden (1982)	3.5	3.2
France (1999)	2.8	1.6	Sweden (1999)	11.6	10.9
Greece (1999)	12.0	9.7	Uganda (2001)	2.1	19.0
Hungary (1999)	2.1	1.2	Ukraine (1999)	0.2	1.1
Iceland (1984)	5.7	3.7	Macedonia, Republic of (2001)	4.8	4.9
Iceland (1999)	3.3	6.0			
India (2001)	4.5	8.9	Great Britain (1981)	4.7	4.6
Ireland (1981)	2.0	3.5	Great Britain (1999)	1.7	1.3
Ireland (1999)	2.7	2.5	Tanzania. United Republic Of (2001)	20.2	20.2
Italy (1981)	0.9	2.7			
Italy (1999)	4.1	3.4	United States (1982)	4.9	6.0
Japan (2000)	2.9	3.5	United States (1999)	16.9	14.4
Republic of Korea (2001)	4.2	8.1	Venezuela (2000)	8.6	15.2
Kyrgyzstan (2003)	1.9	3.4	Germany, West (1981)	2.0	5.2
Latvia (1999)	0.5	0.9	Germany, West (1999)	2.9	2.6
Lithuania (1999)	0.4	1.0	Germany, East (1999)	1.3	3.2
Luxembourg (1999)	14	7.2	Northern Ireland (1981)	2.9	2.5
Malta (1983)	0.8	3.7	Northern Ireland (1999)	0.9	1.6
Malta (1999)	1.6	2.4	Serbia (2001)	0.2	1.4
Mexico (2000)	3.8	5.3	Montenegro (2001)	3.0	5.9

Table 4.10 Gender and unpaid work in conservation and environment groups

Country (year)	*Female %*	*Male %*	*Country (year)*	*Female %*	*Male %*
Austria (1990)	1.1	1.7	Lithuania (1990)	0.9	2.8
Belgium (1990)	1.3	3.9	Malta (1991)	0.6	1.1
Brazil (1991)	1.1	1.7	Mexico (1990)	2.3	2.4
Bulgaria (1990)	2.2	4.7	Netherlands (1990)	2.9	2.8
Canada (1990)	4.0	3.1	Norway (1990)	0.7	0.9
Chile (1990)	0.4	1.4	Poland (1990)	1.2	2.2
China (1990)	0.5	3.0	Portugal (1990)	0.3	1.1
Czech Republic (1991)	1.4	4.3	Romania (1993)	0.5	1.3
Denmark (1990)	0.8	1.0	Russian Federation (1990)	1.5	1.3
Estonia (1990)	1.3	2.9	Slovakia (1991)	1.7	4.4
Finland (1990)	1.8	4.6	Slovenia (1992)	1.1	1.8
France (1990)	1.3	1.7	Spain (1990)	0.7	1.3
Hungary (1991)	0.8	1.9	Sweden (1990)	1.6	3.3
Iceland (1990)	2.0	2.0	Great Britain (1990)	2.0	1.6
Ireland (1990)	1.0	0.2	United States (1990)	4.4	2.8
Italy (1990)	0.9	2.0	Germany, West (1990)	1.0	1.8
Japan (1990)	1.5	0.8	Germany, East (1990)	1.3	2.6
Republic of Korea (1990)	2.6	2.2	Northern Ireland (1990)	1.7	0.0
Latvia (1990)	4.5	5.5			

have a lower simple cost of time. However, it can be argued that women might be more active in community-based and neighborhood organizations which address local environmental issues, while men are more likely to participate in formal environmental organizations. Our survey question captures more of the latter than the former and for this reason, our results may not seriously conflict with findings to the contrary. Moreover, it should be noted that women may experience higher restrictions on the time available for participation in voluntary organizations, especially when younger, as they may be involved in household activities which are time intensive.

Age

As we explained in the previous chapter, it seems than young people are more concerned with environmental problems. However, there are costs of participation (money, time) that make it difficult to imagine a clear argument on age and environmental actions. Tables 4.12 and 4.13 present the first results focusing on membership participation. Table 4.12 reports that the age group 30–49 is more often involved in conservation and environmental groups. The difference between the youngest and oldest group is statistically significant ($t = 2.47$, youngest group; $t = 3.73$ oldest group). Table 4.13 also reports that the age group 30–49 has the highest mean value (5.34) compared to the age 15–29 group (4.98) and the age 50+ group (5.07). However, the differences are not statistically significant.

Table 4.11 Gender and unpaid work in conservation, environment, and animal rights groups

Country (year)	*Female* %	*Male* %	*Country (year)*	*Female* %	*Male* %
Albania (2002)	5.9	8.1	Mexico (2000)	2.8	3.3
Algeria (2002)	4.9	7.1	Republic of Moldova (2002)	4.3	4.2
Argentina (1999)	0.6	2.4			
Austria (1999)	1.7	2.5	Netherlands (1981)	0.6	1.7
Bangladesh (2002)	12.4	25.1	Netherlands (1999)	2.1	2.6
Belgium (1981)	1.2	2.6	Norway (1982)	0.8	1.1
Belgium (1999)	2.6	4.4	Peru (2001)	1.4	3.0
Bosnia and Herzegovina (2001)	1.4	1.6	Philippines (2001)	6.2	11.5
			Poland (1999)	0.4	0.5
Bulgaria (1999)	1.5	0.9	Portugal (1999)	0.1	0.7
Belarus (2000)	2.0	2.4	Puerto Rico (2001)	2.6	2.4
Canada (1982)	1.7	2.0	Romania (1999)	0.0	1.3
Canada (2000)	3.2	5.7	Russian Federation (1999)	0.5	0.3
Chile (2000)	1.9	2.2	Singapore (2002)	1.8	0.7
China (2001)	26.5	28.9	Slovakia (1999)	1.3	2.8
Croatia (1999)	0.3	2.7	Vietnam (2001)	5.7	10.2
Czech Republic (1999)	2.4	4.2	Slovenia (1999)	1.3	4.8
Denmark (1981)	0.2	0.3	South Africa (2001)	1.2	1.7
Denmark (1999)	1.3	3.2	Zimbabwe (2001)	0.3	2.3
Estonia (1999)	0.3	2.1	Spain (1981)	1.2	1.7
Finland (2000)	2.2	1.7	Spain (1999)	1.0	1.0
France (1981)	0.5	1.5	Spain (2000)	1.2	1.2
France (1999)	1.4	0.5	Sweden (1982)	3.3	5.0
Greece (1999)	10.1	8.6	Sweden (1999)	4.2	3.4
Hungary (1999)	1.7	2.1	Turkey (2001)	0.0	0.3
Iceland (1984)	3.0	0.5	Uganda (2001)	1.1	15.6
Iceland (1999)	1.4	1.2	Ukraine (1999)	0.1	0.4
India (2001)	3.6	6.7	Macedonia, Republic of (2001)	3.4	2.8
Ireland (1981)	1.1	1.7			
Ireland (1999)	1.1	0.6	Great Britain (1981)	1.2	0.8
Italy (1981)	0.7	1.2	Great Britain (1999)	5.6	10.2
Italy (1999)	1.5	2.0	Tanzania, United Republic Of (2001)	21.6	20.7
Japan (2000)	1.0	1.6			
Republic of Korea (2001)	3.2	5.8	United States (1982)	1.3	1.9
			United States (1999)	10.0	6.9
Kyrgyzstan (2003)	0.9	1.7	Germany, West (1981)	0.3	1.9
Latvia (1999)	0.7	0.2	Germany, West (1999)	0.9	1.2
Lithuania (1999)	0.5	0.3	Germany, East (1999)	0.6	1.8
Luxembourg (1999)	4.9	3.7	Northern Ireland (1981)	1.8	0.6
Malta (1983)	0.8	0.9	Northern Ireland (1999)	0.6	0.6
Malta (1999)	1.7	1.8	Serbia (2001)	0.0	0.7
			Montenegro (2001)	2.1	2.9

Table 4.12 Age difference and membership in conservation and environment groups

Country (year)	*15–29*	*30–49*	*50 and over*	*Country (year)*	*15–29*	*30–49*	*50 and over*
Austria (1990)	2.7	2.5	2.9	Malta (1991)	4.2	1.4	0.0
Belgium (1990)	7.3	10.1	5.6	Mexico (1990)	2.5	3.0	3.1
Brazil (1991)	2.6	4.4	0.4	Netherlands (1990)	19.1	29.5	19.7
Bulgaria (1990)	2.7	5.2	2.7	Norway (1990)	3.9	5.6	2.5
Canada (1990)	7.1	9.0	6.1	Poland (1990)	1.6	2.0	1.0
Chile (1990)	2.2	1.5	0.8	Portugal (1990)	2.6	1.1	0.5
China (1990)	1.0	1.1	0.8	Romania (1993)	1.1	1.0	0.9
Czech Republic (1991)	4.8	6.6	7.9	Russian Federation (1990)	0.9	2.6	1.2
Denmark (1990)	9.3	15.3	11.8	Slovakia (1991)	4.9	6.2	6.1
Estonia (1990)	2.3	3.3	2.1	Slovenia (1992)	1.6	1.7	1.9
Finland (1990)	2.6	5.6	7.6	Spain (1990)	1.7	1.6	1.0
France (1990)	1.4	1.9	3.3	Spain (1990)	1.7	2.0	0.5
Hungary (1991)	1.2	1.3	1.6	Sweden (1990)	7.9	15.0	7.5
Iceland (1990)	4.6	6.2	2.8	Switzerland (1989)	9.7	11.6	9.9
Ireland (1990)	2.4	2.4	2.1	Great Britain (1990)	1.8	8.0	6.5
Italy (1990)	5.5	3.3	1.0	United States (1990)	7.5	11.4	6.2
Japan (1990)	0.5	1.3	1.3	Germany, West (1990)	7.5	5.2	2.3
Republic of Korea (1990)	1.2	2.0	3.4	Germany, East (1990)	6.2	3.8	2.0
Latvia (1990)	5.5	3.5	4.6	Northern Ireland (1990)	3.9	0.8	2.7
Lithuania (1990)	2.7	2.6	1.1				

Inspecting the results for unpaid work reveals a similar picture in Table 4.14. The age group 30–49 has the highest involvement (2.09 percent), followed by the age group 15–29 (1.79) and the oldest group (1.77). However, we do not observe significant differences between the groups. On the other hand, Table 4.15 shows that the youngest group has the strongest participation (3.35 percent), followed by the group 30–49 (3.19) and the group 50+ (3.07). Nevertheless, again the differences are not statistically significant. In general, the results support the notion that older people are less willing to contribute to the environment through involvement in environmental organizations (Lubell 2002). However, we do not observe a strictly negative correlation. Rather, it is a non-linear relationship with a peak at the age 30–49, results that are in line with some empirical studies (see, e.g., Martinez and McMullin 2004).

Marital status

Now, we turn our attention to the relationship between environmental participation and marital status, since it is commonly included as a control variable in empirical work. Frequent social involvement and higher environmental norms could lead to higher levels of participation. However, married people may not have too much free time, especially if they have children. Hence, we cannot predict the overall effect. Tables 4.16 and 4.17 may give us some clues in order to clarify this issue.

Table 4.13 Age difference and membership in conservation and environment and animal rights groups

Country (year)	*15–29*	*30–49*	*50 and over*
Albania (2002)	9.3	10	11.9
Algeria (2002)	4.0	6.1	1.9
Argentina (1999)	2.8	2.2	1.7
Austria (1999)	9.8	9.4	8.5
Bangladesh (2002)	19.1	20.2	25.4
Belgium (1981)	3.1	4.1	2.5
Belgium (1999)	12.5	10.5	11.7
Bosnia and Herzegovina (2001)	2.2	2.1	1.4
Bulgaria (1999)	2.5	1.7	0.4
Belarus (2000)	2.0	0.8	0.3
Canada (1982)	4.1	5.6	4.2
Canada (2000)	7.8	8.3	10.7
Chile (2000)	3.2	2.8	3.0
China (2001)	2.1	1.2	0.4
Croatia (1999)	3.6	2.2	1.0
Czech Republic (1999)	7.1	5.6	7.3
Denmark (1981)	5.1	6.4	5.2
Denmark (1999)	8.6	11.8	16.8
Estonia (1999)	1.1	1.8	1.9
Finland (2000)	4.5	6.1	3.1
France (1981)	1.9	1.3	1.2
France (1999)	1.4	1.6	3.3
Greece (1999)	15	7.8	8.2
Hungary (1999)	1.7	1.4	1.9
Iceland (1984)	3.4	6.6	3.2
Iceland (1999)	1.2	6.9	4.6
India (2001)	7.9	6.5	7.1
Ireland (1981)	2.0	3.4	3.0
Ireland (1999)	3	1.7	2.9
Italy (1981)	1.3	3.0	1.0
Italy (1999)	4.9	4.3	2.7
Japan (2000)	0.8	2.7	4.5
Republic of Korea (2001)	3.8	6.8	7.5
Kyrgyzstan (2003)	2.8	2.7	1.9
Latvia (1999)	0.5	0.3	1.1
Lithuania (1999)	1.7	0.4	0.2
Luxembourg (1999)	9.4	12.1	9.9
Malta (1983)	2.8	2.3	1.4
Malta (1999)	2.7	2.0	1.5
Mexico (2000)	4.1	4.5	5.0
Republic of Moldova (2002)	5.1	5.1	3.7
Morocco (2001)	0.4	0.4	1.0
Netherlands (1981)	11.9	10.4	12.0
Netherlands (1999)	27.7	46.9	48.5
Norway (1982)	2.8	5.1	4.7
Peru (2001)	2.6	2.5	5.4
Philippines (2001)	6.1	7.7	11.4
Poland (1999)	1.2	1.2	1.3
Portugal (1999)	0.4	0.3	0.7
Puerto Rico (2001)	6.2	4.8	1.9
Romania (1999)	0.8	1.4	0.8
Russian Federation (1999)	0.6	0.7	0.7
Singapore (2002)	1.2	1.0	0.1
Slovakia (1999)	3.0	2.3	2.7
Vietnam (2001)	8.3	8.5	5.6
Slovenia (1999)	3.1	3.6	3.1
South Africa (2001)	3.4	4.8	3.4
Zimbabwe (2001)	2.8	1.3	3.5
Spain (1981)	2.9	0.7	0.8
Spain (1999)	3.7	3.5	1.0
Spain (2000)	4.0	1.1	0.6
Sweden (1982)	2.6	4.6	2.4
Sweden (1999)	10.7	12.6	10.4
Uganda (2001)	12.6	6.7	11.4
Ukraine (1999)	0.0	0.9	0.7
Macedonia, Republic of (2001)	5.3	6.0	3.0
Great Britain (1981)	3.8	7.1	3.4
Great Britain (1999)	2.4	0.9	1.1
Tanzania. United Republic Of (2001)	24.1	19.1	14.3
United States (1982)	4.2	7.0	5.1
United States (1999)	12.9	14.8	19.2
Venezuela (2000)	12.7	12.6	9.0
Germany, West (1981)	2.1	4.1	3.8
Germany, West (1999)	1.8	4.2	1.9
Germany, East (1999)	4.2	0.9	2.6
Northern Ireland (1981)	3	1.8	3.3
Northern Ireland (1999)	0.4	2.0	1.1
Serbia (2001)	1.3	0.6	0.6
Montenegro (2001)	4.4	5.3	3.3

Table 4.14 Age and unpaid voluntary work in conservation and environment

Country (year)	*15–29*	*30–49*	*50 and over*	*Country (year)*	*15–29*	*30–49*	*50 and over*
Austria (1990)	1.4	1.5	1.2	Lithuania (1990)	2.3	2	1.1
Belgium (1990)	2.2	3.9	1.6	Malta (1991)	1	1.4	0
Brazil (1991)	1.8	1.6	0.4	Mexico (1990)	2.4	2.2	2.7
Bulgaria (1990)	3.1	5.2	1.4	Netherlands (1990)	0.4	3.4	4.1
Canada (1990)	3.7	3.2	3.7	Norway (1990)	0	1.2	0.9
Chile (1990)	0.9	1	0.5	Poland (1990)	1.6	1.5	1.8
China (1990)	2.3	1.8	2	Portugal (1990)	1.6	0.6	0
Czech Republic (1991)	2.1	3.2	2.7	Romania (1993)	1.1	1	0.7
Denmark (1990)	0.7	1	0.8	Russian Federation (1990)	0.7	2.2	1
Estonia (1990)	2.3	2.1	1.4	Slovakia (1991)	3.3	3.6	2.1
Finland (1990)	1.7	2.9	5.3	Slovenia (1992)	0.8	1.7	1.6
France (1990)	1.1	1.7	1.7	Spain (1990)	1.6	1.1	0.5
Hungary (1991)	0.6	1.3	1.6	Sweden (1990)	3.2	2.2	1.5
Iceland (1990)	1.4	2.3	2.3	Great Britain (1990)	0.1	2.9	1.8
Ireland (1990)	0.8	1.1	0	United States (1990)	2.4	4.9	2.6
Italy (1990)	3.4	1.2	0.4	Germany, West (1990)	2.6	1.5	0.6
Japan (1990)	0	1.5	1.6	Germany, East (1990)	3.2	1.8	1.2
Republic of Korea (1990)	1	3	3.4	Northern Ireland (1990)	1.3	0	1.8
Latvia (1990)	6.3	2.8	7.4				

Table 4.16 reports the earlier results. The differences between the two groups are not statistically significant. The mean values are very close (4.43 for married and 4.40 for single/never married). However, country values are very heterogeneous; for example, in Denmark, the Netherlands, United States, Great Britain, and Finland married people are actively involved in environmental organizations. On the other hand, single/never married respondents are more frequently members of such organizations in Canada, Latvia, Lithuania, Malta, or Germany. Table 4.17 shows a similar picture. The difference is not statistically significant and single/never married people report an even higher level of participation (5.43 versus 5.26 percent). Again, we observe significant differences between countries. For example, in Canada (2000), Denmark (1999), Republic of Korea, the Netherlands (1999), Norway, Philippines, Sweden (1999), Great Britain (1981), and United States (1999) married people are more actively involved. On other hand, in countries such as Bulgaria, China, Croatia, Czech Republic, Greece, India, Malta (1983), Spain, Uganda, United Republic of Tanzania, Venezuela, and Northern Ireland (1981) singles/never married report a more intensive level of participation. Interestingly, there are more western countries in the former group and more developing/transition countries in the latter one. It is also interesting to note that in countries where two observations are available, there is the tendency for participation rates of singles/never married people to decrease in relation to the participation rates of married couples. It seems that the opportunity costs of participation have changed over time.

Table 4.15 Age and unpaid voluntary work in conservation, environment, and animal rights groups

Country (year)	*15–29*	*30–49*	*50 and over*	*Country (year)*	*15–29*	*30–49*	*50 and over*
Albania (2002)	5	8	7.1	Mexico (2000)	3.3	3.1	2.7
Algeria (2002)	7.7	5.9	2.7	Republic of Moldova (2002)	5.9	4	3.1
Argentina (1999)	2.2	1.4	0.7				
Austria (1999)	2.1	2.4	1.7	Netherlands (1981)	1.3	1.1	1.1
Bangladesh (2002)	18.3	19.2	25.4	Netherlands (1999)	1.6	2.6	2.6
Belgium (1981)	1.8	1.4	2.3	Norway (1982)	0.8	1.3	0.7
Belgium (1999)	5.6	2.7	3.3	Peru (2001)	1.3	2.4	3.8
Bosnia and Herzegovina (2001)	1.1	1.9	1.4	Philippines (2001)	5.9	9.1	12.4
				Poland (1999)	0	0.9	0.2
Bulgaria (1999)	2.5	0.9	0.8	Portugal (1999)	0.2	0.2	0.7
Belarus (2000)	1.6	2.3	2.5	Puerto Rico (2001)	5.5	2.8	0.9
Canada (1982)	1.4	2.2	2.1	Romania (1999)	0	0.7	0.8
Canada (2000)	3.5	4.6	4.8	Russian Federation (1999)	0.4	0.3	0.5
Chile (2000)	2.2	2.2	1.6	Singapore (2002)	1.7	1.1	0
China (2001)	31.4	28.1	23.5	Slovakia (1999)	3.1	1.8	1.5
Croatia (1999)	1.4	2.1	0.8	Vietnam (2001)	10.1	7.9	6.3
Czech Republic (1999)	4.8	2.9	2.6	Slovenia (1999)	1.9	3.3	3.1
				South Africa (2001)	2	0.9	1.9
Denmark (1981)	0.5	0.3	0	Zimbabwe (2001)	1.4	0.5	2.1
Denmark (1999)	1.9	2.2	2.5	Spain (1981)	3.1	1.2	0.5
Estonia (1999)	1.5	0.6	1.4	Spain (1999)	1.3	1.5	0.4
Finland (2000)	3.1	3	0.6	Spain (2000)	2.6	0.7	0.8
France (1981)	1.1	0.9	0.9	Sweden (1982)	1.6	6.2	3.5
France (1999)	0.3	0.7	1.4	Sweden (1999)	2.6	3	5.3
Greece (1999)	12.5	8.2	5.2	Turkey (2001)	0.2	0.2	0
Hungary (1999)	1.2	2.1	2	Uganda (2001)	10.4	4.8	9.1
Iceland (1984)	1	1.8	2.3	Ukraine (1999)	0	0.4	0.2
Iceland (1999)	0.4	2.5	0.7	Macedonia, Republic of (2001)	3.6	3.3	2.4
India (2001)	6.3	4.6	5.9				
Ireland (1981)	1.1	1.6	1.6	Great Britain (1981)	0.8	1.7	0.5
Ireland (1999)	0.4	0.5	1.5	Great Britain (1999)	3.7	11.7	6.7
Italy (1981)	0.6	1.5	0.7	Tanzania, United Republic of (2001)	25.6	20.2	16.1
Italy (1999)	2.9	1.6	1.2				
Japan (2000)	0.4	0.8	2	United States (1982)	0.9	2	1.9
Republic of Korea (2001)	4.1	3.6	7.1	United States (1999)	7.8	7.4	10.6
				Germany, West (1981)	1.1	1.4	0.6
Kyrgyzstan (2003)	1	1.1	1.9	Germany, West (1999)	0.7	1.5	0.6
Latvia (1999)	0	0.5	0.7	Germany, East (1999)	2.8	0.5	1.1
Lithuania (1999)	1	0.3	0.2	Northern Ireland (1981)	1	0	2.5
Luxembourg (1999)	4.7	4.2	4.1	Northern Ireland (1999)	0	0.8	0.8
Malta (1983)	0.7	1.2	0.7	Serbia (2001)	0.4	0.4	0.2
Malta (1999)	2.3	1.2	1.9	Montenegro (2001)	3.2	2.7	1.5

Table 4.16 Marital status and conservation and environment groups

Country (year)	*Married %*	*Single/ never married %*	*Country (year)*	*Married %*	*Single/ never married %*
Austria (1990)	3.3	2.2	Malta (1991)	0.4	5.4
Belgium (1990)	7.8	8.2	Mexico (1990)	3.7	2.0
Brazil (1991)	2.4	2.9	Netherlands (1990)	24.0	18.4
Bulgaria (1990)	4.4	2.2	Norway (1990)	4.0	5.6
Canada (1990)	7.4	9.4	Poland (1990)	1.6	1.5
Chile (1990)	1.1	2.1	Portugal (1990)	1.3	2.4
China (1990)	0.6	2.1	Romania (1993)	0.9	1.6
Czech Republic (1991)	7.0	6.6	Russian Federation (1990)	2.0	2.5
Denmark (1990)	14.2	9.7	Slovakia (1991)	6.4	4.2
Estonia (1990)	3.0	2.2	Slovenia (1992)	1.6	1.1
Finland (1990)	5.9	2.9	Spain (1990)	1.0	2.6
France (1990)	2.7	1.4	Spain (1990)	1.3	1.4
Hungary (1991)	1.3	1.9	Sweden (1990)	10.6	9.9
Iceland (1990)	5.0	5.0	Switzerland (1989)	10.7	10.2
Ireland (1990)	2.1	3.0	Great Britain (1990)	7.4	3.5
Italy (1990)	2.0	5.2	United States (1990)	8.9	6.1
Japan (1990)	1.3	0.5	Germany, West (1990)	3.3	7.2
Republic of Korea (1990)	2.4	1.5	Germany, East (1990)	3.1	4.0
Latvia (1990)	3.8	5.6	Northern Ireland (1990)	1.5	4.3
Lithuania (1990)	1.5	4.6			

Next we are going to explore unpaid work in such organizations. Tables 4.18 and 4.19 present the results. In Table 4.18 we do not observe statistically significant differences and the mean values are also higher in the single/never married group (with values of 2.12 compared to 1.89). In Table 4.19 we do observe a statistically significant difference between these groups ($t = 2.83$) with higher values for the singles/never married people (3.80 versus 3.09). We again observe notable differences among countries.

Correlation with other voluntary organizations

In a next step we are going to expand our analysis slightly, looking at the correlations between participation in environmental organizations and involvement in other organizations. One would predict that societies with a higher rate of environmental participation may also demonstrate higher participation in other areas. Referring back to our discussion on the network dimension of social capital in Chapter 2, we could characterize countries in which there is a high level of participation in many kinds of voluntary organizations as societies in which there is a high level of social capital. This relationship is also linked to the discussion from Chapter 3 in which we explained some of reasons why people are more likely to

Table 4.17 Marital status and conservation, environment, and animal rights groups

Country (year)	*Married %*	*Single/ never married %*	*Country (year)*	*Married %*	*Single/ never married %*
Albania (2002)	11.2	9.5	Republic of Moldova (2002)	4.8	5.0
Algeria (2002)	3.6	4.5	Morocco (2001)	0.6	0.3
Argentina (1999)	2.2	2.0	Netherlands (1981)	12.6	10.5
Austria (1999)	9.8	9.4	Netherlands (1999)	47.0	38.3
Bangladesh (2002)	20.2	22.6	Norway (1982)	5.4	1.8
Belgium (1981)	3.5	3.3	Peru (2001)	4.2	2.5
Belgium (1999)	12.1	12.2	Philippines (2001)	9.1	4.3
Bosnia and Herzegovina (2001)	2.2	1.9	Poland (1999)	0.9	1.8
Bulgaria (1999)	1.1	2.4	Portugal (1999)	0.5	0.5
Belarus (2000)	0.8	1.6	Puerto Rico (2001)	4.5	5.0
Canada (1982)	4.4	4.6	Romania (1999)	1.2	1.0
Canada (2000)	10.5	5.8	Russian Federation (1999)	0.8	0.8
Chile (2000)	3.0	3.5	Singapore (2002)	0.9	1.1
China (2001)	0.9	4.3	Slovakia (1999)	2.6	3.4
Croatia (1999)	1.7	3.1	Vietnam (2001)	6.4	7.2
Czech Republic (1999)	6.7	7.9	Slovenia (1999)	3.9	3.2
Denmark (1981)	6.4	5.3	South Africa (2001)	5.5	4.1
Denmark (1999)	15.1	9.7	Zimbabwe (2001)	2.5	3.3
Estonia (1999)	2.0	1.0	Spain (1981)	1.1	2.5
Finland (2000)	5.0	6.3	Spain (1999)	1.8	4.2
France (1981)	1.6	1.5	Spain (2000)	0.7	4.2
France (1999)	2.3	2.3	Sweden (1982)	3.2	4.5
Greece (1999)	6.8	14.3	Sweden (1999)	12.9	9.0
Hungary (1999)	1.9	1.8	Uganda (2001)	8.6	15.4
Iceland (1984)	5.2	4.7	Ukraine (1999)	0.8	0.0
Iceland (1999)	5.9	4.3	Macedonia. Republic of (2001)	4.8	5.5
India (2001)	5.9	9.8			
Ireland (1981)	3.0	2.3	Great Britain (1981)	5.1	3.6
Ireland (1999)	2.0	3.9	Great Britain (1999)	1.3	2.2
Italy (1981)	1.6	1.9	Tanzania, United Republic Of (2001)	17.8	23.1
Italy (1999)	3.2	5.7			
Japan (2000)	3.1	1.7	United States (1982)	5.6	5.1
Republic of Korea (2001)	6.9	4.3	United States (1999)	15.6	12.2
			Venezuela (2000)	11.6	16.3
Kyrgyzstan (2003)	2.4	2.7	Germany, West (1981)	3.5	2.2
Latvia (1999)	0.8	0.6	Germany, West (1999)	3.2	1.2
Lithuania (1999)	0.3	2.6	Germany, East (1999)	1.6	3.9
Luxembourg (1999)	11.0	10.7	Northern Ireland (1981)	1.8	6.5
Malta (1983)	1.7	3.2	Northern Ireland (1999)	1.5	0.5
Malta (1999)	2.1	2.3	Serbia (2001)	0.7	1.3
Mexico (2000)	4.5	5.4	Montenegro (2001)	4.5	4.7

Table 4.18 **Marital status and unpaid work in conservation and environment groups**

Country (year)	*Married %*	*Single/ never married %*	*Country (year)*	*Married %*	*Single/ never married %*
Austria (1990)	1.6	1.0	Lithuania (1990)	1.5	2.9
Belgium (1990)	2.7	3.0	Malta (1991)	0.4	2.5
Brazil (1991)	1.1	2.0	Mexico (1990)	2.7	2.3
Bulgaria (1990)	3.7	3.0	Netherlands (1990)	3.2	2.1
Canada (1990)	3.3	4.8	Norway (1990)	0.9	1.3
Chile (1990)	0.7	1.1	Poland (1990)	1.8	2.2
China (1990)	1.8	2.6	Portugal (1990)	0.3	1.8
Czech Republic (1991)	3.2	1.8	Romania (1993)	0.8	1.6
Denmark (1990)	0.4	1.9	Russian Federation (1990)	1.8	1.2
Estonia (1990)	2.1	2.7	Slovakia (1991)	3.3	3.5
Finland (1990)	3.2	1.4	Slovenia (1992)	1.6	1.1
France (1990)	1.8	1.4	Spain (1990)	0.6	1.8
Hungary (1991)	1.3	0.9	Sweden (1990)	1.5	4.7
Iceland (1990)	2.4	1.4	Great Britain (1990)	2.1	1.4
Ireland (1990)	0.7	0.7	United States (1990)	3.5	2.5
Italy (1990)	0.8	3.1	Germany, West (1990)	1.2	2.1
Japan (1990)	1.4	0.5	Germany, East (1990)	1.7	2.5
Republic of Korea (1990)	3.4	0.8	Northern Ireland (1990)	1.0	1.4
Latvia (1990)	4.6	5.6			

participate (higher level of personal efficacy and networks), and why people may be unable to participate (lack of capacity). Individuals who are already involved in other organizations may acquire networks, develop capacities and improve personal efficacy, increasing the likelihood that they are involved in environmental organizations (or vice versa). The World Values Survey provides a great opportunity to explore this question in detail while at the same time allowing us to cover a broad set of different activities. Table 4.20 covers the results of belonging to a particular voluntary organization. We observe a strong correlation between environmental participation and participation in human rights, peace movement organizations, professional organizations, consumer groups, voluntary organization focusing on education, arts, music or cultural activities and sports or recreation, and also organizations providing social welfare service for elderly. On the other hand we observe a lower correlation with participation in political parties, local political actions, labor unions, religious, youth and women's groups. Nevertheless, in 29 out of 30 cases the correlation is statistically significant.

Table 4.21 indicates similar tendencies towards participation in many kinds of voluntary organizations, although the coefficients are not statistically significant in many cases (24 out of 30 cases). However, once we include animal rights groups, the correlations tend to be much stronger. The first column of Table 4.21 reports

Table 4.19 Marital status and unpaid work in conservation, environment, and animal rights groups

Country (year)	*Married %*	*Single/ never married %*	*Country (year)*	*Married %*	*Single/ never married %*
Albania (2002)	7.8	5.7	Mexico (2000)	3.0	4.5
Algeria (2002)	3.9	7.7	Republic of Moldova (2002)	4.3	5.3
Argentina (1999)	1.1	2.4			
Austria (1999)	2.3	2.2	Netherlands (1981)	1.5	1.0
Bangladesh (2002)	18.8	23.6	Netherlands (1999)	2.5	1.8
Belgium (1981)	1.8	2.2	Norway (1982)	1.1	0.6
Belgium (1999)	3.5	5.0	Peru (2001)	3.6	1.3
Bosnia and Herzegovina (2001)	1.6	1.3	Philippines (2001)	9.6	5.3
			Poland (1999)	0.3	0.7
Bulgaria (1999)	0.7	2.7	Portugal (1999)	0.5	0.3
Belarus (2000)	1.9	2.6	Puerto Rico (2001)	2.7	5.8
Canada (1982)	1.4	2.4	Romania (1999)	0.8	0.0
Canada (2000)	5.5	2.9	Russian Federation (1999)	0.3	0.6
Chile (2000)	2.1	2.7			
China (2001)	27	37.6	Singapore (2002)	0.8	1.6
Croatia (1999)	1.6	1.6	Slovakia (1999)	1.7	3.4
Czech Republic (1999)	2.9	5.2	Vietnam (2001)	6.4	9.9
			Slovenia (1999)	3.6	2.5
Denmark (1981)	0.0	0.9	South Africa (2001)	1.5	1.9
Denmark (1999)	2.2	2.3	Zimbabwe (2001)	1.3	1.8
Estonia (1999)	1.3	1.3	Spain (1981)	1.0	2.9
Finland (2000)	1.8	3.8	Spain (1999)	0.8	1.4
France (1981)	1.1	1.3	Spain (2000)	0.7	2.6
France (1999)	1.0	0.4	Sweden (1982)	5.6	1.5
Greece (1999)	7.8	11.1	Sweden (1999)	4.0	3.1
Hungary (1999)	2.4	0.9	Turkey (2001)	0.2	0.0
Iceland (1984)	1.7	3.1	Uganda (2001)	6.3	13.2
Iceland (1999)	1.7	0.9	Ukraine (1999)	0.3	0.0
India (2001)	4.5	10.9	Macedonia, Republic of (2001)	2.8	3.6
Ireland (1981)	1.4	1.2			
Ireland (1999)	0.5	0.8	Great Britain (1981)	1.1	0.6
Italy (1981)	0.8	0.9	Great Britain (1999)	8.3	9.2
Italy (1999)	1.5	2.8	Tanzania, United Republic Of (2001)	19.3	24.8
Japan (2000)	1.3	0.8			
Republic of Korea (2001)	4.6	4.3	United States (1982)	1.6	1.5
			United States (1999)	8.7	7.7
Kyrgyzstan (2003)	1.0	2.3	Germany, West (1981)	1.3	0.4
Latvia (1999)	0.4	0.0	Germany, West (1999)	1.1	0.3
Lithuania (1999)	0.2	1.7	Germany, East (1999)	0.5	2.5
Luxembourg (1999)	4.0	4.6	Northern Ireland (1981)	0.9	2.7
			Northern Ireland (1999)	0.6	0.2
Malta (1983)	0.7	1.3	Serbia (2001)	0.4	0.4
Malta (1999)	1.8	2.3	Montenegro (2001)	2.8	2.1

Table 4.20 Correlations regarding participating in different organizations

	Belong to conservation, the environment, groups	*Belong to conservation, the environment, animal rights groups*
Belong to social welfare service for elderly group	0.624*** 0.000	0.691*** 0.000
Belong to religious organization group	0.357** 0.028	0.459*** 0.000
Belong to education, arts, music orcultural activities	0.758*** 0.000	0.874*** 0.000
Belong to labour unions	0.321** 0.049	0.084 0.514
Belong to political parties	0.279* 0.090	0.508*** 0.000
Belong to local political actions	0.389** 0.016	0.645*** 0.000
Belong to human rights groups	0.794*** 0.000	0.873*** 0.000
Belong to professional associations	0.572*** 0.000	0.714*** 0.000
Belong to youth work groups	0.436*** 0.006	0.593*** 0.000
Belong to sports or recreation groups	0.771*** 0.000	0.699*** 0.000
Belong to women's group	0.418** 0.010	0.574*** 0.000
Belong to peace movement groups	0.660*** 0.000	0.603*** 0.000
Belong to organization concernedwith health	0.619*** 0.000	0.817*** 0.000
Belong to consumer groups	0.885*** 0.000	0.917*** 0.000
Belong to other groups	0.567*** 0.000	0.410*** 0.001

Note: Significance levels: * $0.05 < p < 0.10$, ** $0.01 < p < 0.05$, *** $p < 0.01$.

Table 4.21 Correlations among participating in different organizations

	Unpaid work conservation, the environment, ecology groups	*Unpaid work conservation, the environment, ecology, animal rights groups*
Unpaid social service welfare servicefor elderly	0.152 0.369	0.849*** 0.000
Unpaid work religious organization	0.228 0.174	0.452*** 0.000
Unpaid work education, arts, music, orcultural activities	0.449*** 0.005	0.773*** 0.000
Unpaid work labor unions	0.277* 0.098	0.560*** 0.000
Unpaid work political parties	0.220 0.190	0.814*** 0.000
Unpaid work local political actions	0.410** 0.012	0.742*** 0.000
Unpaid work human rights groups	0.477*** 0.003	0.712*** 0.000
Unpaid work professional associations	0.365** 0.026	0.807*** 0.000
Unpaid work youth work	0.291* 0.081	0.695*** 0.000
Unpaid work sports or recreation	0.384** 0.019	0.598*** 0.000
Unpaid work women's group	0.376** 0.022	0.680*** 0.000
Unpaid work peace movement	0.139 0.411	0.717*** 0.000
Unpaid work organization concernedwith health	0.331** 0.045	0.852*** 0.000
Unpaid work consumer groups	0.462* 0.083	0.401 0.124
Unpaid work other groups	0.401** 0.014	-0.003 0.986

Note: Significance levels: * $0.05 < p < 0.10$, ** $0.01 < p < 0.05$, *** $p < 0.01$.

a relatively strong correlation between active participation in environmental organizations and the variables on unpaid work in human rights groups, education, arts, music or cultural activities, local political actions, and consumer groups. The second column reports strong findings for unpaid work in organizations concerned with health, the peace movement, social welfare service for elderly, professional associations, political parties, and local political actions. Thus, the connection to political organizations is much stronger when dealing with unpaid work.

Correlation with pro-environmental attitudes

As discussed in the previous chapter, there is a wide range of studies that have examined individuals' environmental preferences. Interest in environmental attitudes began in the early 1970s (Bord and O'Connor 1997). Preferences for protecting environmental goods have been a controversial issue in the last few years. It is a promising line of inquiry to consider empirical evidence on citizens' environmental preferences and search for factors that shape those preferences. After all, true collective action to solve a public good problem or social dilemma is the result of a group of individuals acting on their shared preferences and intentions. While we might hope that governments will take leadership in such circumstances, they will be hesitant unless they are certain that the majority of voters will support the action, and any democratically elected government always has one eye on re-election. Corporations will not take action that may reduce profits, even if it is the "right" thing to do, and while business has been regarded as "morally neutral" for a long time, that situation that is now changing. Of course, business will take the actions that are legislated by governments, but the problem remains that governments are usually reactive and not proactive (see discussion in Chapter 1). The majority of studies analyzing environmental preferences have focused on specific and limited environmental goods or areas (Whitehead 1991, Stevens *et al.* 1994, Danielson *et al.* 1995, Cameron and Englin 1997, Blomquist and Whitehead 1998, Carlsson and Johansson-Stenman 2000, Popp 2001, Dupont 2004, Bulte *et al.* 2005). It is difficult to find contributions to the literature that relate to a country or a group of countries or that have considered the perspective on environmental damage in general (Engel and Pötschke 1998, Witzke and Urfei 2001, Israel and Levinson 2004).

The disadvantage of some existing studies is an excessive simplification, because individuals are asked about the environment in general. As Witzke and Urfei (2001) pointed out, this is likely to cause a downward bias in reported environmental preferences, because people did not know what they were agreeing to pay for. On the other hand, asking the questions from a general perspective may avoid embedding effects which are usually linked to specific environmental commodities (Diamond and Hausman, 1994). As we saw in the previous chapter, a few studies have considered the participation in voluntary environmental organizations (see, among others, Whitehead 1991, Blomquist and Whitehead 1998, Carlsson and Johansson-Stenman 2000, Lubell 2002, Cappellari and Turati 2004, Martinez and McMullin 2004, Torgler and García-Valiñas 2007). Usually, individuals who participate actively in environmental institutions have higher preferences for environmental protection. The results are mainly based on micro data sets. In this section we are going to take a first pass analysis of the correlation between environmental attitudes and environmental participation. We will make a more detailed analysis of this issue in the next chapters, by means of a micro and macro economic approach.

Not surprisingly, there are (at least) two ways we could argue for the expected direction of the correlation between environmental attitudes and environmental participation. On the one hand, we could suggest that societies reporting higher preferences for environmental protection might be more inclined to contribute by participating in environmental organizations. On the other hand, one can argue that such societies may have established different channels to achieve the preferred environmental outcome (for example, through institutional conditions). Hence, our ability to make a prediction at the macro level is somewhat constrained. The actual process through which societies will express their preferences depends on the trust that citizens have in different institutions or channels to solve environmental problems. A perception of government corruption or unacceptable lags in implementation of public environmental policies could encourage people to transfer money from the public sector to NGOs and vice versa. In this respect, institutional quality is a significant factor in the decision to participate in voluntary organizations, and could explain some of the trade-offs that are made.

Tables 4.22 to 4.24 present the results of the macro-level correlations. Table 4.22 shows that there is a relatively strong correlation between the willingness to give part of one's income for environmental protection and a society's overall level of environmental participation. In most cases the correlation is statistically significant. Inclusion of the extended question in the first two columns of the results also indicates a statistically significant correlation between the willingness to pay higher taxes if the extra money were used to prevent environmental pollution and environmental participation. The next result shows that belonging to an environmental organization is correlated with disagreeing that the government should reduce environmental pollution with own costs (i.e. that the government should pay to reduce environmental pollution). This result would tend to indicate that societies with a higher participation rate are less willing to free-ride. However, the result is no longer robust once we use unpaid work to measure participation.

Surprisingly, the willingness "to buy things at a 20 percent higher price if it helped to protect the environment" and environmental participation returns only a low correlation (not statistically significant). We should note that in the question, it is not clear if the price increase is a tax or not. The results confirm the idea that indirect taxes are usually less visible than income taxes, so sometimes consumers are not able to distinguish the origin of the increase for themselves. It is possible that had the price increase been linked to organically produced food or some other environmentally friendly production process, the answer could have been different. The price of organic produce is usually higher, but pro-environmental individuals would be willing to pay more, due to the lower damage to the environment caused by this method of production.

Table 4.22 Correlations between participating and pro-environmental attitudes

	Belong to conservation, the environment, animal rights groups	*Unpaid work conservation, the environment, ecology, animal rights groups*	*Belong to conservation, the environment, groups*	*Unpaid work conservation, the environment, ecology groups*
Would give part of my income for the environment				
• 1 Strongly agree	–0.308**	–0.349***	–0.275*	–0.186
• 2 Agree				
• 3 Disagree				
• 4 Strongly disagree	*0.018*	*0.007*	*0.099*	*0.271*
I would agree to an increase in taxes if the extra money were used to prevent environmental pollution				
• 1 Strongly agree	–0.340***	–0.481***	–0.184	–0.140
• 2 Agree				
• 3 Disagree				
• 4 Strongly disagree	*0.008*	*0.000*	*0.268*	*0.409*
The Government should reduce environmental pollution, but it should not cost me any money				
• 1 Strongly agree	0.293**	0.058	0.636***	0.179
• 2 Agree				
• 3 Disagree				
• 4 Strongly disagree	*0.024*	*0.661*	*0.000*	*0.290*
I would buy things at a 20% higher price if it helped to protect the environment				
• 1 Strongly agree	–0.111	–0.240	0.037	0.023
• 2 Agree				
• 3 Disagree				
• 4 Strongly disagree	*0.500*	*0.146*	*0.862*	*0.914*

Note: Significance levels: * $0.05 < p < 0.10$, ** $0.01 < p < 0.05$, *** $p < 0.01$, p-values in italics.

Table 4.23 Correlations between participating and environmental values

	Belong to conservation, the environment, animal rights groups	*Unpaid work conservation, the environment, ecology, animal rights groups*	*Belong to conservation, the environment, groups*	*Unpaid work conservation, the environment, ecology groups*
All the talk about pollution makes people too anxious				
• 1 Strongly agree	0.229	0.140	0.246	0.109
• 2 Agree				
• 3 Disagree				
• 4 Strongly disagree	*0.179*	*0.416*	*0.148*	*0.528*
If we want to combat unemployment in this country, we shall just have to accept environmental problems				
• 1 Strongly agree	0.035	-0.041	0.183	0.379**
• 2 Agree				
• 3 Disagree				
• 4 Strongly disagree	*0.842*	*0.810*	*0.286*	*0.023*
Protecting the environment and fighting pollution is less urgent than often suggested				
• 1 Strongly agree	0.051	–0.235	0.214	0.327*
• 2 Agree				
• 3 Disagree				
• 4 Strongly disagree	*0.766*	*0.162*	*0.211*	*0.052*
My country's environmental problems can be solved without any international agreements to handle them.				
• 1 Strongly agree	–0.276*	—0.241	–0.177	–0.016
• 2 Agree				
• 3 Disagree				
• 4 Strongly disagree	*0.058*	*0.107*	*0.388*	*0.939*

Note: Significance levels: * $0.05<p<0.10$, ** $0.01<p<0.05$, *** $p<0.01$, p-values in italics.

The results in Table 4.23 are not as robust. There is no correlation between the level of disagreement about the statement that "talk about pollution makes people too anxious" and environmental participation. Moreover, it is only in the last result column (unpaid work) that we observe a statistically significant correlation between the level of disagreement with the statement "if we want to combat unemployment in this country, we shall just have to accept environmental problems" and environmental participation. A similar result is observable when analyzing the correlations between environmental participation and the statement "protecting the environment and fighting pollution is less urgent that often suggested." In addition, societies with a higher level of membership (see first result column) are more likely to disagree with the statement that "environmental problems can be solved without any international agreements." This result is in line with the finding that people with higher levels of concern for the environment also have knowledge about the global expansion and global impact of several environmental problems (Torgler and García-Valiñas 2007).

Finally, the correlation between environmental participation and environmental behavior is explored in Table 4.24. Membership participation (extended version) is correlated with activities such as attending a meeting or signing a letter or petition aimed at protecting the environment. On other hand, there is no significant correlation between having tried to reduce water consumption for environmental reasons and environmental participation. Societies with a higher membership rate report a higher propensity towards choosing household products that are thought to be better for the environment and are more inclined to reuse or recycle something for environmental reasons rather than throwing it away.

Correlation with environmental outcome

Finally, in this section of the book we are going to look at a diverse range of measures of environmental quality used in this research by covering two key variables: pollution (CO2 and PM10) and conservation (land protected for biodiversity). The measure of CO2 pollution is a global environmental outcome, as the negative externalities can be dispersed across space and time whereas responsibility for controlling emissions is attributed to regional or federal governments. Conservation of the natural environment on the other hand, occurs mainly on a local level, and PM10 pollution can be seen as local pollution. The differing types of environmental outcomes will engender different collective action problems. Global externalities require large-N collective action solutions, that is, global cooperation to address this problem. Of course, the idea of the world as one group would require the incorporation of many different competing interests, cultures, priorities, values, and stages of development. On the other hand, local problems require organization of a much smaller group that is likely to be composed of individuals with similar interests and priorities.

Given its primary concern with the environment, this part of the chapter pays particular attention to the issue of pollution, a problem that has existed throughout recorded history. For example, the Romans complained about the stink of smoky

Table 4.24 Correlations between participating and environmental behavior

	Belong to conservation, the environment, animal rights groups	*Unpaid work conservation, the environment, ecology, animal rights groups*	*Belong to conservation, the environment, groups*	*Unpaid work conservation, the environment, ecology groups*
Which, if any, of these things have you done in the last 12 months, out of concern for the environment?				
Have you chosen household products that you think are better for the environment?				
• 0 Have not	0.159	–0.019	0.491**	0.047
• 1 Have done	*0.355*	*0.914*	*0.015*	*0.827*
Have you decided for environmental reasons to reuse or recycle something rather than throw it away?				
• 0 Have not	0.194	0.024	0.494**	0.178
• 1 Have done	*0.264*	*0.891*	*0.017*	*0.416*
Have you tried to reduce water consumption for environmental reasons?				
• 0 Have not	0.168	0.226	–0.273	–0.209
• 1 Have done	*0.312*	*0.178*	*0.197*	*0.328*
Have you attended a meeting or signed a letter or petition aimed at protecting the environment?				
• 0 Have not	0.430***	0.068	0.314	–0.032
• 1 Have done	*0.006*	*0.684*	*0.135*	*0.883*

Note: Significance levels: * $0.05<p<0.10$, ** $0.01<p<0.05$, *** $p<0.01$, p-values in italics.

chimneys, and not only did their inefficient smelting process for workable metals (e.g., weapons for the legions or commemorative statues) result in air and water pollution, but the water that was used to harden the metals returned to the foundry's main water supply, which the population then consumed. Europe in the Middle Ages also suffered air pollution. For instance, London experienced problems from the burning of soft coal in the thirteenth century, and in the fourteenth century, Edward I of England ordered that the burning of sea coal in craftsman's furnaces be prohibited because of the foul-smelling fumes. In the late nineteenth century, both England and the United States enacted several smoke control ordinances (Frijters *et al.* 2009).

As Figure 4.1 indicates, in the 1990s, Australians saw air pollution as the most relevant atmospheric environmental problem; however, interestingly, this concern has decreased over time.

European citizens generally consider air pollution as one of the most serious current environmental problems that must be solved and controlled. Other issues perceived as serious problems are nuclear power and radioactive waste and disasters caused by industrial activities. On average, around 44 percent of European citizens declared that they are "very worried" about atmospheric emissions (European Opinion Research Group, 2002). That percentage was much higher for some countries who were especially concerned with that issue, such as, Greece (71 percent), Italy (62 percent), Luxembourg (61 percent), France (59 percent) or Portugal (53 percent).

To increase the accuracy in measuring the relationships between pollution and participation in environmental organizations, we are going to differentiate between local and global pollutants. The World Bank's *World Development Indicators*

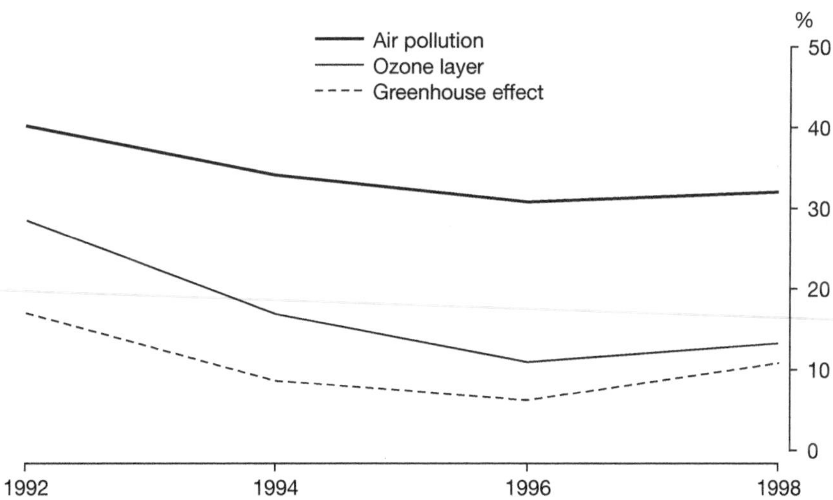

Figure 4.1 Concern about atmospheric problems in Australia

Source: ABS (2001: 156).

provide two measurements of pollution, namely, CO_2 emissions and PM10. The former is measured as CO_2 emissions (kg per 2000 PPP $ of GDP) that result primarily from fossil fuel combustion and cement manufacturing. The latter measure, PM10, is fine particle matter of less than 10 microns in diameter (Di Vita 2007, WDI code book). Particles of this size cause a range of health problems including cancer, respiratory disease, and heart disease as they are able to enter the respiratory system. The measures of PM10 are sourced from the WDI as part of the "environment" evaluation and calculates the concentrations of PM10 (micrograms per cubic meter) on a country level. These estimates represent "the average annual exposure level of the average urban resident to outdoor particulate matter."

We can contrast the very local nature of PM10 pollution against a situation in which the impacts are indivisible and the influences are felt internationally rather than at only the national or regional level. Global warming is just such a global externality: the stratosphere is a public good, and its scarcity is not transferred into higher prices. However, dealing with this issue is a challenge, and nations have had only modest success in agreeing to deal with global public goods or develop efficient policies. Not only is there a strong incentive to free-ride, but it is difficult to estimate and balance the costs and benefits involved. For example, damages are not only imposed on people living in other countries but also on subsequent generations. One major class of global pollutants is greenhouse gases, of which CO_2 is the most relevant.

According to the Eurobarometer 2002 (European Opinion Research Group 2002), 37 percent of European people show a high level of concern in respect to the extinction of species, and around 35 percent were very worried about natural resources overexploitation and ecosystems degradation. Therefore, conservation issues are very important. In order to check several links, we use one proxy for conservation sourced from the UN Millennium Development Goals. The proxy measures the area protected to maintain biological diversity, and is the total area protected divided by total surface area of country/territory, including marine area 12 nautical miles around. This variable has been used, for example, by Neumayer (2002).

Now that we have a description of our environmental outcome measures, let us present results. To maximize the number of observations we will focus on the question that covers the most countries (relating to conservation, the environment, animal rights). One should note that we are exploring simple correlations in order to obtain an overview of relationships rather than to determine a clear causality direction. Figures 4.2 and 4.3 refer to CO_2 pollution. We observe a negative correlation between environmental participation and the pollution level at the country level. These results would indicate a positive relationship between environmental participation and environmental outcomes.

The correlation is statistically significant in Figure 4.2 ($r = -0.33$), but not in Figure 4.3 ($r = -0.09$). Analyzing the linear relationship in a simple regression using environmental outcome as a dependent variable indicates that membership participation can explain 11 percent of the total variance of the variable CO_2

pollution (see Figure 4.2). Thus, from these results, we could suggest that membership participation has consequences for the environmental behavior and outcomes.

However, we obtain a different picture once we look at Figures 4.4 and 4.5 and at local pollution. There is a positive and statistically significant correlation between environmental participation and pollution. Figure 4.4 shows an r-value of 0.54 and Figure 4.5 a value of 0.34. Thus, these figures could indicate that environmental participation is used as a channel for action where pollution levels are relatively high. In other words, one could argue that the possibility of local change induces individuals to invest more energy in potential improvement. This indicates the causality direction is not clear and that there might be differences between local and global pollution.

A higher level of local pollution may induce a higher willingness to participate in environmental organizations. Such an argument is supported by Figures 4.6 and 4.7, which represent conservation values that are largely attributable to local priorities. The correlation is also negative and statistically significant, with r-values of –0.55 and –0.24. Figure 4.7 also reports that in a simple regression, unpaid work explains not less than 30 percent of the total variance of the conservation measure.

Figures 4.4 to 4.7 are interesting insofar as they indicate that individuals may react by increasing their voluntary activities when environmental outcomes are poorer. Thus, this could indicate that some individuals are keen to "privately" solve a collective action problem. We are going to explore this research question

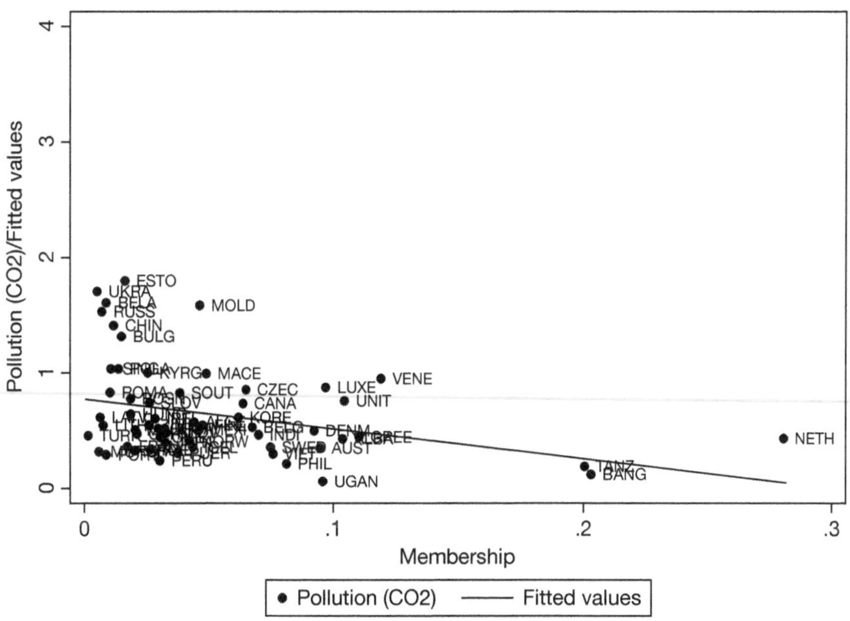

Figure 4.2 Membership and pollution (CO2)

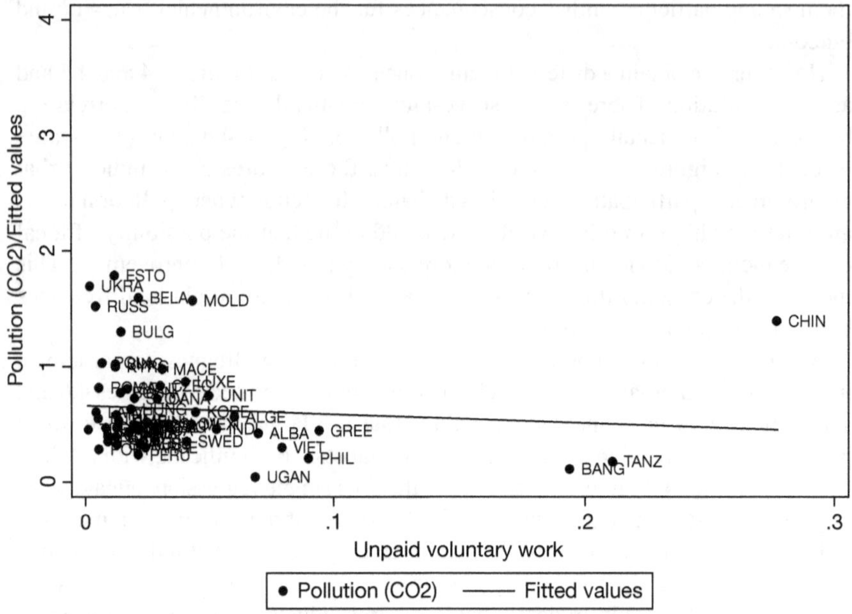

Figure 4.3 Unpaid work and pollution (CO2)

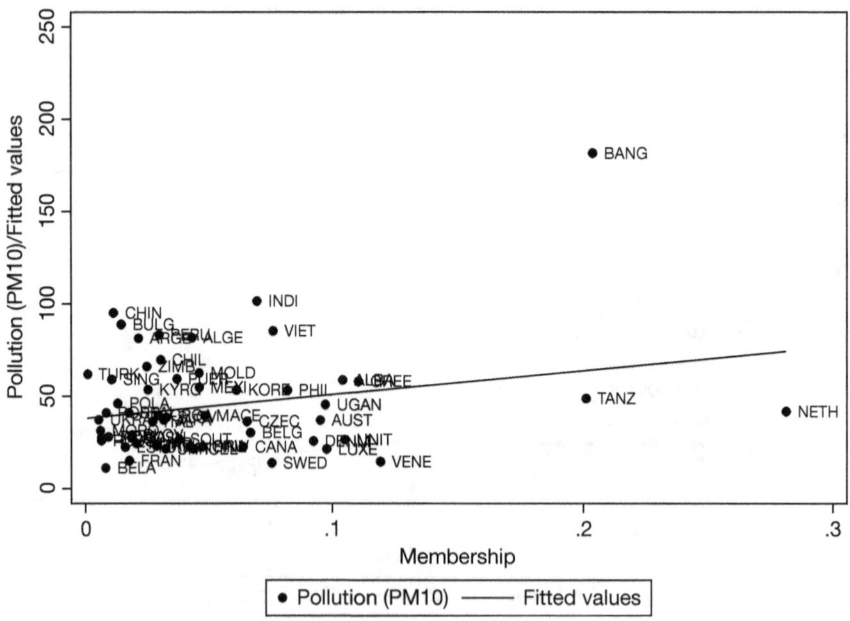

Figure 4.4 Membership and pollution (PM10)

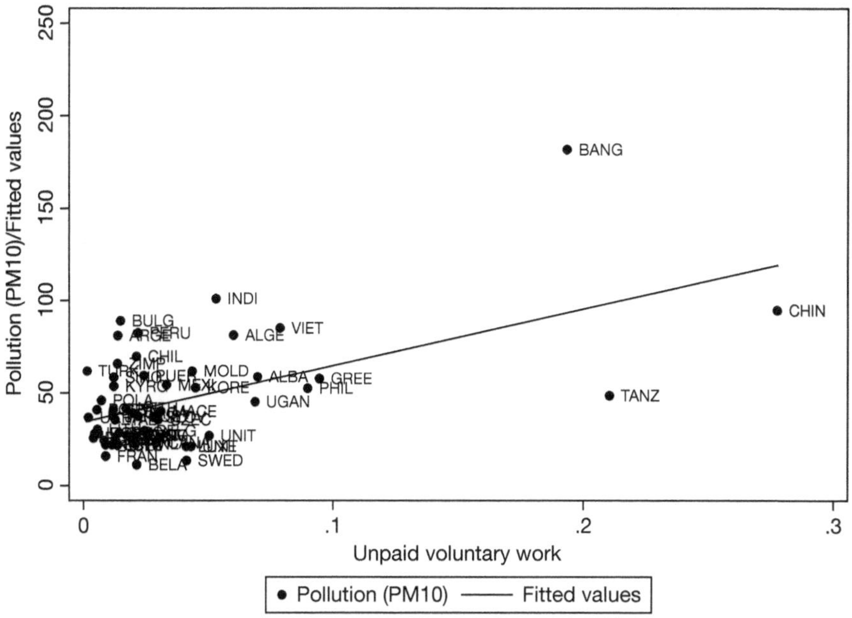

Figure 4.5 Unpaid work and pollution (PM10)

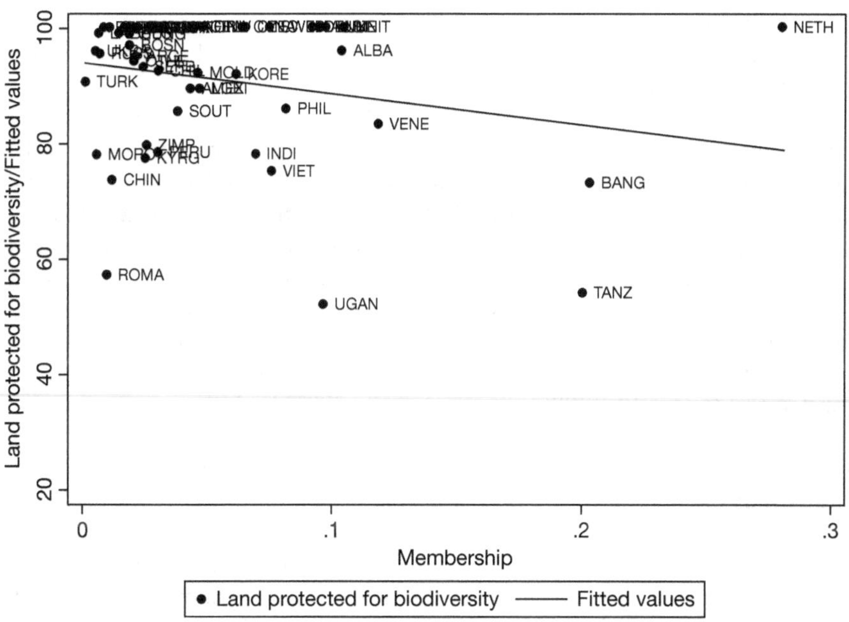

Figure 4.6 Membership and land protected for biodiversity

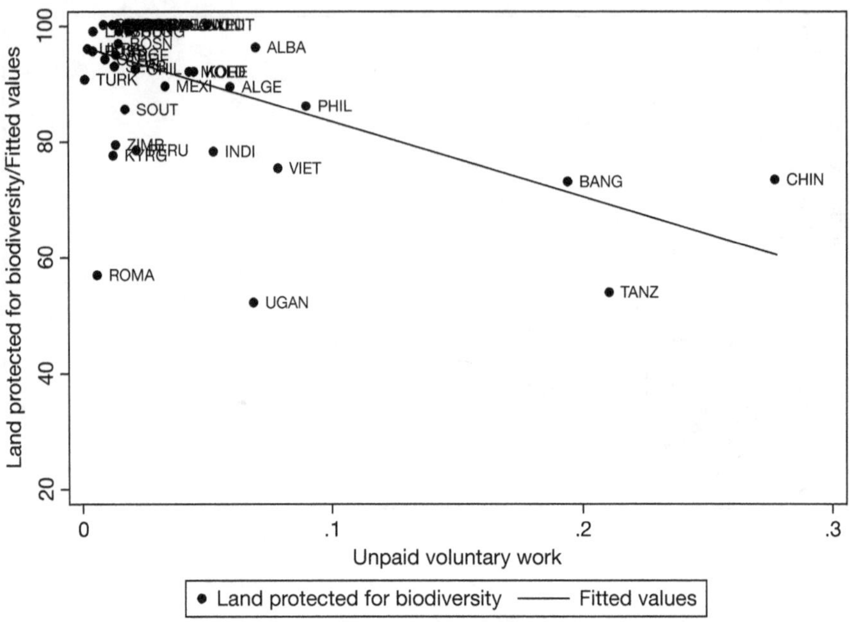

Figure 4.7 Unpaid work and land protected for biodiversity

in the next chapter when we move from a descriptive analysis that gives information about the raw effects to a multivariate analysis that gives an indication about the partial effects. The micro approach in Chapter 5 will be complemented with a multivariate analysis at the macro level in Chapter 8.

To explore whether such a relationship holds, we implement additional sources in the analysis. First, we include the Environmental Sustainability Index (ESI) which was developed by the Yale Center for Environmental Law and Policy and the Center for International Earth Science Information Network at Columbia University. The index measures the ability of nations to protect their environment over the next few decades and integrates a large number of data sets to track natural resource endowments, past and present pollution levels and environmental management efforts. In addition, the ESI reports on the capacity of a society to improve its environmental performance, covering 21 indicators of environmental sustainability (see ESI 2005). Looking at the 2001 database, we observe five core components: environmental systems, environmental stresses (reduction), human vulnerability, social and institutional capacity, and global stewardship (see Table 4.25).

Table 4.26 reports the correlation matrix between these main factors and our two main volunteering variables. We observe the tendency for a lower environmental sustainability to be correlated with a stronger participation rate. This result is clearly visible for the "UNPAID WORK" variable. On the other hand, for membership participation we also observe that private initiatives are positively

Table 4.25 2001 Environmental Sustainability Index (ESI)

Environmental systems	Urban SO2 concentration
	Urban NO2 Concentration
	Urban TSP Concentration
	Water availability per capita
	Water inflow availability per capita
	Dissolved oxygen concentration
	Phosphorus concentration
	Suspended solids
	Electrical conductivity
	Percentage of mammals threatened
	Percentage of breeding birds threatened
	Severity of human-induced soil degradation
	Land area impacted by human activities as a percentage of total land area
Reducing environmental stresses	NOx emissions per populated land area
	SO2 emissions per populated land area
	VOCs emissions per populated land area
	Coal consumption per populated land area
	Vehicles per populated land area
	Fertilizer consumption per ha of arable land
	Pesticide use
	Industrial organic pollutants per available freshwater
	Percent of country's territory under severe water stress
	Change in forest cover
	Percentage of country with acidification exceedance
	Consumption pressure per capita
	Nuclear waste generated
	Total fertility rate
	Project growth rate, present to 2050
Reducing human vulnerability	Daily per capita calories supply as a percentage of total requirements
	Percept of population with access to clean water
	Child death rate from respiratory diseases
	Death rate from intestinal infectious diseases
	Under-5 mortality rate
Social and institutional capacity	Research & Development scientists and engineers per million population
	Expenditure for Research & Development as a percentage of GNP
	Scientific and technical articles per million population
	IUCN members
	Civil and political liberties
	Environmental regulatory stringency
	Environmental regulatory innovation
	Percent of land area under protected status
	Number of Sectoral EIA Guidelines
	Number of ISO 14001 certified companies per GDP
	Dow Jones Sustainability Group Index: percentage of eligible companies in index
	Average Innovest EcoValue rating of firms
	Number of World Business Council on Sustainable
	Development members, per GDP

continued

Table 4.25 Continued

	Environmental competitiveness (WEF Survey)
	Availability of sustainable development information at the national level
	Environmental strategies and action plans
	Percentage of ESI variables missing from public global data sets
	Energy efficiency (total energy consumption per unit GDP)
	Renewable energy production as a percentage of total energy consumption
	Price of premium gasoline (USD per gallon)
	Subsidies for energy or materials usage (WEF Survey)
	Corruption measure (World Bank)
Global stewardship	Number of memberships in environmental intergovernmental organizations
	Percentage of CITES reporting requirements met
	Levels of ratification under the Vienna Convention for the Protection of the Ozone Layer
	Compliance with environmental agreements (WEF Survey)
	Montreal Protocol Multilateral Fund participation
	Global Environmental Facility participation
	FSC accredited forests as percentage of total forest area
	Ecological footprint 'deficit'
	CO2 emissions (total times per capita)
	CFC consumption
	S02 exports
	Historic, cumulative CO2 emissions

Source: http://sedac.ciesin.columbia.edu/es/esi/archive.html

correlated with public initiatives (global stewardship). Table 4.26 also shows the importance of exploring both volunteering factors independently as their relationship in regards to environmental quality differs to some extent.

Summary and conclusions

This chapter constitutes an initial orientation to the data we use to analyze participation in environmental organizations. Through statistical and correlation analysis we have reported some interesting findings. Information taken from several waves of the World Values Survey and the European Values Survey has been very useful in observing several significant relationships both in specific countries and from a global point of view.

First of all, we show the percentage of participation in environmental organizations in several countries around the world, and in some cases we are able to analyze their temporal evolution. In this respect, we have distinguished two kinds of participation, with different intensity levels and also different areas. At first, we consider membership in general, without distinguishing between active and non-active members of environmental organizations. We then make the distinction

Table 4.26 2001 Environmental Sustainability Index (ESI)

Membership	*ESI*	*System*	*Stress*	*Vulner*	*Cap*	*Global*	
Membership	1						
ESI	0.0839	1					
Environmental systems (System)	0.0772	0.7313	1				
Reducing environmental stresses (Stress)	–0.2866	–0.0047	0.1295	1			
Reducing human vulnerability (Vulner)	–0.196	0.5917	0.1896	–0.3412	1		
Social and institutional capacity (Cap)	0.2145	0.8633	0.4599	–0.3822	0.5827	1	
Global stewardship (Global)	0.2461	0.6621	0.3804	–0.0989	0.1888	0.5733	1
Unpaid Work	*ESI Index*	*System*	*Stress*	*Vulner*	*Cap*	*Global*	
Unpaid work	1						
ESI	–0.3732	1					
Environmental systems (System)	–0.3156	0.7313	1				
Reducing environmental stresses (Stress)	–0.0073	–0.0047	0.1295	1			
Reducing human vulnerability (Vulner)	–0.5397	0.5917	0.1896	–0.3412	1		
Social and institutional capacity (Cap)	–0.2309	0.8633	0.4599	–0.3822	0.5827	1	
Global stewardship (Global)	–0.1708	0.6621	0.3804	–0.0989	0.1888	0.5733	1

between members in general and those members who participate actively through unpaid voluntary work in these organizations. As we mentioned in the previous chapter, several empirical papers have drawn attention to the importance of that difference (Olli *et al.* 2001, Martinez and McMullin 2004). A more active participation can lead to greater improvements and developments in social capital, making it easier to solve environmental problems by facilitating, empowering, and giving more effectiveness to achieve environmental outcomes. In fact, we have found that active participation shows a strong and positive relationship with the conservation of natural areas.

Due to the higher costs of active participation, the percentage of people who donate time and work to environmental organizations is lower than the percentage corresponding to membership. This result is in accordance with our expectations. However, in both cases we found that in the top of the ranking there are countries whose citizens are well-informed about environmental topics. In Europe, Denmark is a very good example of this, and the increase in participation there is notable in the last few decades. The quality of available environmental information could be a key factor in explaining why people are motivated to contribute in this context. In the next chapter we are going to explore this question more thoroughly. In particular we are keen to explore whether political interest affects environmental participation, since a higher level of political interest is correlated with better informed citizens. Additionally, the proximity to and seriousness of the environmental problem can also be a determining factor. We will explore those issues in more detail in the coming chapters. The relationships and correlations we observe in this chapter give us a place to start for the empirical work to follow. We are especially interested in the results presented in Chapter 5 regarding whether private initiatives increase when the government is not able or willing to deal with environmental issues.

Regarding the socio-demographic profile of those citizens who tend to contribute in environmental organizations, we have found that, in general, men present higher rates of participation than women. This finding does not contradict the generalized idea that women are more concerned about environmental problems, as it may only indicate that women have less spare time available to donate. Additionally, it seems than people aged 30–49 years contribute more intensively to protect the environment. Finally, the results on marital status remain non-conclusive. It will be valuable to explore the impact of socio-demographic factors in a multivariate analysis at the micro level to better disentangle the effect of such elements.

Moreover, we observe networking effects within countries that is consistent with the social capital theory. We have found a significant and positive correlation between membership of an environmental organization and participation in other kinds of organizations, such as human rights, consumer groups, voluntary organizations centered around education, arts, music or cultural activities, sports or recreation, and organizations providing social welfare service for elderly. The correlations decrease slightly in significance when we consider active participation, probably because time is more costly and scarce than money. Additionally, the link between environmental participation and participation in political organizations is more intense when we consider unpaid work.

As we have shown in the previous chapter, attitudes matter too. Several pro-environmental intentions and behaviors help to predict why people decide to participate in environmental organizations. In Chapter 7 we will explore the link between environmental motivation and environmental participation in more detail. We also observe a positive relationship between environmental participation and other pro-environmental behaviors. For example, nationals who are more actively recycling are also more active participants in environmental organizations. At the same time, we have observed a trade-off between environmental participation and other economic contributions (especially taxes), which means that people who are contributing are less willing to pay additional money to preserve the environment. It may be that they think their contribution is already enough.

Finally, some interesting results have been generated when we look at environmental outcomes. On the one hand we found that local environmental problems may be related to higher efforts in terms of participation. Of course, proximity to a problem can tend to heighten concern about discovering the solution. Such an argument is enforced when exploring the relationship between environmental participation and environmental sustainability. On the other hand, it seems that participation in environmental organizations is related to solution of some environmental problems. We find that the higher the participation in environmental organizations, the lower the CO2 emissions. These findings reinforce the idea that higher levels of social capital in the country may also lead to improved environmental outcomes and the effectiveness of environmental policies. However, one should note that such an analysis does not provide any causal implications.

Notes

1 On rare occasions we observe individuals who are younger (15 and above).
2 For a review see Zelezny *et al.* (2000).
3 Results of Eurobarometer to EU15.

References

ABS (2001) *Australia's Environment: Issues and trends*, Canberra: Australian Bureau of Statistics.

Bekkers, R. (2005) "Participation in voluntary associations: relations with resources, personality, and political values," *Political Psychology*, 26: 439–54.

Blomquist, G.C. and Whitehead, J.C. (1998) "Resource quality information and validity of willingness to pay in contingent valuation," *Resource and Energy Economics*, 20: 179–96.

Bord, R.J. and O'Connor, R.E. (1997) "The gender gap in environmental attitudes: the case of perceived vulnerability to risk," *Social Science Quarterly*, 78: 830–40.

Bulte, E., Gerking, S., List, J.A., and De Zeeuw, A. (2005) "The effect of varying the causes of environmental problems on stated WTP values: evidence from a field study," *Journal of Environmental Economics and Management*, 49: 330–42.

Cameron, T.A. and Englin, J. (1997) "Respondent experience and contingent valuation of environmental goods," *Journal of Environmental Economics and Management*, 33: 296–313.

Cappellari, L. and Turati, G. (2004) "Volunteer labour supply: the role of workers' motivations," *Annals of Public and Cooperative Economics*, 75: 619–43.

Carlsson, F. and Johansson-Stenman, O. (2000) "Willingness to pay for improved air quality in Sweden," *Applied Economics*, 32: 661–69.

Clark, A.E., Frijters, P., and Shields, M.A. (2008) "Relative income, happiness, and utility: an explanation of the Easterlin paradox and other puzzles," *Journal of Economic Literature*, 46: 95–144.

Danielson, L., Hoban, T.J., Van Houtven, G., and Whitehead, J.C. (1995) "Measuring the benefits of local public goods: environmental quality in Gaston County, North Carolina," *Applied Economics*, 27: 1253–60.

Diamond, P.A. and Hausman, J. (1994) "Contingent valuation: is some number better than no number?" *Journal of Economic Perspectives*, 8: 45–64

Di Vita, G. (2007) "Legal families and environmental protection: is there a causal relationship?" Fondazione Eni Enrico Mattei, Working Paper 2007–78.

Frijters, P., Dulleck, U., and Torgler B. (2009) *Introductory Economics for Decision Makers: What you need to know to make economic decisions in Australia*, Melbourne: Thomson Learning Australia.

Dupont, D.P. (2004) "Do children matter? An examination of gender differences in environmental valuation," *Ecological Economics*, 49: 273–86.

Engel, U. and Pötschke, M. (1998) "Willingness to pay for the environment: social structure, value orientations and environmental behavior in a multilevel perspective," *Innovation*, 113: 315–32.

European Opinion Research Group (2002) *The Attitudes of Europeans towards the Environment* (Eurobarometer 58.0), Brussels: EU.

Frey, B.S. (1997) *Not Just for Money: An economic theory of personal motivation*, Cheltenham, Glos.: Edward Elgar.

——and Stutzer, A. (2002) *Happiness and Economics*, Princeton, NJ: Princeton University Press.

Inglehart, R. *et al.* (2000) *Codebook for World Values Survey*, Ann Arbor, MI: Institute for Social Research.

Israel, D. and Levinson, A. (2004) "Willingness to pay for environmental quality: testable empirical implications of the growth and environmental literature," *Contributions to Economic Analysis and Policy*, 31: art. 2.

Lubell, M. (2002) "Environmental activism as collective action," *Environment and Behavior,* 34: 431–54.

Martinez, T.A. and McMullin, S.L. (2004) "Factors affecting decisions to volunteer in nongovernmental organizations," *Environment and Behaviour*, 36: 112–26.

Neumayer, E. (2002) "Do democracies exhibit stronger international environmental commitment? A cross-country analysis," *Journal of Peace Research*, 39: 139–64.

Olli, E., Grendstad, G., and Wollebaek, D. (2001) "Correlates of environmental behaviours. Bringing back social context," *Environment and Behaviour*, 33: 181–208.

Popp, D. (2001) "Altruism and the demand for environmental quality," *Land Economics*, 77: 339–49.

Putnam, R.D. (2000) *Bowling Alone: The collapse and revival of American Community*, New York: Simon and Schuster.

Stevens, T.H., More, T.A. and Glass, R.J. (1994) "Interpretation and temporal stability of CV bids for wildlife existence: a panel study," *Land Economics*, 70: 355–63.

Torgler, B. (2007) *Tax Compliance and Tax Morale: A theoretical and empirical analysis*, Cheltenham, Glos.: Edward Elgar.

——and García-Valiñas, M.A. (2007) "The determinants of individuals' attitudes towards preventing environmental damage," *Ecological Economics*, 63: 536–52.

Whitehead, J.C. (1991) "Environmental interest group behaviour and self-selection bias in contingent valuation mail surveys," *Growth and Change*, 22: 10–21.

Witzke, H.P. and Urfei, G. (2001) "Willingness to pay for environmental protection in Germany: coping with the regional dimension," *Regional Studies*, 353: 207–14.

Zelezny, L.C., Chua, P.P., and Aldrich, C. (2000) "Elaborating on gender differences in environmentalism," *Journal of Social Issues*, 56: 443–57.

5 The determinants of environmental participation

An empirical analysis

> Volunteer behavior raises questions about tastes and social pressure that do not arise in standard analyses of work for pay.
>
> (Freeman 1997: S141)

Introduction

This chapter constitutes an initial approach to the determinants of participation in environmental organizations, from a general point of view. After reviewing the literature on environmental participation in Chapter 3 and providing a detailed introduction to the data in Chapter 4, it is useful to now explore empirically the determinants of environmental participation. Additionally, we would like to emphasize the importance of the institutional context, an aspect that we have discussed in Chapter 2 and will discuss again in Chapter 8. It is proposed that high quality political institutions and a transparent government are especially significant in motivating or facilitating citizens to provide public goods. Due to the importance of institutional and governmental issues, we have also focused on the impact of corruption on the individual participation decision. Moreover, a further aim of this chapter is to characterize the kind of people who usually participate in environmental organizations from a *microeconomic* perspective. This micro-oriented perspective will continue through the next two empirical chapters before we finalize the book in Chapter 8 with a more macro-oriented approach.

Corruption, political interest, and environmental participation

Throughout Chapters 1 and 2, and particularly in the second part of Chapter 2, we covered the proposition raised by recent literature, that the link between quality of institutions and quality of the environment has generally identified a positive relationship. This represents a paradigm shift since the 1960s and 1970s, when democracy and hence market economies (since they often go together) were regarded as the antithesis to environmental protection (Ehrlich 1968, Hardin 1968, Heilbroner 1974). The "no growth" movement of that era sought to contain growth and various economic freedoms with the aim of protecting common goods. However, some environmental disasters in the past 30 years have resulted from dictatorships, weakening this argument against democracies (Pellegrini and Gerlagh 2006). In addition, recent work establishing the connection between the quality of institutions and several other factors (including trade, fiscal responsibility, and globalization) has paved the way for a literature examining the links with economic and environmental welfare. The increasing interest in institutions has begun to address the deficiency in previous empirical work, which largely focus on the relationships between income and pollution, or on some variation of the Environmental Kuznet's Curve (EKC).

Among the many arguments reviewed in Chapter 2, we reported findings from Pellegrini and Gerlagh (2006), that corruption is even more significant than democracy in explaining environmental outcomes. Disproportionate influence from special interest groups may also be a symptom of corruption; hence Fredriksson and Svensson (2003: 1401) examine these groups, and find that interaction "between corruption and political instability is important in determination of other forms of economic policy." We take the perspective in our contribution that corruption leads to inefficiency, which can generate environmental exploitation. On the other hand, if people perceive that institutions and/or government are not able to be trusted, they may try to achieve environmental goals on their own. Thus, weak and dysfunctional states can induce people to pursue their goals via the non-governmental sector, perhaps cooperating through environmental organizations.

The inclusion of political interest in the empirical work is of particular significance, and in Chapter 3 we covered in detail the rationale behind use of this characteristic for our analysis. We represent the level of informal education with the self-reported measure of political interest. As mentioned, it is surprising that this aspect has been largely neglected in the literature. We propose that a higher level of political interest allows citizens to better supervise the government, resulting in a stronger sense of civic awareness that may lead to a higher level of environmental contribution or participation. The level of interest in politics will determine the extent to which individuals go about collecting, processing, and interpreting political matters. A government could operate with impunity if no one is motivated to analyze the available information regarding its activities (Rose-Ackerman 1999). To a certain extent, political interest leads to better supervision and scrutiny of the administration and governance performance, increasing the individual's knowledge of political matters. This increased knowledge may augment the ability to acquire political information, allowing the collection of more information at lower costs, which in turn increases the individual incentive to be informed and to discuss political issues. This may enhance the perception of environmental problems. Thus, political interest may increase the outside pressure from the public to improve environmental standards or may provide politicians with the incentive to act pro-environmentally. A politically interested population could also demand a higher level of transparency and may be able to monitor and control politicians better, potentially reducing the perceived complexity of the political process, environmental issues, and environmental policies.

Politically interested citizens will associate with one another and engage in discussion. Exchange of arguments and face-to-face interaction enhances group identification and gives citizens the opportunity to identify others' preferences. As others' preferences become visible, the moral costs of free-riding or not behaving in line with society's rules increase, which strengthens the incentive to participate in environmental activities. This discussion process also displays something of the social capital dimension of networks, building trust and reducing free-riding by identifying preferences of others. The outcome resembles the trust that can be developed in the cognitive dimension of social capital.

If political discussion is common in a society, citizens are confronted with arguments from both sides – those favoring and those opposing certain political outcomes that affect the environment – increasing the overall level of available information. In addition, once citizens become involved in an issue, they feel responsible for the result, which may create a sense of civic duty and a higher willingness to comply or to even participate in environmental organizations. Thus, discussion provides the opportunity to clarify the benefits and costs of political issues and thereby increases cooperation among group members. This increases the human capital involved in and developed by political matters. Such a higher stock of human capital may reduce the tolerance of environmental degradation. Several studies have found that political interest contributes to the probability of being involved in the political process (Verba *et al.* 1995). Political interest becomes an important explanatory factor in models of political behaviors, from political sophistication (Carpini and Keeter 1996) to voting (Verba *et al.* 1995).

With respect to the effects of communicating preferences, Alm *et al.* (1999) analyze tax compliance, arguing that there is a social norm of compliance affecting individual reporting decisions. Their findings indicate that communication combined with the vote influences tax compliance, so that paying taxes becomes the accepted mode of behavior. Discussion gives the chance to clarify benefits and costs of a behavior and thus increases cooperation among group members. After surveying experimental findings Alm (1996: 123) argues that "I believe that cheap talk in combination with the vote allows individuals to change the social norms, in this case to demonstrate that evasion will not be accepted." Similar results were found by Torgler and Schaltegger (2005).

Kuenzi (2006) has empirically demonstrated that civic education (non-formal education) has a significant and positive impact on political participation. This kind of education is the result of an informal process that is not necessarily a part of an individual's formal education. Nevertheless, individuals certainly invest energy, time, and money in this informal education, and in fact the expenses incurred by being politically interested (represented by the costs of informal education) may outweigh the benefits (represented by increased accountability and transparency of the administration).

Politically interested persons may find channels to reveal their environmental preferences by demonstrating a higher willingness to use instruments for voicing complaints that threaten to undermine the political support for a government. In addition, politically interested citizens' processes of informal education will uncover political information, helping them understand what is expected of a legitimate and environmentally friendly government. Such understanding opens the door to potential complaints and puts pressure on the government and the bureaucrats to act in the public interest. This is especially important in countries where other means of constraining bureaucrats and politicians may be lacking, as pointed out by Rose-Ackerman (1999: 144) – political interest and political understanding may increase effective avenues for challenging official actions. Although policies that enhance accountability and openness "are likely to be more acceptable to democratically elected leaders, these reforms can also have an effect in undemocratic systems whose leaders nevertheless need public support to retain power." However, it is possible that the government could stonewall any process until the protest groups have exhausted their energy and resources (Rose-Ackerman 1999). Bureaucrats could ignore the threats of lobbyists and protestors in expectation of succeeding with such a strategy.

Interestingly, few studies have explored the link between political interest and the environment. Torgler and García-Valiñas (2007) have shown that political interest has a strong impact on environmental preferences, and we explained in Chapter 3 that there are some studies exploring the impact of informal education in environmental participation. Thus, it is not only formal education that should have an impact on whether an individual participates in an environmental organization. We will use several proxies to measure political interest, helping us to check the robustness of the results, and will discuss the proxies in the next section.

The model and methodology

The question on environmental participation that is of primary interest in this chapter is phrased as follows:

> Now I am going to read off a list of voluntary organizations; for each one, could you tell me whether you are an active member, an inactive member or not a member of that type of organization? Environmental organization

Our dependent or response variable (y) has the value 1 if an individual is an active member of an environmental organization, otherwise 0. Thus, we are going to use a probit model for the analysis of binary outcomes. We will also use a probit model in Chapter 6 and 7, hence a short discussion on the probit model is warranted at this point. In binary response models, the interest lies in the response probability (see Wooldridge 2002, Baum 2003). In our binary-participation model, we are interested in the participation probability

$$\Pr(y=1\,|\,\boldsymbol{x}) = \Pr(y=1\,|\,x_1, x_2, \ldots, x_k) \qquad (5a)$$

where x refers to a full set of explanatory variables such as political interest, perceived corruption, gender, age, education, etc. To take non-linearity into account we consider a binary-participation model that has the following form:

$$\Pr(y=1\,|\,\boldsymbol{x}) = D(\beta_0 + \beta_1 x_1 + \beta_k x_k) = D(x_i \beta_i). \qquad (5b)$$

In our probit model, D is the standard normal cumulative distribution function (cdf):

$$D(z) = \int_{-\infty}^{z} \phi(v)dv. \tag{5c}$$

D ensures that (5c) is between 0 and 1. An OLS model, on the other hand, is likely to produce point predictions that are outside the unit interval. We derive our probit model from an underlying latent variable model:

$$y_i^* = x_i\beta_i + e_i \tag{5d}$$

where y_i^* is the unobserved magnitude and e_i the disturbance process using the following decision rules:

$$\begin{aligned} y_i &= 0 \text{ if } y_i^* \leq 0 \\ y_i &= 1 \text{ if } y_i^* > 0. \end{aligned} \tag{5e}$$

We assume e_i has a standard normal distribution which also means that e_i is symmetrically distributed about zero. We can now derive the following participation probability for y:

$$\begin{aligned} \Pr(y=1 \mid x) &= \Pr(y_i^*=1 \mid x_1) = \Pr(e > x_i\beta_i \mid x) \\ &= 1 - \mathrm{D}(-x_i\beta_i) = \mathrm{D}(x_i\beta_i). \end{aligned} \tag{5f}$$

We estimate the parameters of binary-participation model by using maximum likelihood techniques. The log likelihood for observation i can be written as

$$l_i(\beta) = y_i \log[G(x_i\beta_i)] + (1 - y_i)\log[1 - G(x_i\beta_i)]. \tag{5g}$$

The log likelihood of the sample is $L(\beta) = \sum_{i=1}^{N} l_i(\beta)$, numerical maximized with respect to the k elements of β.

To find the marginal effect of a continuous variable x_j on the participation probability, we use the following partial derivative:

$$\frac{\delta \Pr(y=1 \mid x)}{\delta x_j} = \frac{\delta \Pr(y=1 \mid x)}{\delta x\beta} \cdot \frac{\delta x\beta}{\delta x_j} = \mathrm{G}'(x\beta)\cdot \beta_j = \mathrm{g}(x\beta)\cdot \beta_j. \tag{5h}$$

As G is the cdf of a continuous random variable, g is a probability density function that is strictly increasing. In our estimations we report the marginal effects at the multivariate point of means. The marginal effect indicates the change in the share of individuals (or the probability of) belonging to a voluntary environmental organization when the independent variable increases by one unit (marginal change in x from the average). If the independent variable is a dummy variable, the marginal effect is evaluated in regard to the reference group.

In our tables we report the maximum likelihood estimates of the coefficients (first value), the z-statistics,[1] and the marginal effects. To find an analogous measure of goodness of fit we show pseudo R^2 values estimated by maximum likelihood. The pseudo R^2 is defined as $(1-L_1/L_0)$ where L_0 is the log-likelihood value for the null model excluding all explanatory variables and L_1 the log-likelihood value for the fitted model. Moreover, we also present chi^2 statistics (p-values) for the overall significance of our regressions.

In general, our models use standard errors adjusted for the clustering on countries (except the first and third estimations in Table 5.1), thus taking into account unobservable country specific characteristics. Clustering leads to a decrease in the *z*-values, but has no impact on the marginal effects. A weighting variable has been applied to correct the samples and thus to obtain a reflection of the national distribution. In the estimations where several countries have been pooled, we have integrated an additional weighting variable. The original weight variable has been multiplied by a constant for each country to get an equal number of weighted observations (around 1,500) for each survey. The World Values Survey provides the weighting variables. Furthermore, "I don't know" answers and missing values were omitted from all estimations. We will also use this approach in future chapters.

Data and variables

In this chapter we will work with a cross-section of individuals using the World Survey wave III (1995–97). Now one could protest (with good reason) that this is not the newest or the most recently available wave. Of course, we have our reasons for implementing this particular dataset, one of which is that key variables for our analysis (in particular "perceived corruption") were only collected in this wave. Since very few studies have worked at the individual level with a "perceived corruption" variable, we feel compelled to address such a shortcoming. Furthermore, many environmental studies are case studies focusing on a single country or a single region. Another advantage of this wave is that it contains measures on a large set of interesting countries from all around the world (including a substantial number of transition countries). Hence, this particular wave has been widely used among social scientists, proving to be a valuable source, particularly in relation to developing countries for which it is challenging to collect reliable data. We take advantage of these characteristics of the dataset, and analyze different cultural regions which also help to investigate the cross-cultural robustness of our key variables. Thus, in this chapter, we will focus on a multi-country analysis for the third WVS wave. The following chapters will then work with more recent data.

Countries with fewer than 750 observations (Montenegro, the Dominican Republic, Ghana, Pakistan, and Tambov) were excluded from the sample to reduce possible biases due to a lack of representativeness. Several other countries were excluded as they do not provide information regarding the dependent and independent variables integrated in our estimations.[2] Finally, Sweden could not be included as one of the control variables (education) is coded differently. We therefore proceed with a sample of 38 countries.[3] The estimations are also performed for various geographic sub-samples to compare the relevance of our independent variables in different environments.

A multivariate analysis sheds some light on who is going to participate, whose priorities and values are forwarded through voluntary activities, and to what extent voluntary participation can achieve representativeness. We have chosen the independent variables based on the previous literature on pro-environmental behaviors and volunteerism outlined in Chapter 3. First of all, we consider several socio-demographic and economic variables. This allows us to take the first step by focusing on "external" factors, avoiding the inclusion of preferences and values in the model. We are aware that such an approach has its limitations and that it does not provide a complete picture of the determinants of environmental engagement: we would refer the reader to our attempts at addressing this issue in Chapter 7. With regard to these external factors, or socio-demographic and socio-economic variables, a traditional economic approach would suggest that volunteers would mostly be individuals with low opportunity costs of time. However, the empirical results demonstrate that the opportunity cost argument fails to consistently predict the probability of participating in environmental organizations. While the results do not bear out the traditional "opportunity cost of time" argument, they are consistent with several previous findings that investigate environmental behavior and environmental preferences.

In a second step, we include political interest in the regression, using three different proxies as a robustness check. Tables A5.1 in the Appendix provides descriptions of these variables. We are going to use (in line with Torgler and García-Valiñas 2007) the following proxies for political interest:

> Political interest: How interested would you say you are in politics?
> (1 = Not at all interested, 2 = Not very interested, 3 = Somewhat interested, 4 = very interested).
>
> Discussing politics: When you get together with your friends, would you say you discuss political matters frequently, occasionally or never?
> (1 = Never, 2 = Occasionally, 3 = Never).
>
> Importance of politics: How important is politics in your life?
> (Not all important = 1, Not very important = 2, Rather important = 3, 4 = Very important).

We have also defined a variable which approximates the state's capacities regarding environmental participation. In developed countries the state offers many valid channels for citizens' actions and expression of preferences. The democratic structure allows individuals to control and influence the government (to a certain extent). Furthermore, the government has a higher incentive to take citizens' preferences into account when formulating policy and making decisions. Thus, we have considered an index of perceived corruption, constructed from the WVS by using the following question:

How widespread do you think bribe taking and corruption is in this country?
Almost no public officials are engaged in it (1)
A few public officials are engaged in it (2)
Most public officials are engaged in it (3)
Almost all public officials are engaged in it (4)

Our analysis uses a variable that is available at the micro level rather than working with country averages, providing an advantage over most of the previous studies on corruption. Use of the variable "perceived corruption" could be criticized as inappropriate measure of actual corruption, as it is merely self-reported perceptions. However, as Tanzi (2002: 38) points out: "If corruption could be measured, it could probably be eliminated." Participants in corruption are not going to admit to its existence, and there are no reliable measures analogous to those used in the legitimate sector of the economy. Use of perceived corruption at the individual level is in line with other indexes such as that from Transparency International which also measures perceptions. Treisman (2000) analyzes the Transparency International measurements and raises what we believe are valid arguments as to why data based on perceptions should be taken seriously. Components of the various surveys and ratings are highly correlated among themselves, even though they have been established with different methodologies, different inputs and in different time periods. Such a consistency allows the conclusion that factors are almost free of biases such as a "temporal mood" or guesses. There is also a consistency in the Transparency International over time, even though the construction of the index varies over time. A strong test of whether the World Values Survey question about corruption is a useful proxy is to check whether the variable is correlated with other well-known indexes on corruption. Thus, we compare our variable with the corruption indexes TI (Transparency International), International Country Risk Guide (ICRG) and Quality of Government (Control of Corruption) developed by Kaufmann *et al.* (2003). The World Values Survey Corruption ratings are highly correlated with the TI ($r = -0.878$), the ICRG ($r = -0.680$) and the Quality of Government rating ($r = -0.827$).[4] Of course, one can still criticize that perceptions are not objective, nor are they quantitative measures of the actual degree of corruption. Perceptions are rather an indirect way of measuring corruption (Tanzi 2002). Nevertheless, we proceed with our analysis, keeping in mind and accepting the limitations of the data as outlined above.

The models also include regional dummy variables for the CEE and FSU (Central and Eastern Europe and Former Soviet Union countries), Latin America, Asia, and Africa,[5] leaving the industrialized economies of Western Europe, USA, and Australia in the reference group.

Now, for the control factors: instead of using age as a continuous variable, we use four dummy variables for age cohorts: <30, 30–49, 50–64, and >65, with <30 as a reference group, to better investigate the impact of age. It is expected that the number of individuals who are actively involved in environmental organizations falls with an increase in age, since older people will not live to enjoy the benefits of preserving resources for later years. However, as people age, they can become more cautious, more risk averse, and more conservative, and they have more free time, so the expectation can be also positive. Gender and marital status enter the regression as dummy variables. From the results of previous studies no clear prediction can be formulated for gender, while for marital status, a positive relation is expected. Finally, education (continuous variable, 1 = no formal education, 9 = university degree) may also be a key variable, and we expect to find that it has a positive impact. In Chapter 3 we have discussed in detail the way in which formal education can affect environmental participation or environmental behavior and attitudes. General knowledge and even specific abilities related to environmental sciences are acquired through the educational system. Moreover, education may bring about an increase in social awareness and civil skills and reduce the costs of environmental activism. It will be interesting to explore the effect of education versus the effect of political interest that can be seen as a proxy for informal education (in line with Chapter 3).

As a proxy for income we use the economic situation of an individual (dummy variable for Upper Class with the remaining individuals in the reference group). Using the exact income would produce biases, because this variable is not comparable across different countries. On one hand, it is expected that wealthier citizens may have a higher demand for a clean environment and less environmental damages (assuming that these are normal goods) and thus a stronger incentive to actively contribute to the environment by participating in a voluntary organization. On the other hand, the opportunity cost of time may be high, thus losing money if they spend their time in voluntary organizations. Furthermore, we control for financial satisfaction (scale 1 = dissatisfied to 10 = satisfied). Participation may depend on the perceived restrictions of an individual. If a person is not satisfied with their financial situation, they have a stronger incentive to spend more time and resources in the accumulation of additional wealth rather than spending time in voluntary organizations.

Finally, another variable that represents and complements the economic situation of individuals is the occupational status (employment status). In addition to a dummy variable for unemployment, we use a dummy variable for self-employed individuals. Self-employed people may have higher opportunity costs of being involved in a voluntary organization. On the other hand, involvement may facilitate the establishment of connections that could positively influence their business. Generally speaking, the likelihood of participation is supposed to strongly depend on the type of sector and company a person is active in. Thus, it is not possible to derive a clear prediction.

Empirical evidence

This section reports two groups of estimation results: a cross-sectional analysis of all 38 countries (Tables 5.1, 5.2, and 5.7) and estimates from four geographic regions (Tables 5.3 to 5.6). The primary objective is to investigate the robustness of our independent variables across countries with different cultural and institutional characteristics and with different levels of economic development.

Table 5.1 presents the first results using the entire panel of countries. We observe that all age groups from 30 to 65+ report a significantly lower probability of participation in environmental organizations than the reference group (below 30 years of age). However, only the coefficient age >65 is statistically significant in the first two estimations. Being at the age >65 reduces the probability of participating in environmental organizations by 1.3 percent (see specifications 1 and 2). Interestingly, the marginal effects increase consistently with each additional increase in the age variables. This result supports our prediction of a negative correlation between age and environmental participation. The lower probability of reaping long-term benefits from preserving resources appears to strongly reduce the incentives of older people to participate in environmental organizations. On the other hand, for the third estimation (including regional dummy variables) the coefficient is no longer statistically significant. Interestingly, women report a lower probability of participating in environmental organizations. Being a woman reduces the probability of participating in voluntary environmental organizations by almost 1 percent. One can argue that these results contradict some previous findings that women are more concerned with environmental issues. The results also appear to contradict the opportunity cost argument that supposes women on average have a lower simple *cost* of time. However, as discussed in Chapter 4, women might be more active in community-based and neighborhood organizations which address local environmental issues, while men are more likely to participate in formal environmental organizations. Our survey question captures more of the latter than the former, and for this reason, our results may not greatly conflict with findings to the contrary. Moreover, it should be noted that women have higher restrictions on participation in voluntary organizations, especially at younger ages, as they are often more involved in time-intensive household activities. However, there may be cultural differences, insofar as gender differences may be less visible in western societies where women are more independent.

A positive relationship is observed between formal education and environmental participation, reporting a highly statistically significant coefficient in all three estimations. Similarly, there is a positive correlation between the economic variables and participation in voluntary environmental organizations. It is only in the second estimation that the coefficient "upper class" loses its statistical significance; but in general the marginal effects are quite substantial. Being a member of the upper class increases the probability of participation by 1.5 percent. There is also the tendency for self-employed persons to report a higher level of participation in environmental organizations. In the first two regressions the coefficients are statistically significant with relatively high marginal effects of 1.7 percent. However, when including regional dummies (in the third specification), the coefficient loses its significance, indicating that we may expect cultural differences. On the other hand, the coefficient "unemployed" has a negative sign and is not statistically significant, even though it could be argued that unemployed individuals have lower opportunity costs of participating in voluntary organizations. Our findings provide hardly any empirical foundation to the theoretical argumentation about individuals' opportunity costs of time.

Table 5.1 Determinants of environmental participation

Weighted Probit	*Coeff.*	*z-Stat. (1)*	*Marg. effects*	*Coeff.*	*z-Stat. (2)*	*Marg. effects*	*Coeff.*	*z-Stat. (3)*	*Marg. effects*
				Clustering on countries					
Independent variables									
(a) Demographic factors									
Age 30–49	–0.020	–0.63	–0.001	–0.020	–0.54	–0.001	0.025	0.74	0.001
Age 50–64	–0.047	–1.15	–0.003	–0.047	–0.80	–0.003	0.066	1.57	0.004
Age 65+	–0.250***	–4.33	–0.013	–0.250***	–2.63	–0.013	–0.095	–1.58	–0.005
Female	–0.134***	–5.22	–0.009	–0.134***	–3.89	–0.009	–0.147***	–5.61	–0.008
Education	0.024***	3.82	0.002	0.024	1.32	0.002	0.050***	8.49	0.003
(b) Marital status									
married	–0.035	–1.20	–0.002	–0.035	–1.04	–0.002	–0.016	–0.54	–0.001
(c) Economic variables									
Financial satisfaction	0.062***	11.92	0.004	0.062***	6.75	0.004	0.033***	5.86	0.002
Upper class	0.190**	2.07	0.015	0.190	1.46	0.015	0.198**	2.03	0.013
(d) Employment Status									
Self-employed	0.221***	5.73	0.017	0.221**	2.40	0.017	0.039	1.00	0.002
Unemployed	–0.058	–1.23	–0.004	–0.058	–1.10	–0.004	–0.051	–1.03	–0.003
(e) Regions									
CEE and FSU							–0.461***	–11.31	–0.024
Latin America							0.188***	5.18	0.011
Asia							0.204***	5.51	0.013
Africa							0.992***	14.14	0.131
Pseudo R2	0.030			0.030			0.082		
Number of observations	48362			48362			48362		
Prob > chi2	0.000			0.000			0.000		

Notes: Robust standard errors and standard errors adjusted for clustering on countries. In the reference group are age<30, male, other married status, other classes, other employment status, Western Europe + USA + Australia. Significance levels: * 0.05<p<0.10, ** 0.01<p<0.05, *** p<0.01. CEE: Central Eastern European Countries. FSU: Former Soviet Union Countries.

We also find regional differences with regard to participating in environmental organization (see specification 3) although one should interpret these results with caution as the number of countries in each region is limited. Interestingly, inhabitants of Latin America, Asia and Africa have a higher probability of participating in voluntary environmental organizations than those of western societies. Only the coefficient CEE and FSU show a statistically significant negative sign with relatively high marginal effects of around 2.4 percent. The results somehow support the argument of Dekker and Van den Broek (1998), who report that there is a

> widespread concern about the presumed decline in social and political engagement in Western society, which is claimed to affect volunteering too. Civic commitment to the common good is supposed to be eroding, due to various interconnected trends associated with modernization: rationalization, at the expense of traditional religious values and moral obligations; the ascent of individualism, manifesting itself in values of autonomy, self-realization, and personal freedom; and the concomitant rise of the "calculative citizen," which hampers pro-social behavior in general and volunteering in particular.
>
> (Dekker and Van den Broek 1998: 16)

However, the authors also stress that against such a pessimistic interpretation it can be argued that individualistic concepts of self-realization and responsibility might just as effectively stimulate pro-social behavior. The low participation in CEE and FSU is no surprise. It can be seen as an indicator of the transition process, where the socio-economic conditions confronting the citizens suddenly deteriorated on a massive scale and quality of life declined even further. As explained by Kasper and Streit,

> modern economic life depends rather precariously on numerous written and unwritten rules. If they are widely violated – as when society collapses after a lost war or in internal chaos – many of the human interactions on which we depend for our wellbeing are no longer possible.
>
> (Kasper and Streit 1999: 3)

The rapid collapse of institutional structures produced a vacuum in these countries, followed by worsening income inequality and poverty rates (Alm *et al.* 2006). In such an institutional vacuum there are diminished incentives to participate in environmental organizations over other (primarily material and survival oriented) considerations. Individuals require time to adapt to such rapid and drastic changes and this adaptation process requires substantial human resources that may crowd out alternative motivations.

In Table 5.2 we extend the previous model by adding three different measurements of political interest, including one behavioral variable (the degree of political discussion). One of the key findings in this study is the fact that political interest is highly correlated with the willingness to contribute. An increase in the level of discussing politics by one unit increases the probability of participating

Table 5.2 Environmental participation and political interest

Weighted probit	*Coeff. (4)*	*z-Stat. Effects*	*Marg.*	*Coeff. (5)*	*z-Stat. Effects*	*Marg.*	*Coeff. (6)*	*z-Stat. Effects*	*Marg.*
Independent variables									
(a) Demographic factors									
Age 30–49	0.006	0.18	0.000	0.005	0.15	0.0003	0.018	0.53	0.001
Age 50–64	0.038	0.90	0.002	0.033	0.77	0.002	0.052	1.22	0.003
Age 65+	–0.113*	–1.83	–0.005	–0.113*	–1.83	–0.005	–0.107*	–1.75	–0.005
Female	–0.117***	–4.30	–0.006	–0.118***	–4.34	–0.006	–0.138***	–5.18	–0.007
Education	0.040***	6.57	0.002	0.037***	5.95	0.002	0.043***	7.07	0.002
(b) Marital status									
Married	–0.018	–0.58	–0.001	–0.014	–0.44	–0.001	–0.014	–0.46	–0.001
(c) Economic variables									
Financial satisfaction	0.034***	5.95	0.002	0.033***	5.73	0.002	0.033***	5.69	0.002
Upper class	0.207**	2.07	0.013	0.196*	1.96	0.012	0.198**	1.99	0.013
(d) Employment status									
Self-employed	0.039	0.99	0.002	0.016	0.40	0.001	0.024	0.59	0.001
Unemployed	–0.048	–0.96	–0.002	–0.064	–1.25	–0.003	–0.061	–1.20	–0.003
(e) Regions									
CEE and FSU	–0.453***	–11.05	–0.023	–0.420***	–10.13	–0.021	–0.442***	–10.64	–0.022
Latin america	0.225***	6.08	0.014	0.277***	7.28	0.017	0.213***	5.81	0.013
Asia	0.210***	5.58	0.013	0.290***	7.37	0.019	0.186***	4.94	0.011
Africa	1.008***	14.30	0.133	1.008***	14.72	0.131	0.961***	13.72	0.122
f) Political Interest									
Discussing politics	0.174***	7.89	0.009						
Interest in politics				0.153***	9.60	0.008			
Importance of politics							0.116***	8.12	0.006
Pseudo R2	0.088			0.095			0.089		
Number of observations	47547			46500			47432		
Prob > chi2	0.000			0.000			0.000		

Notes: Robust standard errors. In the reference group are age<30, male, other married status, other classes, other employment status, Western Europe + USA + Australia. Significance levels: * 0.05<p<0.10, ** 0.01<p<0.05, *** p<0.01. CEE: Central Eastern European Countries. FSU: Former Soviet Union Countries.

by almost 1 percent (see specification 4). This result is confirmed when using two further proxies ("interest in politics" and "importance of politics," see specification 5 and 6). Hence, the results obtained in this chapter demonstrate that we would do well to extend future analyses beyond merely including formal education and that we should also include individuals' interest for current political matters. This aspect has been neglected in many previous studies. It is worthwhile mentioning that the impact of the variable "education" is not affected by the inclusion of political interest.

Next, we report the effect of the independent variables in the four regions.[6] It can be argued that the observed effects in the panel of countries reported in Tables 5.1 and 5.2 are driven by one of the regions. It is also possible that some variables act differently in the different regions. Tables 5.3 to 5.6 present the results of our cross-check of these effects. There are no statistically significant differences between the age categories except for Asia, where the age group 50–64 has the highest probability of participating in voluntary environmental organizations. Gender differences are observable in all regions except in western societies, with the strongest marginal effects for Asia. Education is positively correlated with participation and is mostly statistically significant in the reference group (Western Europe, USA, and Australia), Latin America and Asia.

Financial satisfaction affects the participation in western societies, in Latin America and in CEE and FSU countries but not in Asian countries. In fact, for Asia, the coefficient "upper class" is statistically significant with a negative sign showing marginal effects of around 2.5 percent. In general, the strongest positive impact of the economic variables is visible in Latin America. On the other hand, Latin America also reports the strongest impact of the employment status variables, but the sign is negative. Being self-employed reduces the probability of participating in environmental organizations by around 1.7 percent. Finally, we observe very consistent findings for the impact of political discussion and political interest. In all four regions the coefficients are always statistically significant, with relatively high marginal effects compared to the other variables.

The results obtained in Tables 5.3 to 5.6 showed that inhabitants of the developing continents were more likely to participate in environmental organizations than those living in western societies. Thus, in the light of those findings it would be interesting to investigate the impact of the state's capacities regarding environmental participation. The results of an analysis including our corruption variable are presented in Table 5.7. To check for robustness, we present three estimations. The first one is without the regional dummy variables (specification 29), the second one includes the regional dummy variables (specification 30) and the third one includes the political interest variable with the strongest marginal effects ("discussing politics", specification 31). As can be seen, the coefficient of "corruption" remains highly statistically significant, with marginal effects between 0.4 and 0.8 percent. Thus, a higher perceived corruption is correlated with a stronger incentive to participate in environmental organizations. If individuals perceive a lack of institutional quality they seemed to be willing to find alternative ways to pursue their goals.

Table 5.3 Determinants of environmental participation in Western Europe, USA, and Australia

Weighted Probit Clustering on countries	*Coeff.*	*z-Stat.* (7)	*Marg. Effects*	*Coeff.*	*z-Stat.* (8)	*Marg. Effects*	*Coeff.*	*z-Stat.* (9)	*Marg. Effects*
Independent variables									
(a) Demographic factors									
Age 30–49	0.076	1.55	0.005	0.079	1.63	0.005	0.064	1.18	0.004
Age 50–64	–0.028	–0.28	–0.002	–0.035	–0.34	–0.002	–0.039	–0.35	–0.003
Age 65+	–0.073	–0.67	–0.005	–0.075	–0.66	–0.005	–0.101	–0.85	–0.006
Female	–0.024	–0.45	–0.002	–0.015	–0.29	–0.001	–0.032	–0.62	–0.002
Education	0.076***	4.62	0.005	0.074***	5.32	0.005	0.071***	4.37	0.005
(b) Marital status									
Married	–0.035	–0.79	–0.002	–0.031	–0.70	–0.002	–0.033	–0.71	–0.002
c) Economic variables									
Financial satisfaction	0.036**	2.06	0.002	0.035**	2.03	0.002	0.035**	2.02	0.002
Upper class	0.090	0.63	0.007	0.085	0.58	0.006	0.077	0.54	0.006
(d) Employment status									
Self–employed	0.042	0.44	0.003	0.046	0.48	0.003	0.043	0.44	0.003
Unemployed	–0.131	–0.82	–0.008	–0.152	–1.06	–0.009	–0.110	–0.69	–0.007
(e) Political interest									
Discussing politics	0.099**	2.29	0.007						
Interest in politics				0.093***	2.72	0.006			
Importance of politics							0.131***	4.52	0.009
Pseudo R2	0.034			0.037			0.039		
Number of observations	10757			10785			10706		

Notes: Standard errors adjusted for clustering on countries in the reference group are age<30, male, other married status, other classes, other employment status. Significance levels: * 0.05<p<0.10, ** 0.01<p<0.05, *** p<0.01.

Table 5.4 Determinants of environmental participation in CEE and FSU countries

WEIGHTED PROBIT Clustering on countries	*Coeff.*	*z-Stat.* (10)	*Marg. effects*	*Coeff.*	*z-Stat.* (11)	*Marg. effects*	*Coeff.*	*z-Stat.* (12)	*Marg. effects*
Independent variables									
(a) Demographic factors									
Age 30–49	–0.013	–0.15	–0.0003	–0.006	–0.07	0.000	0.038	0.51	0.0008
Age 50–64	0.026	0.25	0.0006	0.037	0.35	0.001	0.081	0.82	0.0018
Age 65+	–0.046	–0.77	–0.0010	–0.070	–1.12	–0.001	–0.028	–0.41	0.0006
Female	–0.187***	-3.01	–0.0041	–0.191***	-3.01	–0.004	–0.221***	-3.67	0.0049
Education	0.019	1.15	0.0004	0.019	1.06	0.000	0.020	1.00	0.0004
(b) Marital status									
Married	–0.014	–0.22	–0.0003	–0.007	–0.11	0.000	0.006	0.09	0.0001
(c) Economic variables									
Financial satisfaction	0.038**	2.55	0.0008	0.036**	2.49	0.001	0.038**	2.47	0.0008
Upper class	0.440	1.39	0.0161	0.430	1.36	0.016	0.412	1.31	0.0145
(d) Employment status									
Self–employed	0.031	0.23	0.0007	0.044	0.31	0.001	–0.005	–0.04	–0.0001
Unemployed	–0.024	–0.25	–0.0005	–0.043	–0.39	–0.001	–0.083	–0.81	–0.0017
(e) Political interest									
Discussing politics	0.266***	4.11	0.0058						
Interest in politics				0.157***	3.86	0.003			
Importance of politics							0.148**	2.26	0.0032
Pseudo R2	0.039			0.034			0.037		
Number of observations	20597			20748			20510		

Notes: Standard errors adjusted for clustering on countries in the reference group are age<30, male, other married status, other classes, other employment status. Significance levels: * 0.05<p<0.10, ** 0.01<p<0.05, *** p<0.01.

Table 5.5 Determinants of environmental participation in Latin American countries

Weighted Probit Clustering on countries	*Coeff.*	*z-Stat.* (13)	*Marg. effects*	*Coeff.*	*z-Stat.* (14)	*Marg. Effects*	*Coeff.*	*z-Stat.* (15)	*Marg. effects*
Independent variables									
(a) Demographic factors									
Age 30–49	–0.020	–0.35	–0.002	–0.023	–0.41	–0.002	–0.022	0.18	–0.002
Age 50–64	0.052	0.87	0.005	0.034	0.57	0.003	0.055	1.49	0.005
Age 65+	–0.128	–1.15	–0.011	–0.144	–1.32	–0.012	–0.126	–1.64	–0.011
Female	–0.112*	–1.69	–0.011	–0.104	–1.53	–0.010	–0.120*	–1.87	–0.012
Education	0.037***	2.71	0.004	0.029**	1.99	0.003	0.039***	2.93	0.004
(b) Marital status									
Married	0.007	0.13	0.001	0.006	0.11	0.001	0.011	–0.01	0.001
(c) Economic variables									
Financial satisfaction	0.042***	5.35	0.004	0.041***	5.23	0.004	0.042***	5.73	0.004
Upper class	0.684**	2.13	0.112	0.628*	1.79	0.097	0.642	1.10	0.102
(d) Employment status									
Self-employed	–0.172*	–1.72	–0.015	–0.207**	–2.17	–0.017	–0.203**	–1.98	–0.017
Unemployed	–0.118*	–1.70	–0.010	–0.104	–1.48	–0.009	–0.130**	–2.03	–0.011
(e) Political interest									
Discussing politics	0.085**	2.18	0.008						
Interest in politics				0.152***	4.44	0.014			
Importance of politics							0.071**	2.09	0.007
Pseudo R2	0.026			0.037			0.028		
Number of observations	7392			7410			7385		

Notes: Standard errors adjusted for clustering on countries in the reference group are age<30, male, other married status, other classes, other employment status. Significance levels: * 0.05<p<0.10, ** 0.01<p<0.05, *** p<0.01.

Table 5.6 Determinants of environmental participation in Asian countries

Weighted Probit Clustering on countries	*Coeff.*	*z-Stat.* (16)	*Marg. Effects*	*Coeff.*	*z-Stat.* (17)	*Marg. Effects*	*Coeff.*	*z-Stat.* (18)	*Marg. Effects*
Independent variables									
(a) Demographic factors									
Age 30–49	0.029	0.60	0.003	0.034	0.60	0.004	0.037	0.80	0.004
Age 50–64	0.170***	2.64	0.017	0.171*	1.87	0.020	0.147**	2.14	0.015
Age 65+	–0.285	–1.17	–0.021	–0.148	–0.66	–0.014	–0.241	–1.31	–0.019
Female	–0.170**	–2.18	–0.015	–0.212***	–2.94	–0.022	–0.226***	–3.05	–0.022
Education	0.039	1.63	0.004	0.034	1.55	0.004	0.046**	2.19	0.004
(b) Marital status									
Married	0.032	0.60	0.003	0.057	1.21	0.006	0.020	0.42	0.002
(c) Economic variables									
Financial satisfaction	–0.002	–0.30	0.000	0.001	0.10	0.000	–0.006	–0.84	–0.001
Upper class	–0.360**	–2.27	–0.024	–0.363**	–2.23	–0.029	–0.347**	–2.30	–0.025
(d) Employment status									
Self-employed	0.185*	1.83	0.019	0.117	1.14	0.013	0.165	1.54	0.017
Unemployed	0.155	1.46	0.016	0.058	0.68	0.006	0.128	1.19	0.013
(e) Political interest									
Discussing politics	0.334***	7.67	0.030						
Interest in politics				0.171**	2.17	0.018			
Importance of politics							0.115***	2.94	0.011
Pseudo R2	0.045			0.033			0.030		
Number of observations	7065			5798			7087		

Notes: Standard errors adjusted for clustering on countries in the reference group are age<30, male, other married status, other classes, other employment status. Significance levels: * 0.05<p<0.10, ** 0.01<p<0.05, *** p<0.01.

Table 5.7 Environmental participation and corruption

Weighted Probit	*Coeff. (19)*	*z-Stat.*	*Marg. Effects*	*Coeff. (20)*	*z-Stat.*	*Marg. Effects*	*Coeff. (21)*	*z-Stat.*	*Marg. Effects*
Independent variables									
(a) Demographic factors									
Age 30–49	–0.009	–0.24	–0.001	0.034	0.88	0.003	0.020	0.50	0.002
Age 50–64	–0.009	–0.18	–0.001	0.078	1.58	0.008	0.056	1.13	0.005
Age 65+	–0.206***	–2.93	–0.017	–0.087	–1.22	–0.008	–0.108	–1.47	–0.009
Female	–0.125***	–4.06	–0.012	–0.135***	–4.41	–0.013	–0.112***	–3.53	–0.010
Education	0.036***	4.73	0.003	0.053***	7.66	0.005	0.044***	6.25	0.004
b) Marital status									
Married	0.013	0.37	0.001	–0.013	–0.38	–0.001	–0.013	–0.36	–0.001
(c) Economic variables									
Financial satisfaction	0.031***	4.67	0.003	0.035***	5.27	0.003	0.036***	5.44	0.003
Upper class	0.216*	1.80	0.025	0.137	1.08	0.014	0.145	1.11	0.015
(d) Employment status									
Self-employed	0.146***	3.28	0.015	0.014	0.32	0.001	0.017	0.38	0.002
Unemployed	–0.032	–0.55	–0.003	–0.074	–1.27	–0.006	–0.076	–1.29	–0.007
(e) Regions									
Latin America				0.181***	4.63	0.018	0.210***	5.27	0.020
Asia				0.246***	6.08	0.026	0.248***	6.02	0.026
Africa				0.996***	13.28	0.187	1.003***	13.31	0.187
(f) Political interest									
Discussing politics							0.144***	5.62	0.013
(g) Institutional quality									
Corruption	0.088***	4.82	0.008	0.035*	1.86	0.003	0.039**	2.02	0.004
Pseudo R2	0.017			0.042			0.047		
Number of observations	24672			24672			24313		
Prob>chi2	0.000			0.000			0.000		

Notes: Robust standard errors. In the reference group are age<30, male, other married status, other Classes, other employment status, Western Europe + USA + Australia. Significance levels: * 0.05<p<0.10, ** 0.01<p<0.05, *** p<0.01. CEE and FSU countries not included.

Concluding remarks

Since the 1970s, the number of environmental studies has been growing. However, there is still a lack of papers that investigate the determinants of participating in voluntary environmental organizations. The rapid growth of the social capital literature inspired our efforts to make a detailed inquiry into the determinants of this variable (see Chapters 2 and 3). In a policy-making context, social capital seems to improve the effectiveness of public environmental policies. However, non-active forms of participation in environmental groups (such as financial membership without volunteering) do not generate positive environmental outcomes (Pretty and Smith 2004).

Furthermore, it is a promising line of research to search empirically for factors such as political discussion and political interest that are mostly neglected in previous studies. We provide evidence that political interest has a positive impact on active environmental participation. In this chapter we have worked with a cross-section of individuals using the World Values Survey wave III (1995–97) covering 38 countries. The estimations not only investigate regional differences but are also performed for various geographic sub-samples to compare the relevance of our independent variables in different environments. One of the major advantages of the data set is that different cultural regions can be investigated, i.e. we can assess the cross-cultural robustness of our variables and explore different institutional conditions.

The results indeed indicate that there are differences between regions. Interestingly, inhabitants of Latin America, Asia, and Africa have a higher probability of participating in voluntary environmental organizations than those of western societies, but although we work with an extensive survey, regional differences should be interpreted cautiously, as there is only a limited number of countries available for each category. We observe the tendency that environmental participation is used as a channel for action in developing countries, where weak and dysfunctional states could induce citizens to pursue their goals through activities in the non-governmental sector. Such an argument is supported when investigating the impact of corruption on individuals' active participation in environmental organizations. A higher perceived corruption leads to an increased participation, which shows that individuals are able to find alternative ways to express their preferences and take action. Hence, it seems that we have a higher quality of institutions encouraging voluntary participation by facilitating collective action, but at the same time we have a lower quality of institutions (as measured by perceived corruption) providing the impetus for voluntary collaboration to solve public good problems. However, one should also note that a rapid and drastic collapse of the institutional structure hinders private participation in environmental organizations. The results show that transition countries experience difficulty in coordinating environmental participation. The rapid reordering of institutions precludes voluntary participation. The energy required to negotiate the chaos dominates individual concerns, crowding out willingness to contribute to the environment.

In general, what process are we observing? Is it bearing out the pre-Olson notion that groups would cooperate to solve their own dilemmas? Or is this evidence of Olson's assertion that interest groups do not provide public goods, that they only cooperate in order to seek advantages for themselves? It could be argued that local groups willingly cooperating to solve local problems, whether they are in the presence of a deficient state or not, are seeking to capture the benefits of a better environment for themselves.

However, this chapter provides further significant findings. It sheds some light on who is likely to participate, whose priorities and values are forwarded through voluntary activities, and to what extent voluntary participation can become representative. The findings in the pooled estimations indicate the tendency of a negative correlation between age and environmental participation. Women report a lower probability of participating in environmental organizations. Interestingly, gender differences are observable in all regions except in western societies, with the strongest marginal effects for Asia. The variables education, financial satisfaction, upper class, and self-employed indicate a positive correlation with the probability of participating in environmental organizations, suggesting that theories of volunteering based on individuals' opportunity cost are not empirically well founded.

In sum, Chapter 5 shows that socio-demographic and socio-economic variables help to understand what shapes individuals' propensity to participate in a voluntary environmental organization. This chapter also shows the relevance of political discussion and political interest, variables that have mostly been neglected in the previous environmental literature. These variables have a strong impact on the probability of participating in environmental organizations. All three proxies for political interest and political discussion have a statistically significant positive impact with relatively high marginal effects.

These findings can be useful in order to create and maintain social capital to better preserve the environment. As Pretty and Smith (2004) pointed out, it is important that international agencies, governments, and other organizations accept and understand that investment in the creation of social capital pays off. Thus, all efforts made to characterize the kind of people who participate actively in environmental organizations help assure the success of such investments.

Appendix

Table A5.1 Description of variables

Variable	*Derivation*
Age	Dummies Age 30–49, age 50–64, 65+ (reference group, age < 30)
Gender	Female (male in the reference group)
Education	Continuous variable What is the highest educational level that you have attained? 10. No formal education 11. Incomplete primary school 12. Completed primary school

continued

Table A5.1 Continued

Variable	*Derivation*
	13. Incomplete secondary school: technical/vocational type 14. Complete secondary school: technical/vocational type 15. Incomplete secondary: university-preparatory type 16. Complete secondary: university-preparatory type 17. Some university-level education, without degree 18. University-level education, with degree
Marital status	Dummy: married = 1; all other classes (divorced, separated, widowed, single) in the reference group.
Financial satisfaction	How satisfied are you with the financial situation of your household? (scale 1 = dissatisfied to 10 = satisfied)
Economic class	People sometimes describe themselves as belonging to the working class, the middle class, or the upper or lower class. Would you describe yourself as belonging to the: Dummy: upper class, the rest (middle class, working class and lower class) is the reference group.
Employment status	Two dummies: self-employed, unemployed, the rest (part time employed, at home, student, retired, other) is in the reference group.
Corruption	To assess the level of perceived corruption from the WVS, we use the following question: How widespread do you think bribe-taking and corruption is in this country? Almost no public officials are engaged in it (1) A few public officials are engaged in it (2) Most public officials are engaged in it (3) Almost all public officials are engaged in it (4)

Source: Inglehart *et al.* (2000).

Table A5.2 Descriptive statistics

Variables	*Obs.*	*Mean*	*Std.*	*Dev.*	*Min.*
Participation in environmental organization	67478	0.035	0.185	0	1
Age 30–49	61015	0.429	0.495	0	1
Age 50–64	61015	0.181	0.385	0	1
Age 65+	61015	0.099	0.299	0	1
Female	68735	0.518	0.500	0	1
Education	64067	5.329	2.302	1	9
Married	65630	0.602	0.489	0	1
Financial satisfaction	65006	5.235	2.750	1	10
Upper class	64382	0.018	0.131	0	1
Self-employed	65388	0.098	0.297	0	1
Unemployed	65388	0.093	0.291	0	1
Discussing politics	64627	1.849	0.654	1	3
Interest in politics	67349	2.279	0.955	1	4
Importance of politics	63520	2.320	0.947	1	4
Corruption	59078	2.936	0.826	1	4

Notes

1 Comparable to t-statistics in a linear model.
2 These countries are Poland, Japan, South Africa, Puerto Rico, Turkey, and Columbia.
3 Western European Countries & USA & Australia (USA, West Germany, East Germany, Switzerland, Australia, Norway, Finland, Spain), CEE and FSU (Bulgaria, Belarus, Estonia, Georgia, Latvia, Lithuania, Moldova, Armenia, Russia, Slovenia, Ukraine, Azerbaijan, Serbia, Macedonia, Croatia, Bosnia-Herzegovina), Latin America (Mexico, Argentina, Brazil, Chile, Peru, Venezuela, Uruguay) Asia (South Korea, India, Taiwan, China, Philippines, Bangladesh), Africa (Nigeria).
4 The sign is negative because for all three ratings used (TI, ICRG, and Quality of Government), a higher score corresponds to a lower corruption.
5 Only one country represents Africa (Nigeria).
6 Africa has not been considered independently, as Nigeria was the only African country in the data set.

References

Alm, J. (1996) "Explaining tax compliance," in S. Pozo (ed.) *Exploring the Underground Economy*, Kalamazoo, MI: W.E. Upjohn Institute for Employment Research.

——, Martinez-Vazquez, J. and Torgler, B. (2006) "Russian attitudes toward paying taxes – before, during, and after the transition," *International Journal of Social Economics*, 33: 832–57.

——, McClelland, G.H., and Schulze, W.D. (1999) "Changing the social norm of tax compliance by voting," KYKLOS, 52: 141–71.

Baum, C.F. (2003) *An Introduction to Modern Econometrics Using Stata*, Texas: Stata Press.

Carpini, D. and Keeter, S. (1996) *What Americans Know about Politics and Why It Matters*, New Haven, CT: Yale University Press.

Dekker, P. and Van den Broek, A. (1998) "Civil society in comparative perspective: involvement in voluntary associations in North America and western Europe," *Voluntas: International Journal of Voluntary and Nonprofit Organizations*, 9: 11–38.

Ehrlich, P.R. (1968) *The Population Bomb*, New York: Ballintine Books.

Fredriksson, G. and Svensson, J. (2003) "Political instability, corruption and policy formation: the case of environmental policy," *Journal of Public Economics*, 87: 1383–1405.

Freeman, R.B. (1997) "Working for nothing: the supply of volunteer labor," *Journal of Labor Economics*, 15: S140–66.

Hardin, G. (1968) "The tragedy of the commons," *Science*, 162: 1243–48.

Inglehart, R. *et al.* (2000) *Codebook for World Values Survey*, Ann Arbor: Institute for Social Research.

Heilbroner, R.L. (1974) *An Enquiry into the Human Prospect*, New York: W.W. Norton.

Kasper, W. and Streit, M.E. (1999) *Institutional Economics: Social order and public policy*. Cheltenham, Glos.: Edward Elgar.

Kaufmann, D., Kraay, A., and Mastruzzi, M. (2003) *Governance Matters III: Governance indicators for 1996–2002*, World Bank, June, 30.

Kuenzi, M. (2006) "Non-formal education and community development in Senegal," Community Development Journal, *41: 210–20.*

Pellegrini, L. and Gerlagh, R. (2006) "Corruption, democracy and environmental policy: an empirical contribution to the debate," *Journal of Environment Development*, 15: 332–54.

Pretty, J. and Smith, D.J. (2004) “Social capital in biodiversity conservation and management,” *Conservation Biology*, 18: 631–38.

Rose-Ackerman, S. (1999) *Corruption and Government: Causes, consequences and reform*, Cambridge: Cambridge University Press.

Tanzi, V. (2002) “Corruption around the world: causes, consequences, scope, and cures,” in G.T. Abed and S. Gupta (eds), *Governance, Corruption and Economic Performance*. Washington: International Monetary Fund.

Torgler, B. and García-Valiñas, M.A. (2007) “The determinants of individuals’ attitudes towards preventing environmental damage,” *Ecological Economics*, 63: 536–52.

—— and Schaltegger, C.A. (2005) “Tax amnesties and political participation,” *Public Finance Review*, 33: 403–31.

Treisman, D. (2000) “The cause of corruption: a cross-national study,” *Journal of Public Economics*, 76: 399–457.

Verba, S., Schlozman, K.L., and Brady, H.E. (1995) *Voice and Equality: Civic volunteerism in American politics*, Cambridge, MA: Harvard University Press.

Wooldridge, J. M. (2002) *Introductory Econometrics*: *A modern approach*, South-Western, Ohio: Thompson.

6 Littering and environmental participation

> Over recent years, the notion of "civil society" has experienced tempestuous times, swiftly developing from a slogan used in opposition to totalitarian regimes in East-Central Europe into one of the catchwords in worried reflections on issues such as social fragmentation, political alienation, and the erosion of community life in Western society. In the process, the idea of civil society has been used in various ways, taking on several connotations, though voluntary organizations and volunteering appear to be core elements of civil society everywhere.
>
> (Dekker and van den Broek 1998: 11–12)

Introduction

This chapter focuses on the environmental behaviors associated with littering. One might expect that economists would have already explored this phenomenon, as the decisions on whether or not to litter may be related to literature on the economics of crime that is based on the costs of littering and the costs of avoiding littering. The negative externalities of a littered environment could also have attracted economists' attention before now. However, the reality is somewhat different. Despite recognition of littering in public places as a major public health and safety hazard through such effects as water pollution, fire hazards, rodent and insect infestations, highway accidents, injuries suffered from discarded cans and broken bottles, and also as diminishing the aesthetic appearance of public places (Cialdini et al. 1990, Ackerman 1997), few studies have addressed this issue. As an example, a search for "littering" in the key economics database ECONLIT returns only eight hits. If we search for "litter" we obtain only 36 results.[1] A better understanding of why people litter or whether people think that littering is justifiable would be quite valuable.

As Huffman *et al.* (1995: 153) pointed out, "one of our society's enduring enigmas is its propensity to litter." Litter differs from other kinds of pollution in that it is produced by the collective action of many individuals rather than by a small number of firms (Feld 1978). Since the production of litter is a collective action, from a socio-economic point of view *not* littering can be seen as a kind of cooperative and social behavior which can contribute to improved social capital. Keeping outdoor public places clean provides public benefits in maintaining a public good character, while costs are private (Anand 2000). This kind of pro-environmental behavior is clearly aligned with participation in environmental organizations. It is an individual behavior that contributes to the improvement of the environment as a public good.

Much of this book is interested in voluntary compliance and behavior, as it offers a solution to social dilemmas (as discussed at length in Chapter 1). The decision to litter or not to litter is an observable, common, and ubiquitous decision that almost everyone faces almost every day. If only for this reason, littering behavior is interesting. The proper disposal of litter incurs a personal cost that could have been avoided by simply leaving the rubbish behind. What would induce people to incur such a cost (without the threat of omnipresent police officers)? We have discussed in Chapters 1 and 2 how voluntary compliance is primarily being driven by social norms or preferences for environmental protection, and in this chapter we will discuss the importance of these factors for the littering decision.

Background

While economics may have neglected the study of littering, other disciplines have been investigating the topic for decades; the psychology literature on littering started to emerge in the 1970s and 1980s with studies such as Finnie (1973), or Geller et al. (1977). Several of these studies used an experimental approach to investigate the processes that influence the littering decision. For example, Geller et al. (1977) explored whether instructions at the bottom of a handbill (antilitter message versus no antilitter message) given in a grocery store affected individuals' littering. Such approaches are quite valuable as they provide an opportunity to control for and manipulate the variables of interest. This reduces causality problems and returns useful information not only about the relationship between two variables but also about the direction of the effect. While psychologists had started to use experiments by the beginning of the twentieth century, economists started relatively late (the first economics experiments were carried out in the 1950s and 1960s). Instead of using laboratory experiments, many of these psychology studies were conducted as field experiments in "the outside world," in the usual environment where social and economic interactions occur. This assists in generating realism and external validity. The advantage of this approach is the absence of observable experimental effect as individuals are completely unaware they have taken part in the field experiment. However, early studies provided only limited insights to the understanding of the process of littering, covering elementary questions such as "why people litter" (Meeker 1997). They also provided limited information regarding the extent to which individuals' heterogeneity affects either the action of littering or the willingness to litter. This situation has now changed, with recent studies providing a better theoretical foundation for their investigations (for example, Keizer et al. 2008, Cialdini et al.1990). Keizer et al. (2008) have explored the spreading of disorder ("broken window theory") in regards to littering by testing whether the signs of existing disorderly and petty criminal behavior trigger more disorderly and petty criminal behavior. Their key aim was to produce a disorderly setting such that it was linked to a process of spreading norm violation. The strength of such a study lies in the exploration of cross-norm inhibition effects in a controlled field-experimental environment. In three small field experiments on littering they compared disorder and order conditions. Their results show that if norm-violating behavior becomes more common, it negatively affects compliance in other areas. The findings show that the presence of graffiti more than doubled the number of people littering. Similarly, almost twice as many people littered when four unreturned shopping carts were standing around in disarray at a parking garage compared to a situation where the garage was clear. Moreover, these results were also confirmed when individuals witnessed others committing an offense against the national law (setting off fireworks in the week before New Year's Eve). Thus, their results suggest that when a certain norm violation becomes more common, other norm deviances are also more frequently observable. Litter and unkempt lawns have also been linked with crime (Brown et al. 2004). Recently, experiments have tried to determine (albeit in a somewhat limited manner) whether socio-demographic factors matter (Meeker 1997).

In contrast to such experimental studies, the exercise in this chapter uses the survey information provided by the European Values Survey (EVS) 1999/2000, the database described in Chapter 4. The empirical work will consider 32 representative national samples of at least 1,000 individuals in each country. While the analysis in Chapter 5 included 38 countries, in this chapter we restrict the scope to include only European countries but we focus on more recent data. To a certain extent, this will allow us to control for unobserved cultural and institutional factors, in light of findings from the previous chapter indicating that we have substantial regional differences. The use of survey data to explore environmental behaviors in Europe should provide a good source of information regarding potential factors that shape attitudes towards littering. Furthermore, surveys are valuable in cross-country and cross-regional comparisons and offer insights regarding what happens over time. Certainly, we acknowledge potential limitations in the use of survey data and will discuss these in the following sub-sections, along with possible solutions for those limitations. One should note that EVS is not a panel survey. We regard this as unfortunate, since a survey that follows individuals over time would have allowed us to study the dynamics of adjustment and causality problems far more accurately. However, to our knowledge, the only available data-set that covers this many countries is cross-sectional. Panel data is often country specific (e.g. GSOEP in Germany or HILDA in Australia), which reduces the generalizability of the results. Nevertheless, we work with the information available, and the remainder of this chapter will proceed as follows: the next section provides a brief overview of the existing literature on littering. We then present our empirical model and develop our hypotheses. The fourth section presents the main results and the final section provides concluding remarks for this chapter.

Environmental participation and littering

Before providing a brief overview of the relevant literature on the determinants of littering, we will first discuss the notion of littering and consider some of the different types of littering.

What is litter?

Litter has been defined as misplaced waste material (Geller *et al.* 1982) or "the careless, incorrect disposal of minor amounts of waste" (Hansmann and Scholz 2003: 753).[2] Littering is considered as "one of the most neglected, yet it is one of the most visible, forms of environmental degradation" (Finnie 1973: 123). There are several places in which litter is commonly found, such as parks, roads, paths, camping grounds, cafes, stores, or other public buildings. Litter may consist of items such as cigarettes, bottles and other glass or plastic containers, serviettes, bags, tissues, take-away food packages and snack wrappers. All of these items are frequently discarded and can seriously harm the environment, especially as some are non-degradable.[3] The destruction of the environment will incur several costs, including reduced environmental amenity and function, as well as any costs involved in removing the litter and cleaning the area. Furthermore, there are additional environmental costs to take into account, since some forms of litter are more dangerous than others. For example, a live cigarette or a piece of glass left behind in a forested area may cause a destructive fire and significant environmental damage (Crump *et al.* 1977).

Other forms of environmentally harmful behaviors, such as illegal dumping, are related to littering. Illegal dumping is the unlawful deposit of waste larger than litter onto land. It includes waste materials that have been dumped, tipped or otherwise deposited onto private or public land where no license or approval exists to accept such waste. Illegal dumping varies from small bags of rubbish in an urban environment to larger scale dumping of waste materials in isolated areas, such as bushland. If not addressed, illegal dumps often attract more waste, potentially including hazardous wastes such as asbestos, household chemicals and paints, automotive fluids, and commercial or industrial wastes.

Types of littering: active and passive

The literature has distinguished between active and passive littering, the difference being the lapse of time between when litter was placed in the area and when the individual vacated the area. The distinction is very similar to that made between un-intentional and intentional littering, demonstrated clearly in the examples described by Sibley and Liu (2003). If a person drops some packaging on the ground and continues walking on a path, that littering behavior could be considered active because there is no lag between the placement of litter and the vacation of the area. In this respect, active littering may be considered an "overt form of behavior because the act of littering occurs the moment the litter is deposited in the environment" (Sibley and Liu 2003: 417). In comparison, passive littering occurs when there is a lapse between the placement of litter and vacation of the area. An example would be if a person placed packaging on a park bench where they were sitting, and later, when vacating the park bench, left the packaging there as litter. Thus, passive littering can be considered a less noticeable form of behavior than active littering. On the other hand, active non-littering occurs when the litter is kept in hand during the whole period that the territory is occupied and the litter is either taken away or put in the correct place upon vacating the area.

Survey respondents have given several reasons for engaging in either active or passive littering, including carelessness, laziness, the inconvenience of keeping the litter, or accidental disposal. In a survey about illegal dumping carried out in New South Wales, Australia (DECC 2004) most people admitted to dumping materials from time to time, claiming that it was too much of an effort to try to dispose of things properly and that they did not have anything else to do with used items but put them out and hope someone takes them.

Key factors that influence littering

One of the main aspects of interests in the study of littering is voluntary compliance. It is noteworthy because non-littering individuals are engaging in a voluntary behavior to conserve an environment, despite there being very little punishment if they were to litter.[4] As we have mentioned on several occasions, voluntary compliance eliminates free-rider behavior and provides the foundation of cooperation and public good provision. We are interested in the factors behind this voluntary behavior, and recognize that social norms and environmental morale are influences on the littering decision. In previous chapters, (particularly in Chapter 1), we have discussed the literature suggesting that social norms help to explain the high degree of compliance (Torgler 2007). Prevailing social norms tend to generate increased individual cooperation in public good situations and, in some instances, of private goods as well. Violation of social norms has negative consequences, such as internal sanctions (e.g. guilt, remorse) or external legal and social sanctions, such as gossip and ostracism.

As Polinsky and Shavell (2000) point out, the corresponding literature focuses on the influence that social norms have on individual behavior, and their role as a substitute for, or a supplement to, formal laws. In fact, laws can also influence social norms. Rege and Telle (2001: 3) suggest that social norms may explain why many individuals do not litter public places. If littering is not acceptable in a society, a "person throwing his ice-cream-paper on the street will feel social disapproval from people observing him . . . many people do not litter even if they know that nobody is observing them, because littering imposes a feeling of guilt." Feelings of guilt or shame restrict behavior, and can increase the costs of non-compliance with the law in the same way as legal sanctions (Grasmick *et al.* 1991).

Additionally, environmental morale can be seen as a necessary pre-condition in order to develop environmentally friendly behaviors. According to Frey (1997), the net costs faced by individuals lead to a price effect that changes behavior. If the net costs are small, more individuals are likely to make the required behavioral change. When the net costs are larger, only those individuals with a high environmental morale are likely to make the changes to their behavior. In fact, it may be the case that

> in important areas, economic incentive instruments cannot be applied at all or would be too costly to overcome cooperation problems . . . This is the case when the costs of control are extremely high due to many diffuse sources of pollution, or due to a large number of individuals causing environmental damage in small ways (e.g. spitting, throwing away batteries, pieces of paper or used cigarettes). In these cases voluntary contributions must be relied upon in order to prevent negative environmental externalities.
>
> (Frey and Stutzer 2006: 3)

In light of the above arguments, we expect that it may be quite valuable to explore what it is that shapes the justifiability of littering.

Attempts to affect or reduce littering

Attempts at external influences to reduce littering include signs, education, taxes, and fines. Social sanctions may also play a part, but in order for people to "feel" social sanctions, littering must be perceived as an unacceptable behavior, which returns us to our discussion on social norms. Littering behavior may be targeted at different points in the decision process (Geller *et al.* 1982, Huffman *et al.* 1995). On one hand, it would be possible to change the antecedent conditions of littering behavior by using verbal or written messages (prompts), signals, education sessions, demonstration, community involvement, or goal-setting strategies (Geller 1992, Dwyer *et al.* 1993). Some studies have shown the effectiveness of education in encouraging environmentally responsible behaviors. For example, Taylor *et al.* (2007) found that education campaigns led to reduced litter loads in stormwater.

Signs

As an antecedent-based procedure, the importance of the design of prompt, sign or advertisement design has been demonstrated. Geller *et al.* (1982) pointed out several attributes that prompts should possess in order to be effective. Thus, according to those authors,

> (1) the prompt should be administered in close proximity with the opportunity to provide the associated response, (2) the prompt should specifically state the desired response, (3) the desired response should be relatively convenient, and (4) the prompt should be conveyed in polite non-demanding language.
>
> (Geller *et al.* 1982: 65)

In the empirical context, Reich and Robertson (1979) found that the polite wording of a sign is very important in achieving reductions in littering. Similarly, Reiter and Samuel (1980) also concluded that the wording of prompts has a significant impact on littering. They found that while threatening messages are more effective at reducing litter than control situations in which there were no signs, the most effective strategy appeared to be the use of signs encouraging cooperation. In this respect, Durdan *et al.* (1985) discovered that written prompts espousing positive messages such as "Please be helpful!" achieved litter reduction in a cafeteria setting. Additionally, techniques involving more social involvement led to more significant littering reductions. This is certainly the case when using verbal prompts, which seem to be more effective than written prompts or signals. Higher proximity and interaction with people necessitates higher efforts and costs, but usually produces better results in reduction of littering. For example, community involvement is considered a socio-intensive procedure (Huffman *et al.* 1995). When some people collaborate to inform their neighbors about the places to deposit waste and to point out the negative consequences of littering, the results tend to be more positive and intense, reducing littering behaviors.

Taxes and fines

On the other hand, it is possible to find interventions that change littering behavior through either offering rewards for abstinence or imposing penalties/taxes (Fullerton and Wolverton 2000, Ackerman 1997, Huffman *et al.* 1995, Dobbs 1991). While rewards can be applied ex-ante, penalties are applied ex-post. The imposition of a fine or a penalty on littering is a more direct approach to reduction of littering.

However, these kinds of behaviors are difficult to implement in practice. It is complicated and costly to control littering, because sometimes it is not possible to observe litter at the moment it is produced. As noted by one researcher,

> local authorities are often criticised for overzealous enforcement and using fines as a means to generate revenue. Nonetheless, the public are very big supporters of the use of enforcement to prevent littering and it was suggested by all groups that took part in this research. Enforcement could mean handing out fines. It could also mean community service. Either way, people had to believe there was a strong possibility they would be caught for littering and that enforcement would be carried out strictly.
>
> (Campbell 2007: 26)

Thus, there are alternative ways to achieve reductions in littering. Due to the difficulty of applying a direct tax to litter, some indirect instruments have been proposed (Dobbs 1991). For example, a tax on the use of plastic bags in retail outlets was introduced in Ireland during 2002. This change brought about a significant reduction in littering (around 90 percent), and resulted in positive landscape effects (Convery *et al.* 2007). Another possible instrument is the use of monetary incentives to encourage people to recycle some non-degradable items. Thus, the positive effects of recycling policies on littering reduction have been observed (Naughton *et al.* 1990; Huffman *et al.* 1995).

Social sanctions

At the same time, we cannot forget the social impact that these kind of behaviors can have. It is possible that the "penalty" of littering could be incurred in the social dimension, by means of non-acceptance, disapproval, or even isolation. Yet, it may be that some kinds of litter are more socially tolerable than others. For example, some authors think that disposing of items such as cigarettes on the street (Cope *et al.* 1993) or organic litter in green areas (Beck 2007) must be perceived as more socially acceptable than other kinds of littering.

The perception of what is acceptable and what is not may change over time. We previously mentioned some research based on several surveys conducted during the period 2001–6 in the UK (Campbell 2007) which found evidence of an increase in general awareness about litter and even the material of which it was made. Awareness of the two biggest components of litter (smokers' materials and chewing gum) had increased, although attitudes had yet to change. Worryingly, more people than before reported throwing litter from their car and also dropping fast food litter on the streets.

It is possible that the perception of what constitutes acceptable littering increases when people think that the responsibility of cleaning public areas is not theirs, and rather it is an issue to be solved by public sector. Thus, it can be acceptable to litter in areas where someone else cleans up (Beck 2007). This may be the case in urban areas, where Cialdini *et al.* (1991) conducted their study; however it can be contrasted with the results obtained by Crump *et al.* (1977) on littering behavior in a forest environment. Their experiments found the opposite to be true: people visiting a heavily littered picnic area would pick up the majority of the rubbish before starting their lunch. The researchers propose that this difference in behavior can be partly attributed to the different settings: there is quite a marked psychological difference between 60 pieces of litter in an urban environment and 60 pieces of litter in a forest environment. Picnickers are also likely to remain in a picnic area for a longer period of time than they would remain in a city street, and Crump *et al.* suggest that this difference could be responsible for the discrepancy in littering behaviors between urban environments and forest environments. Similar to Cialdini *et al.* (1991) and Keizer *et al.* (2008), Torgler *et al.* (2009) also observe that the environmental behavior of individuals is systematically influenced by the perception of others' behavior: people act in a conditionally cooperative way with respect to littering. If an individual believes that throwing away litter in a public place is common, then the environmental morale of the individual decreases. In contrast, if an individual believes others to be compliant, then the environmental morale increases.

Determinants of littering

Socio-demographic and socio-economic factors

Previous literature has identified several socio-economic and socio-demographic features with respect to those people who usually litter (Beck 2007). On one hand, it seems that young people litter more than older people (Durdan *et al.* 1985, Huffman *et al.* 1995), and that men litter more than women, which supports the idea that women are more concerned with environmental issues (Zelezny *et al.* 2000, Campbell 2007).

Norms of littering

Sometimes there is a higher probability of littering in places where there is already litter rather than in clean areas (Cialdini *et al.* 1991). According to Campbell (2007),

> it was most acceptable to drop litter when an area was already dirty and run-down, but not when it was tidy and presentable. It was most excusable to drop litter when everyone else was doing it, but not when in respectable company.
> (Campbell 2007: 19)

This would suggest that if people notice other individuals are littering, their willingness to litter increases, reducing the moral constraints which would otherwise compel individuals to behave in an (ordinarily) socially accepted manner.

Finnie (1973) and Heberlein (cited in Cialdini *et al.* 1991) also conclude that clean areas remain clean. Krauss *et al.* (1976: 112) offer an explanation for this phenomenon: "any norm violation that is observed tends to weaken the norm by detracting from its social validity." In general, the presence of prior litter is linked to a significant increase in several litter items. Thus, litter leads to more litter.

Proper receptacles

The presence of proper trash receptacles can significantly reduce littering. Campbell (2007) reports that a lack of bins, or bins that were full or overflowing, was one of the most common excuses for littering. It is very important that people are able to find trash receptacles for convenient deposit of litter. If there are many receptacles and they are well-located, then the individual costs of putting rubbish in the correct place will decrease. Those lower costs lead to important littering reductions. Those reductions are even higher in the case of decorated containers (Huffman *et al.* 1995).

Community education

Existing studies have also examined the role that education can play in reducing public litter (Taylor *et al.* 2007), and the instruments (e.g. taxes, fines, charges, and market incentives) that can be used to minimize the problem of public littering (Fullerton and Wolverton 2000, Ackerman 1997, Dobbs 1991).

Environmental activism

Krauss *et al.* (1976) obtained a significant relationship between some kinds of environmental activism and littering. They found that people who were asked to sign a petition about cleaning public areas would litter less often than other people. Roales-Nieto (1988) observed a significant littering reduction when some volunteers cleaned the dirtiest areas of their neighborhood. Active participation by citizens in cleaning and maintaining their neighborhoods is one of the features that lead to reduced littering. It has been recognized that environmental organizations "have been successful in changing public attitudes and norms regarding many issues such as recycling, littering, and energy conservation and in affecting public policy by creating public awareness" (Handy 2001: 654).

Our contribution is particularly interesting because it examines the kind of factors that influence the justification or acceptability of littering from an international point of view. Most of the previous studies have applied in small or medium geographic areas. Comparing different areas of the world can give us some clues with respect to individual environmental preferences and morale, and we will be able to characterize people who do not display these kinds of behaviors. We will also examine the impact of environmental participation in this respect. At the same time, we would like to check for similarities in the characteristics of those who undertake several cooperative and environmentally friendly behaviors.

Empirical model

To assess the justifiability of littering, we use the following question:

> Please tell me for each of the following statements whether you think it is always justified, never justified, or somewhere in between: . . . Throwing away litter in a public place.

A ten-scale index is used for this question, with the two extremes being "never justified" and "always justified." The natural cut-off point is the value 1, where a high amount of respondents assert that throwing away litter in a public place is "never justified" (68.3 percent). Previous studies on "other justifiability variables" that are not related to littering use WVS data and find support for a similar cutoff point by applying a probit model in their empirical model (e.g., Swamy *et al.* 2001). Thus, our attitudinal anti-littering variable takes the value 1 if the respondent says that discarding litter in a public place is "never justified," and zero otherwise. Thus, in line with the process used in Chapter 5 we will implement a probit model in the empirical section.

According to Beck (2007), previous surveys which have analyzed attitudes to littering are "not always comparable, due in part to the way in which questions were framed.[5] In some cases, the report did not indicate details of the survey questions as much as hoped." In only four of those surveys was the justification or acceptability of littering asked about, and the results were different, which make it difficult to draw any general conclusions.[6] In addition, there is a complete lack of papers addressing the issue of environmental participation and its impact on littering.

Even though previous field experiments study littering behavior directly, there are many advantages to using such a large database. Besides the strength of exploring this large data source, working with such an attitudinal variable can help to reduce the effect of potentially spurious factors. If we were to investigate littering directly, it would be necessary to control for aspects such as the rule of law or the deterrence system (e.g., fines and penalty of getting caught).

Several economists are skeptical about using an attitudinal question as the dependent variable. Due to the measurement-error problems Bertrand and Mullainathan (2001) advise against using survey answers as dependent variable. However, as we will discuss in this chapter, there are methods that one can apply to deal with such potential biases (see also Torgler *et al.* 2009). It is important to generate more knowledge and better methodologies on how to work with such data and how to better deal with such shortcomings. An increasing number of economists are exploring attitudinal questions, which should gradually lead to further methodological innovations. It would be a pity to neglect interesting research questions due to such problems. For example, research that deals with social capital, corruption, happiness, and tax compliance has produced interesting insights in exploring the causes of attitudes (Diener and Suh 2000, Brewer *et al.* 2002, Uslaner 2004, Brewer *et al.* 2004, Chang and Chu 2006, Torgler 2007, 2008). Moreover, if the justifiability of littering is endogenous, it is useful to explore its determinants to be able to derive policy implications.

Data

Despite the obvious advantage of using justifiability of littering as a dependent variable rather than using littering, it is common to criticize the subjective characteristics of survey data. It is not possible to ascertain whether respondents are truthful in their answers with survey data, since truth is not observable by the interviewers (Kanazawa 2005). To validate the statements made by respondents, one could explore the correlation between respondents' statements and observed behavior. However, this is only possible for specific questions (e.g., voting behavior). Using an attitudinal question, such as in our case, reduces the possibilities of conducting such a validation analysis. Nevertheless, we could explore the correlation between our justifiability of littering variable and environmental performance/outcome at the macro (country) level. Therefore, we explore the relationship between our dependent variable and the Environmental Sustainability Index (ESI) developed by the Yale Center for Environmental Law and Policy and the Center for International Earth Science Information Network at Columbia University. The index measures the ability of nations to protect the environment over the next few decades, integrating 76 data sets tracking natural resource endowments, past and present pollution levels, environmental management efforts and the capacity of a society to improve its environmental performance covering 21 indicators of environmental sustainability (see the ESI 2005).

To increase the number of observations we work with the World Values Survey (WVS) as it contains the same questions as the EVS.[7] The results are reported in Figure 6.1. We take the country mean values of all the waves to generate our justifiability of littering variable. In this case, we do not recode the variable. This means that higher values are correlated with a higher level of the justifiability of littering. In the ESI index, higher values are correlated with a higher level of environmental sustainability. The index ranges from 0 to 100. The highest values can be found in Scandinavian countries, such as Finland, Norway, and Sweden (with a score of more than 70). Figure 6.1 shows an expected negative correlation relationship (Pearson r = –0.373) that is statistically significant at the 0.01 level. Analyzing the linear relationship in a simple regression indicates that the justifiability of littering variable can explain approximately 15 percent of the total variance of the dependent variable (ESI). Such results indicate the usefulness of working with attitudinal questions, despite the potential survey biases.

In addition, we compare the original scale with an ordered probit model and an OLS with standardized/beta coefficients to test the relative strength of a variable. We will also use an ordered probit after re-coding the ten-scale variable into a

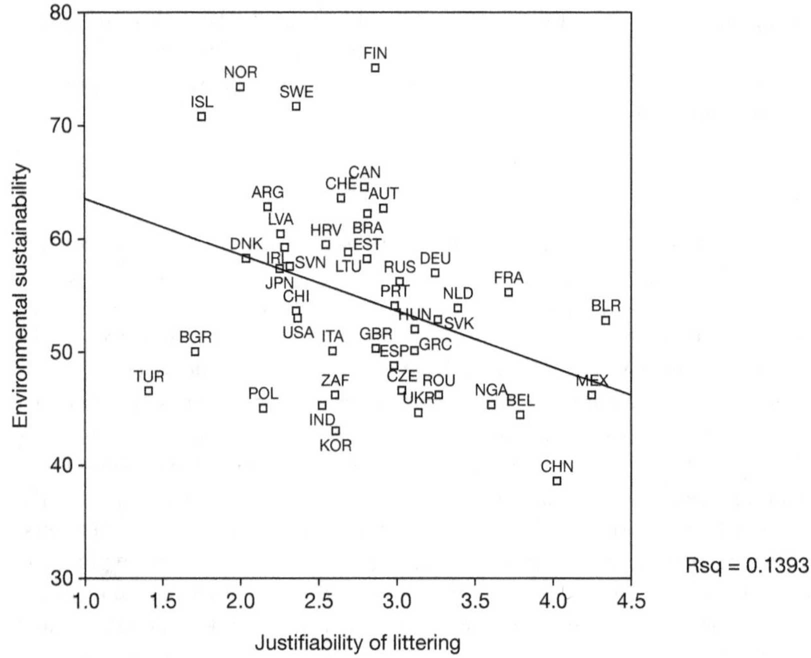

Figure 6.1 Environmental sustainability and justifiability of littering

four-point scale (0, 1, 2, 3), with the value 3 assigned for "never justified." The scale numbering from 4–10 is assigned the value 0 due to lack of variance (2 = 2, 3 = 1). Such an approach is standard practice and has been used, for example, in the happiness and tax compliance literature (Frey and Stutzer 2002, Torgler 2007). It is important to go beyond the original probit model (1 = never justified) since the answer to the question could be biased. It is obvious that the "socially correct" answer would be "never justified." In other words, if the respondents want to give the "socially acceptable" answer they would say "1" and, if not, they would answer truthfully. In this latter case, an answer of "0" might be indicative of a much lower justifiability than an answer of "1." In the interview situation, it could be that respondents want to avoid looking bad in front of the interviewer (Bertrand and Mullainathan 2001). If this was indeed the case, we would observe systematic biases rather than just random errors. To deal with this problem, we try different cutoff points. We check, for example, what happens if we run a probit model, where we convert the values 1 and 2 to 1 (all other values = 0).[8] We will not report all these robustness tests but one should note that our environmental participation variable is always highly statistically significant with comparable quantitative effects.

The experimental literature has shown that manipulations (e.g., order of the questions, exact wording or scales) can affect how people process and interpret questions. The problem arises because "respondents may make little mental effort in answering the question, such as by not attempting to recall all the relevant information or by not reading through the whole list of alternative responses" (Bertrand and Mullainathan 2001: 68). To check this point, we explore the correlation between two similar questions asked in the EVS during different parts of the interview. These were previously described in Chapter 5. However, let us remember them:

> How interested would you say you are in politics? (PI) Very interested (value 1), somewhat interested (value 2), not very interested (value 3), not the least interested (value 4).

> How important is politics in your life? (IMP) Very important (value 1), quite important (value 2), not very important (value 3), not the least important (value 4).

The correlation at the individual level is 0.614. Moreover, we also explore the correlation with the question:

> When you get together with your friends, would you say you discuss political matters frequently (value 3), occasionally (value 2) or never (value 1)? (DP)

The correlation between the IMP and the DP is 0.451 and between the PI and the DP is 0.564. Thus, all the variables are highly correlated. Face-to-face interviews may also help to guarantee that subjects are aware of the whole list of alternative responses. The EVS has the advantage of being a wide-ranging survey covering a large number of different topics. The data for the environmental question used in this chapter were only a part of the large EVS survey. Hence, this further reduces the environmental framing biases, an argument that is relevant for all the empirical chapters in this book.

Our key independent variable (environmental participation) was introduced in Chapter 4, and is going to be measured with the following question:

> Please look carefully at the following list of voluntary organizations and activities and say which, if any, you belong to. Conservation, the environment, ecology, animal rights (1 = mentioned, 0 = not mentioned).

Additionally, the previous literature on social norm of compliance has indicated the need to control for socio-demographic and socio-economic factors. As we have reviewed the environmental literature in Chapter 3 we will now confine our discussion primarily to the evidence generated in the compliance and social norm literature. Occasionally, we will also refer to the littering literature.

Age

Following the process used in Chapter 5, we have formed several classes. The difference is that in this case, we have extended the number of categories: <30, 30–39, 40–49, 50–59, 60–69, >70, with <30 as reference group. It is argued that social position is key in the explanation of an age effect. Tittle (1980) explains that older persons have acquired greater social stakes such as material goods, status, and a stronger dependency on the reactions from others. The desire to avoid exclusion produces a motivation for compliance behavior, representing both compliance with social norms and a recognition of socially appropriate behavior (Bamberg and Möser 2007). The literature on tax morale provides support for this age effect (see Torgler 2007), as does the criminology literature through extensive exploration of the impact of age on crime (for an overview see Torgler and Valev 2006).

Gender

As mentioned in Chapter 3, experimental and empirical studies have established gender differences in several fields of behavior. The social norm literature clearly indicates that women are more willing to comply with society's rules (Torgler 2007). Additionally, women demonstrate more concern about environmental problems (Zelezny *et al.* 2000). The irony is, as mentioned previously, that some women do not have the time to engage in pro-environmental activities, especially those who work intensively both in and out of the home. In this respect, choosing to correctly dispose of litter can be seen as a "minimal cost" pro-environmental behavior in terms of the time needed to carry it out. So, we would expect to find that women litter less and have a lower acceptance of littering. Campbell (2007) reported that those who justified littering were a predominantly male segment, and that, in general, women feel guiltier than men do when they litter.

Formal and informal education and income

Torgler and García-Valiñas (2007) stress that formal education impacts on environmental preferences, as does informal education. The work in the previous chapter provides strong support for the idea that informal education matters. However, one should note that the relationship between education and rule compliance is not robust in the compliance literature.

Marital status

Tittle (1980) states, "a long tradition in sociology, extending back to Durkheim, postulates that proneness toward rule breaking varies inversely with the extent to which individuals are involved in social networks with constraining content." This would imply that married people are more compliant than others, especially compared to singles, because they are more constrained by their social network.

Employment status

An additional variable that complements the measurement of an individual's economic situation is their employment status. Chapter 3 has shown that we may observe differences between those of different employment status. For example, unemployed individuals have lower preferences for environmental protection policies. Similarly, the literature on crime has shown that unemployment is an important factor for crime (Entorf and Spengler 2002).

Religious belief

We use the frequency of church attendance as a proxy for religious belief. The advantage of this measure is the ability to make an approximation of how much time individuals devote to religion, instead of asking them to directly rate their degree of religious faith. The church as an institution instills behavioral norms and moral constraints in the members of the community. Some papers in the criminology literature have found a negative correlation between religious membership and crime (see, e.g., Hull 2000, Hull and Bold 1989, Lipford *et al.* 1993). Religious belief seems to affect the degree of rule breaking and the social norm of compliance, and has been found to restrict engagement in tax evasion (Torgler 2006).

Results

Our multivariate analysis includes the vector of control variables discussed. In some estimates we differentiate between two different regions of Europe (i.e. western and eastern Europe) because of the reform process in the transition countries and due to the fact that our work in the previous chapter has shown differences between both regions. Additionally, in this way we show the importance of institutional context in the explanation of environmentally cooperative behaviors.

Table 6.1 presents the first results of the multivariate analysis. We exclude income from these initial estimates, because the ten-point income scale in the EVS is based on national currencies, which reduces the ability to make a cross-country comparison.[9] The self-classification of the respondents' economic situation into various economic classes may be used as a proxy. However, data for this purpose has not been collected in all countries, so we include economic status sequentially in the specification (see Table 6.2). In line with previous chapters, a probit estimation is appropriate for this analysis as it takes into account the ranking information of the scaled dependent variables. Here we also report the marginal effects. Moreover, weighted estimates are conducted to make the samples correspond to the national distribution.[10] Again, answers such as "don't know" and missing values are eliminated in all estimations.

Our first specification (1) is presented in Table 6.1. This regression uses a regional dummy variable, namely Western Europe. The second specification (2) goes a step further by including country fixed effects. Controlling for individual country effects allows us to eliminate (to a certain extent) some unobserved factors at the country level (e.g., institutional conditions). Certainly, looking at the descriptive statistics presented in Chapter 4, there is a risk that we might under-estimate the effect of environmental participation owing to the fact that it might be partly absorbed by the countries' culture and institutional conditions. However, such an approach is useful to check the robustness of the relationship between environmental participation and anti-littering attitudes. Similarly, in the third specification (3) we present standard errors adjusted for the clustering on 30 countries. This approach was introduced in the previous chapter. If we compare the results to those from the first specification (1), we can see that the coefficient and marginal effect values remain the same. Adding country fixed effects lead to a strong increase in the Pseudo R2 value. Consistent with our main prediction, the estimation results in Table 6.1 indicate that being a member in an environmental organization increases the probability of stating that littering is never justifiable by around 4 percent. The coefficient is statistically significant in all three specifications and the size of the effect is substantial. As Table 6.2 indicates, the results remain robust when the proxies for an individual's economic situation are included. Thus, there is a strong relationship between participating in an environmental organization and not littering.

In general, the results on the justifiability of littering are in line with the literature on social norms or morality, such as tax morale (Torgler 2007). Age is negatively correlated with the justifiability of littering; that is, as people get older, the justifiability decreases. The results indicate that the peak is reached between 50 and 69 (see marginal effects) in both tables. Women are more willing to comply than men. For example, specification two (2) reports that being a woman rather than a man increases the probability of stating that littering is never justifiable by 5.4 percent. Moreover, married people show the highest level of opposition to littering. Less robust findings are observed for the formal education and church attendance. The coefficients on education are mostly not statistically significant and church attendance is only statistically significant in specification one (1) and four (4). Interestingly, students report the lowest willingness to litter, followed by part-time employees. On the other hand, unemployed people report a high level of compliance. It should be noted that the results in the tables are always in relation to the reference group (full-time employed). Finally, specification one (1) also reports significant differences between east and west Europe. However, once the clustering method is implemented or the economic situation is controlled for, the significant difference disappears.

Endogeneity problems

However, the causality in these relationships is not clear. There may be a potential selection bias as people who are opposed to littering may choose to participate in a voluntary environmental organization. Such an argument would imply a reverse causality. However, due to the fact that everyone is confronted with the decision to litter or not, and taking into account that littering only covers one small part of environmental protection, one could argue that having a strong preference against littering may not provide sufficient incentive to participate in an environmental organization. Nevertheless, to control for such a potential problem, we will use an instrumental approach in the empirical part to check the robustness of the results. It is difficult to find a suitable proxy at the micro level that is entirely exogenous. A suitable instrument must be contemporaneously uncorrelated with the error term but must be highly correlated with membership in a voluntary environmental organization. We use an index of concerns regarding the living conditions of others that fits such a requirement, although one can argue that from a theoretical point of view, there might be a link between interdependent preferences (concern about the situation of others) and compliance (littering).[11] From this perspective we agree that we do not have the best instrument to work with. Table 6.3 reports the results of two-stage least squares (2SLS) estimations together with the first stage regressions. It shows that the instruments and the F-tests for the instrument exclusion set in the first-stage regression are statistically significant. We also report the Anderson canonical correlations LR test for the relevance of the instruments, checking the relevance of the excluded instruments. A rejection of the null hypothesis indicates that the model is identified and that the instruments are relevant (see Hall *et al.* 1996). We also report the Anderson-Rubin test result, showing that the endogenous variables are jointly statistically significant. The test has the advantage of being robust to the presence of weak instruments. Table 6.3 reports that in all cases the Anderson canonical correlations LR test shows rejection of the null hypothesis, which supports the choice of the instrument used. The Anderson-Rubin test is also statistically significant. Consistent with our previous results, we find that environmental participation is correlated with a lower justifiability of littering. The relationship is quite strong and robust. Thus, although we cannot fully depend on consistent estimates when working with such a micro data set, the strong relationship is a good indicator that environmental participation matters.

Table 6.1 Determinants of the justifiability of littering (1)

	Coeff.	*z-Stat.*	*Marg. effects*	*Coeff.*	*z-Stat.*	*Marg. effects*	*Coeff.*	*z-Stat.*	*Marg. effects*
	Weighted probit			*Weighted probit*			*Weighted probit*		
Dependent variable	*Justifiability of littering*			*Justifiability of littering*			*Justifiability of littering*		
	Robust standard errors			*Country fixed effects*			*Standard errors adjusted for the clustering on 30 countries*		
	(1)			*(2)*			*(3)*		
Voluntary organization									
Environ. Organization	0.119***	3.49	0.041	0.111***	3.03	0.038	0.119**	2.26	0.041
Demographic factors									
Age 30–39	0.108***	4.16	0.038	0.102***	3.82	0.035	0.108***	3.05	0.038
Age 40–49	0.173***	6.29	0.060	0.170***	5.95	0.058	0.173***	4.49	0.060
Age 50–59	0.237***	7.87	0.081	0.262***	8.42	0.086	0.237***	5.02	0.081
Age 60–69	0.285***	7.66	0.096	0.330***	8.56	0.107	0.285***	4.09	0.096
Age 70+	0.244***	5.59	0.082	0.319***	7.08	0.103	0.244***	2.92	0.082
Woman	0.100***	6.10	0.036	0.154***	9.08	0.054	0.100***	3.60	0.036
Formal and informal education									
Education	–0.001	–0.46	0.000	0.002	1.20	0.001	–0.001	–0.14	0.000
Political discussion	–0.018	–1.55	–0.007	0.019	1.55	0.007	–0.018	–0.74	–0.007

Marital status									
Widowed	–0.052*	–1.71	–0.019	–0.072**	–2.26	–0.025	–0.052	–1.13	–0.019
Divorced	–0.091***	–3.08	–0.033	–0.068**	–2.26	–0.024	–0.091**	–2.33	–0.033
Separated	–0.132**	–2.26	–0.048	–0.170***	–2.78	–0.061	–0.132**	–2.24	–0.048
Never married	–0.132***	–5.70	–0.048	–0.162***	–6.72	–0.058	–0.132***	–3.23	–0.048
Employment status									
Part-time employee	–0.122**	–4.00	–0.044	–0.085***	–2.72	–0.030	–0.122**	–2.44	–0.044
Self-employed	0.034	0.99	0.012	0.000	–0.01	0.000	0.034	0.74	0.012
Unemployed	0.118***	3.83	0.041	0.091***	2.84	0.031	0.118***	2.66	0.041
At home	0.152***	4.96	0.052	0.002	0.07	0.001	0.152**	2.08	0.052
Student	–0.152***	–4.05	–0.056	–0.177***	–4.56	–0.064	–0.152***	–3.53	–0.056
Retired	0.012	0.40	0.004	–0.004	–0.13	–0.001	0.012	0.30	0.004
Other	0.058	0.99	0.020	0.028	0.48	0.010	0.058	0.66	0.020
Religious belief									
Church attendance	0.011***	3.54	0.004	–0.003	–0.75	–0.001	0.011	0.76	0.004
Region									
Western Europe	–0.065***	–4.24	–0.023	Country fixed eff.			–0.065	–0.50	–0.023
Pseudo R2	0.021			0.085			0.021		
Number of observations	37356			37356			37356		
Prob > chi2	0.000			0.000			0.000		

Notes: The reference group consists of AGE<30, MAN, MARRIED, FULL-TIME EMPLOYEE, EASTERN EUROPE. The symbols *, **, *** represent statistical significance at the 10%, 5% and 1% levels, respectively.

Table 6.2 Determinants of the justifiability of littering (2)

	Coeff.	*z-Stat.*	*Marg. Effects*	*Coeff.*	*z-Stat.*	*Marg. Effects*
	Weighted probit			*Weighted probit*		
Dependent variable	*Justifiability of littering*			*Justifiability of littering*		
	Robust standard errors			*Country fixed effects*		
	(4)			*(5)*		
Voluntary organization						
Environmental organization	0.115**	2.28	0.040	0.116**	2.25	0.039
Demographic factors						
Age 30–39	0.085**	2.33	0.030	0.097**	2.57	0.033
Age 40–49	0.136***	3.46	0.047	0.135***	3.28	0.046
Age 50–59	0.201***	4.75	0.069	0.230***	5.21	0.076
Age 60–69	0.155***	3.00	0.054	0.225***	4.16	0.075
Age 70+	0.026	0.43	0.009	0.149**	2.36	0.050
Woman	0.039	1.63	0.014	0.113***	4.60	0.039
Formal and informal education						
Education	–0.006**	–2.26	–0.002	–0.004	–1.36	–0.001
Political discussion	–0.030*	–1.79	–0.011	0.027	1.51	0.009
Marital status						
Widowed	–0.035	–0.77	–0.012	–0.052	–1.10	–0.018
Divorced	–0.158***	–3.54	–0.058	–0.112**	–2.45	–0.040

Separated	–0.181**	–2.10	–0.067	–0.263***	–2.88	–0.097
Never married	–0.094***	–2.84	–0.034	–0.149***	–4.27	–0.053
Economic situation						
Upper class	–0.047	–1.37	–0.017	–0.070*	–1.91	–0.024
Middle class	–0.109***	–4.39	–0.039	–0.059**	–2.26	–0.021
Employment status						
Part-time employee	–0.037	–0.80	–0.013	–0.016	–0.35	–0.006
Self-employed	0.095**	2.00	0.033	–0.004	–0.08	–0.001
Unemployed	0.211***	4.96	0.073	0.181***	4.08	0.061
At home	0.221***	5.39	0.075	0.013	0.29	0.004
Student	–0.124**	–2.22	–0.045	–0.138**	–2.37	–0.049
Retired	–0.021	–0.48	–0.008	–0.026	–0.58	–0.009
Other	0.041	0.53	0.015	0.016	0.21	0.006
Religious belief						
Church attendance	0.021***	5.19	0.008	–0.003	–0.62	–0.001
Region						
Western Europe	0.011	0.46	0.004			
Pseudo R2	0.021			0.102		
Number of observations	19305			19305		
Prob > chi2	0.000			0.000		

Notes: The reference group consists of age<30, man, married, full-time employee, lowest class, eastern Europe. The symbols *, **, *** represent statistical significance at the 10%, 5% and 1% levels, respectively.

Table 6.3 Determinants of the justifiability of littering (3)

	Coeff.	*t-Stat.*	*Coeff.*	*t-Stat.*	*Coeff.*	*t-Stat.*	*Coeff.*	*t-Stat.*
	Weighted 2SLS		*First stage regression*		*Weighted 2SLS*		*First stage regression*	
Dependent variable	*Justifiability of littering*				*Justifiability of littering*			
	(6)				*(7)*			
Voluntary organization								
Environmental organization	5.364***	5.83			3.701	4.57		
Demographic factors								
Age 30–39	0.017	0.70	0.003	0.69	0.047*	1.86	–0.004	–0.69
Age 40–49	0.018	0.71	0.006	1.49	0.042	1.55	0.001	0.09
Age 50–59	–0.012	–0.37	0.017***	3.50	0.021	0.64	0.014*	1.89
Age 60–69	0.037	1.03	0.012**	2.11	0.066*	1.95	0.002	0.22
Age 70+	0.048	1.20	0.009	1.41	0.065	1.62	–0.005	–0.50
Woman	0.008	0.45	0.007***	2.70	0.007	0.41	0.007*	1.75
Formal and informal education								
Education	–0.013***	–4.47	0.003***	8.40	–0.011***	–3.59	0.003***	5.01
Political discussion	–0.066***	–3.92	0.012***	6.03	–0.049***	–2.77	0.014***	4.66
Marital status								
Widowed	0.037	1.38	–0.010**	–2.41	0.009	0.31	–0.005	–0.87
Divorced	0.026	0.95	–0.009*	–1.90	0.011	0.34	–0.012*	–1.71
Separated	–0.042	–0.75	–0.002	–0.16	–0.131**	–2.05	0.013	0.84
Never married	–0.091***	–3.96	0.007*	1.71	–0.076***	–3.14	0.007	1.25

Economic situation								
Upper class					–0.103***	–3.15	0.021***	3.15
Middle class					–0.050***	–2.72	0.008**	2.04
Employment status								
Part-time employee	–0.092***	–2.59	0.010*	1.72	–0.073*	–1.85	0.016*	1.70
Self-employed	–0.060*	–1.66	0.012*	1.89	–0.040	–1.11	0.011	1.29
Unemployed	0.062**	2.28	–0.007	–1.61	0.068**	2.50	–0.005	–0.76
At home	0.042	1.59	–0.008*	–1.94	0.004	0.17	–0.002	–0.26
Student	–0.036	–0.93	–0.006	–0.94	–0.007	–0.16	–0.014	–1.51
Retired	0.026	1.14	–0.006	–1.51	–0.027	–0.96	0.003	0.49
Other	–0.045	–0.72	0.010	0.92	–0.044	–0.72	0.012	0.83
Religious belief								
Church attendance	–0.002	–0.60	0.000	–0.05	0.000	–0.05	–0.001	–0.70
Regions	country fixed effects				country fixed effects			
Instrument:								
Care index			0.001***	6.30			0.001***	5.22
Test of excluded instruments			39.67***				27.29***	
Anderson canon. cor. LR statistic	40.091***				30.65***			
Anderson-Rubin test	216.98***				80.82***			
Number of observations	35229				18433			
Prob > F	0.000				0.000			

Notes: The reference group consists of age<30, man, married, full-time employee. The symbols *, **, *** represent statistical significance at the 10%, 5% and 1% levels, respectively.

Conclusions

In this chapter, we investigate the determinants of littering, exploring the relationship between environmental participation and the justifiability of littering. Using recent EVS data for western and eastern European countries, we find strong empirical support for such a relationship. The results remain robust after dealing with potential causality issues. We have decided to present an analysis on public littering due to the lack of empirical evidence in the area – especially in the field of economics – and to supplement experimental studies that have mainly been conducted by social psychologists. When considering other independent factors, this exercise may underline the importance of using a rich set of methods to fully understand individuals' justifiability of littering. An innovative approach would be to combine survey and experimental evidence. So far, we have established that encouraging individuals to be active in environmental organizations helps to keep the environment clean and promote anti-littering attitudes. We have also found a positive impact of such social capital on littering attitudes. Thus, we have shown the connections between participation in environmental organizations and the reduced justifiability of littering, which is significant in improving environmental outcomes.

To our knowledge, only a limited number of studies have empirically explored the determinants of littering with such a large data set. The majority of these have focused on a very small area. This relationship can be used to bring about positive environmental outcomes in other areas. The interesting and attractive feature of this behavior is its voluntary nature. Such behavior is not only cost effective but can be more effective in areas where law enforcement and market incentives fail (e.g., where it is very costly to control littering behavior).

Certainly, it seems that social capital matters in determining people's anti-littering attitudes. Higher environmental involvement leads to higher preferences and more friendly attitudes towards the environment. We tried to check the causality relationship and our analysis confirms such an idea, although one should note – as mentioned previously – that providing a clear causality relationship is quite problematic. This point is relevant for this chapter and all the other chapters in this book. It would be more appropriate to refer to an observable correlation. We recognize that it is also problematic to interpret our results and observed correlations throughout the chapter as causal effects. As mentioned in the introduction and in line with Guiso *et al.* (2003), we do not disregard the traditional latent variable critique and see the results as more precisely estimated partial correlations. For simplicity, we use the notion of "impact" or "effect" when discussing the results, the model and comparable papers in the literature review.

Not surprisingly, we can conclude that the understanding of what shapes the justifiability of littering needs to be investigated further. Still, only a relatively limited number of studies have explored the relevance of social norms in the area of littering. A good understanding of the interactions between environmental morale and preferences, actions and perceived environmental cooperation, and the factors strengthening these relationships, may have the potential to bring about better environmental outcomes.

Appendices

Table A.6.1 Countries

Western Europe	*Eastern Europe*
Germany	Belarus
Austria	Bulgaria
Belgium	Croatia
Denmark	Czech Republic
Finland	Estonia
France	Greece
Great Britain	Hungary
Iceland	Latvia
Ireland	Lithuania
Italy	Poland
Luxembourg	Romania
Malta	Russia
Netherlands	Slovak Republic
North Ireland	Slovenia
Portugal	Ukraine
Spain	
Sweden	

Table A6.2 Description of control variables

Variable	*Derivation*
Age	Age 30–39, age 40–49, age 50–59, age 60–69, age +70 (age <30 in the reference group)
Gender	Woman (man in the reference group)
Formal and informal education	Education: What is the highest educational level that you have attained? 1. No formal education 2. Incomplete primary school 3. Completed primary school 4. Incomplete secondary school: technical/vocational type 5. Completed secondary school: technical/vocational type 6. Incomplete secondary: university-preparatory type 7. Completed secondary: university-preparatory type 8. Some university-level education, without degree 9. University-level education, with degree Political discussion: When you get together with your friends, would you say you discuss political matters? 1 Never 2 Occasionally 3 Frequently
Marital status	Widowed; divorced; separated; never married (married in the reference group)
Economic situation	People sometimes describe themselves as belonging to the working class, the middle class, or the upper or lower class. Would you describe yourself as belonging to the:

continued

Table A6.2 Continued

Variable	*Derivation*
	upper class, middle class (the rest, working class and lower class, in the reference group).
Employment status	Part-time employee, self-employed, unemployed, at home, student, retired, other (full-time employed in the reference group).
Religious belief	Church attendance: Apart from weddings, funerals and christenings, how often do you attend religious services these days? 1 Practically never or never 2 Less often than once a year 3 Once a year 4 Only on special holy days/Christmas/Easter days 5 Other specific holy days 6 Once a month 7 Once a week 8 More than once a week

Table A6.3 Descriptive statistics

Variables	*Obs.*	*Mean*	*Std. Dev.*	*Min*	*Max*
Key variables					
Environmental organization	41125	0.049	0.216	0	1
Justifiability of littering	40674	0.683	0.465	0	1
Control variables					
Age 30–39	40963	0.197	0.398	0	1
Age 40–49	40963	0.191	0.393	0	1
Age 50–59	40963	0.15	0.357	0	1
Age 60–69	40963	0.135	0.342	0	1
Age 70+	40963	0.102	0.302	0	1
Woman	41114	0.54	0.498	0	1
Education	39840	18.712	5.125	5	74
Political discussion	40713	1.886	0.654	1	3
Upper class	21335	0.136	0.343	0	1
Middle class	21335	0.338	0.473	0	1
Widowed	39861	0.097	0.295	0	1
Divorced	39861	0.07	0.256	0	1
Separated	39861	0.016	0.124	0	1
Never married	39861	0.228	0.42	0	1
Part-time employed	40919	0.068	0.252	0	1
Self-employed	40919	0.052	0.222	0	1
Unemployed	40919	0.229	0.42	0	1
At home	40919	0.095	0.293	0	1
Student	40919	0.061	0.24	0	1
Retired	40919	0.073	0.261	0	1
Other	40919	0.018	0.131	0	1
Church attendance	40762	3.871	2.456	1	8
Instrument					
Care	38540	34.863	7.727	11	55

Notes

1 Accessed on July 7, 2009.
2 According to Huffman *et al.* (1995: 154), "discarded items may not be uniformly perceived as litter; for example, a hamburger bag versus an abandoned automobile."
3 A recent survey carried out by ENCAMS in the UK (Campbell 2007) showed that the most frequently mentioned items of litter were: (i) fruit debris, (ii) small pieces of paper, sweet wrappers, tissues, and tickets, (iii) take-away food wrappers, (iv) plastic bags, (v) chewing gum, (vi) nappies, condoms, needles and sanitary products, (vii) glass bottles and cans, (viii) cigarette butts, papers and packets.
4 In resolving the free-rider problem, one possible solution is to "force" people to cooperate. This is in line with deterrence policy based on the economics-of-crime approach. The individual maximizes their utility from a behaviour or action, taking into account the probability of detection and the degree of punishment. However, empirical and experimental findings indicate that deterrence models predict far less compliance than is actually observed. Using the economics-of-crime approach, it is still not possible to explain this level of compliance, even if we take into account the amount of risk aversion expressed by the participants.
5 Beck (2007) reported some previous surveys carried out primarily in the US and Australia.
6 For example, in surveys in Australia (1997) and Georgia, US (2006) surveys, high percentages of non-acceptability were found (76 percent and 95 percent respectively). However, people from Iowa, US (2001) considered littering as a minor issue, so the acceptability was high. In the Washington survey (1999) the majority of people thought that littering was acceptable if there was no receptacle nearby. According to Campbell (2007), in UK nearly half of the general population (48 percent) admitted to dropping some form of litter. Additionally several differences among the explanatory factors can be observed among the surveys.
7 We used country average values over the available waves.
8 The results remain robust when testing alternative cutoffs.
9 Moreover, income is coded on a scale from 1 to 10 and these income intervals are not fully comparable across countries.
10 The weighting variable is provided by the EVS.
11 Concerned about the living conditions of elderly, unemployed, immigrants, sick and disabled people, immediate family, people in your neighborhood, people of the region you live in, your fellow countrymen, Europeans, humankind (for each factor: 1 = not all, 5 = very much). We define this variable as care index.

References

Ackerman, F. (1997) *Why Do We Recycle? Markets, values, and public policy*, Washington, DC: Island Press.

Anand, P.B. (2000) "Cooperation and the urban environment: an exploration," *The Journal of Development Studies,* 36: 30–58.

Bamberg, S. and Möser, G. (2007) "Twenty years after Hines, Hungerford and Tomera: a new meta-analysis of psycho-social determinants of pro-environmental behaviour," Journal of Environmental Psychology, *27: 14–25.*

Beck, R.W. (2007) *Literature Review – Litter: A review of litter studies, attitude surveys and other litter-related literature. Final report*, Keep America Beautiful.

Bertrand, M. and Mullainathan, S. (2001) "Do people mean what they say? Implications for subjective survey data," *American Economic Review* (Papers and Proceedings), 91: 67–72.

Brewer, P.R., Steenbergen, M.R., and Marco, R. (2002) "All against all: how beliefs about human nature shape foreign policy opinions," *Political Psychology,* 23: 39–58.

——, Gross, K., Aday, S., and Willnat, L. (2004) "International trust and public opinion about world affairs," *American Journal of Political Science,* 48: 93–109.

Brown, B., Perkins, D., and Brown, G. (2004) "Crime, new housing, and housing incivilities in a first-ring suburb: multilevel relationships across time," *Housing Policy Debate,* 15: 301–45.

Campbell, F. (2007) *People who Litter*, ENCAMS Research Report. <http://www.keepbritaintidy.org/ImgLibrary/people_who_litter percent20litterseg2006_763.pdf>.

Chang, E.C.C. and Chu Y. 2006, "Corruption and trust: exceptionalism in Asian democracies?" *Journal of Politics,* 68: 259–71.

Cialdini, R.B., Reno, R.R., and Kallgren, C.A. (1990) "A focus theory of normative conduct: Recycling the concept of norms to reduce littering in public places," *Journal of Personality and Social Psychology*, 58: 1015–26.

——, Kallgren, C.A., and Reno, R.R. (1991), "A focus theory of normative conduct: a theoretical refinement and re-evaluation," *Advances in Experimental Social Psychology,* 24: 201–34.

Convery, F., McDonnell, S., and Ferreira, S. (2007) "The most popular tax in Europe? Lessons from the Irish plastic bags levy," *Environmental and Resource Economics,* 38: 1–11.

Cope, J. G., Huffman, K.T, Allred, L.J., and Grossnickle, W.F. (1993) "Behavioral strategies to reduce cigarette litter," *Journal of Social Behavior and Personality,* 8: 607–19.

Crump, S.L., Nunes, D.L., and Crossman, E.K. (1977) "The effects of litter on littering behavior in a forest environment," *Environment and Behavior,* 9: 137–46.

DECC (2004) *An Assessment of Attitudes and Behaviour amongst Multi Unit Dwelling Residents in Relation to Illegal Dumping, Final Report,* Department of Environment and Climate Change of New South Wales Government <http://www.environment.nsw.gov.au/resources/warr/spd_gov_0504_mudresrpt.pdf>.

Diener, E. and Suh, E.M. (2000) *Culture and Subjective Well-Being*, Cambridge: MIT Press.

Dobbs, I. (1991) "Litter and waste management: Disposal taxes versus user charges," *Canadian Journal of Economics,* 24: 221–27.

Durdan, C.A., Reeder, G.D., and Hecht, P.R. (1985) "Litter in a University cafeteria: demographic data and the use of prompts as an intervention strategy," *Environment and Behavior,* 17: 387–404.

Dwyer, W.O., Leeming, F.C., Cobern, M.K., Porter, B.E., and Jackson, J.M., (1993) "Critical review of behavioural interventions to preserve the environment: research since 1980," *Environment and Behavior,* 25: 275–321.

Entorf, H. and Spengler, H. (2002) *Crime in Europe: Causes and consequences*, Berlin: Springer.

ESI (2005) *Environmental Sustainability Index: Benchmarking national environmental stewardship.* Yale Center for Environmental Law and Policy and Center for International Earth Science Information Network, Yale University and Columbia University.

European Values Survey (1999) *Questionnaire*, Tilburg University, The Netherlands.

Feld, S.L. (1978) "Deterrence: for the prevention and cure of litter," *Evaluation Review,* 2: 547–60.

Finnie, W.C. (1973) "Field experiments in litter control," *Environment and Behavior,* 5: 123–44.

Franzen, A. (2003) "Environmental attitudes in international comparison: an analysis of the ISSP Surveys 1993 and 2000," *Social Science Quarterly,* 84: 297–308.

Frey, B.S. (1997) *Not Just for Money: An economic theory of personal motivation,* Cheltenham, Glos.: Edward Elgar.

—— and Stutzer, A. (2002) *Happiness and Economics,* Princeton: Princeton University Press.

—— and —— (2006) "Environmental morale and motivation," CREMA Working Paper 2006–17.

Fullerton, D. and Wolverton, A. (2000) "Two generalizations of a deposit-refund system," *American Economic Review,* 90: 238–42.

Geller, E.S. (1992) "Solving environmental problems: a behaviour change perspective," in S. Staub and P. Green (eds), *Psychology and Social Responsibility: Facing global challenges,* New York: New York University Press.

——, Witmer, J.F., and Tuso, M.A. (1977) "Environmental interventions for litter control," *Journal of Applied Psychology,* 62: 344–51.

——, Winett, R.A., and Everett, P.B. (1982) *Preserving the Environment: New strategies for behaviour change,* Elmsford, NY: Pergamon.

Grasmick, H.G., Bursik Jr., R.J., and Kinsey, K.A. (1991) "Shame and embarrassment as deterrents to noncompliance with the law: the case of an antilittering campaign," *Environment and Behavior,* 23: 233–51.

Guiso, L., Sapienza, P., and Zingales, L. (2003) "People's opium? Religion and economic attitudes," *Journal of Monetary Economics,* 50: 225–82.

Hall, A., Rudebusch, G., and Wilcox, D. (1996) "Judging instrument relevance in instrumental variable estimation," *International Economic Review,* 37: 283–98.

Handy, F. (2001) "Advocacy by environmental nonprofit organizations: An optimal strategy for addressing environmental problems?" *International Journal of Social Economics,* 288: 648–66.

Hansmann, R. and Scholz, R.W. (2003) "A two-step informational strategy for reducing littering behavior in a cinema," *Environment and Behavior,* 35: 752–62.

Huffman, K.T., Grossnickle, W.F., Cope, J.G., and Huffman, K.P. (1995) "Litter reduction: a review and integration of the literature," *Environment and Behavior,* 27: 153–83.

Hull, B.B. (2000) "Religion still matters," *Journal of Economics,* 26: 35–48.

—— and Bold, F. (1989) "Towards an economic theory of the church," *International Journal of Social Economics,* 16: 5–15.

Kanazawa, S. (2005) "Who lies on surveys, and what can we do about it?" *Journal of Social, Political and Economic Studies,* 30: 361–70.

Keizer, K., Lindenberg, S., and Linda, S. (2008) "The spreading of disorder," *Science,* 322: 1681–84.

Krauss, R.M., Freedman, J.L., and Whitcup, M. (1976) "Field and laboratory studies of littering," *Journal of Experimental Social Psychology,* 14: 109–22.

Lipford, J., McCormick, R.E., and Tollison, R.D. (1993) "Preaching matters", *Journal of Economic Behavior and Organization,* 21: 235–50.

Meeker, F.L. (1997) "A comparison of table-littering behavior in two settings: a case for a contextual research strategy," *Journal of Environmental Psychology,* 17: 59–68.

Naughton, M., Sebold, F., and Mayer, T. (1990) "The impacts of the California beverage container recycling and litter reduction Act on consumers," *The Journal of Consumers Affairs,* 24: 190–20.

Polinsky, M.A. and Shavell, S. (2000) "The economic theory of public enforcement of law," *Journal of Economic Literature,* 38: 45–76.

Rege, M. and Telle, K. (2001) "An experimental investigation of social norms," Discussion papers No. 310, Statistics Norway, Research Department.

Reich, J.W. and Robertson, J.L. (1979) "Reactance and norm appeal in anti-litter messages," *Journal of Applied Social Psychology*, 9: 91–101.

Reiter, S.M. and Samuel, W. (1980) "Littering as a function of prior litter and the presence or absence of prohibitive signs," *Journal of Applied Social Psychology*, 64: 104–12.

Roales-Nieto, J.G. (1988) "A behavioural community program for litter control," *Journal of Community Psychology*, 16: 107–18.

Sibley, C.G. and Liu, J.H. (2003) "Differentiating active and passive littering: a two-stage process model of littering behaviour in public spaces," *Environment and Behaviour,* 35: 415–33.

Swamy, A., Knack, S., Lee., Y., and Azfar, O. (2001) "Gender and corruption," Journal of Development Economics, 64: 25–55.

Taylor, A., Curnow, R., Fletcher, T., and Lewis, J. (2007) "Education campaigns to reduce stormwater pollution in commercial areas: do they work?," *Journal of Environmental Management,* 84: 323–35.

Tittle, C. (1980) *Sanctions and Social Deviance: The question of deterrence*, New York: Praeger.

Torgler, B. (2006) "The importance of faith: tax morale and religiosity," *Journal of Economic Behavior and Organization*, 61: 81–109.

—— (2007) *Tax Compliance and Tax Morale: A Theoretical and Empirical Analysis*, Cheltenham, UK: Edward Elgar.

—— (2008) "Trust in international organizations: an empirical investigation focusing on the United Nations," *Review of International Organizations*, 3: 65–93.

—— *and García-Valiñas, M.A. (2007) "The determinants of individuals' attitudes towards preventing environmental damage,"* Ecological Economics, *63: 536–52.*

—— *and Valev, N.T. (2006) "Corruption and age,"* Journal of Bioeconomics, *8: 133–45.*

——*, Frey, B.S., and Wilson, C. (2009) "Environmental and pro-social norms: evidence on littering,"* The B.E. Journal of Economic Analysis & Policy, *9: art. 18.*

Uslaner, E.M. (2004) 'Trust and corruption', in J.G. Lambsdorf, M. Taube, and M. Schramm (eds), *Corruption and the New Institutional Economics*, London: Routledge.

Zelezny, L.C., Chua, P.P., and Aldrich, C. (2000) "Elaborating on gender differences in environmentalism," *Journal of Social Issues,* 56: 443–57.

7 Participation in environmental organizations

Environmental motivation

> 80 per cent of success is just showing up.
>
> Woody Allen

Introduction

Now the question remains whether there is a link between environmental attitudes and environmental behavior. Substantial research on the relationship between attitudes and behavior in psychological and sociological journals dates back to the 1930s and even further (for example, LaPiere 1934). However, economists have not really contributed to the area, perhaps due to the fact that many are still reluctant to work with attitudinal questions. This literature has already generated many papers establishing that attitudes predispose individuals to behave in a certain manner. According to Ajzen and Fishbein (1980) and Lewis (1982), behavior can be predicted from behavioral intentions which may be attributed to attitudes and subjective norms, which in turn can be predicted from beliefs. However, after reviewing the literature concerning the direct path from attitudes to behavior, Bagozzi *et al.* (1989) state that the existing findings give a mixed picture, with some studies finding a significant direct effect and others not. Ajzen and Fishbein (1977) reviewed 109 investigations and discovered that 84 displayed either low (mostly non-significant), partial (inconsistent or low but statistically significant), or high correspondence (statistically significant, considerable magnitude) between attitudinal and behavioral entities. The authors stress that "inappropriate measures tend to reduce the obtained relations between attitude and behavior, but appropriate measures invariably produce strong relationships" (Ajzen and Fishbein 1977: 913). Our justifiability of littering variable is closely linked to the compliance literature that has focused on tax morale proxied by the justifiability of paying taxes (Torgler 2007) or the justifiability of corruption (Torgler and Valev 2006, 2009). A recent study on tax compliance uses field, survey, and experimental data (Torgler *et al.* 2007) and finds strong evidence that attitudes affect behavior.

What does the environmental literature have to say? Hines *et al.* (1986/87) report that the correlation between pro-environmental attitudes and pro-environmental behavior is 0.38 (based on nine studies). A more recent meta-study conducted a literature search focusing on the period from 1995 to 2006 and covered a total sample of 57 effect sizes from 46 independent studies (Bamberg and Möser 2007). The conclusions of this meta-analysis confirm the view that pro-environmental behavior is a mixture of self-interest and pro-social motives. We will take a closer look at this claim. It is relevant because empirical support for a theoretical foundation depends not only on the validity of the theory but also on the quality of the data.

These studies suggest that more evidence is required to study empirically whether some pro-environmental attitudes have a positive effect on environmental behavior or (in our case) the involvement in environmental organizations. Thus, more empirical evidence is required in order to see whether environmental attitudes affect environmental participation in particular. We therefore consider environmental motivation or pro-environmental attitudes as a key independent variable in this chapter. One should note that we use the concepts of motivation and attitudes as substitutes, although one may argue that there are significant differences between the two. Our key point is that both factors have a direct impact on environmental behavior. Moreover, our proxies are not really able to isolate either element in an adequate manner. Our analysis explores whether self-reported willingness to contribute to environmental quality is correlated with self-reported environmental behavior. In this respect, the microeconomic approach allows us to extend the analysis that we have conducted in Chapter 5, and so far we have included some interesting variables in the analysis, developing an intuitive model and obtaining several interesting findings.

The strength of this chapter lies in the exploration of the impact of environmental motivation on environmental behavior. The previous chapters have stressed that environmental motivation or pro-environmental attitudes are particularly important when economic incentive instruments cannot be applied at all or would be too costly to overcome cooperation problems. Now, by focusing on individuals' voluntary engagement in environmental organizations we test its impact with the use of a large micro data set covering 32 European countries. In Chapter 8 we also check the robustness of this relationship by working with a macro data set. Such breadth and depth of data allows exploration of the different channels through which individuals express their environmental motivation via pro-environmental attitudes, and we capitalize on this opportunity by exploring two variables that measure voluntary environmental participation (i.e. membership and voluntary work).

The outline of the rest of the chapter is as follows. The next section begins with a discussion of the theoretical background and proposes a very simple model of volunteering. We then introduce the data set and the key variables. We follow this with a presentation of the empirical findings, and then finally offer some concluding remarks.

Theoretical framework

In previous chapters, we have mentioned several definitions of environmental participation from an economic perspective. Let us remember the one proposed by Clark *et al.* 2003: 23, who defined it as "an individual's voluntary effort to provide an environmental public good." An economic analysis also prompts the question: why do people carry out actions (incurring private costs) that lead to collective outcomes? We previously observed that, although some theoretical models will predict free-rider effects, in practice we observe several altruistic behaviors. Andreoni (1990) developed an important model of impure altruism as a means of understanding donations to public goods. He assumes an economy with only one private good and one public good. The individual utility donation function depends on the consumption of a private good (x_i), the total amount of a public good (G), and the individual's gift to the public good (g_i). Thus, $U_i = U(x_i, G, g_i)$. This allows the author to differentiate two cases, namely a purely altruistic situation $U(x_i, G_i)$ when the individual cares nothing for the private gift, and $U(x_i, g_i)$ when the individual is motivated to give only by a "warm-glow" outcome (purely egoistic). The cases in between are defined as an impurely altruistic behavior. However, he acknowledges that there are important alternative approaches to such an impure altruism model, namely moral or group-interested behavior. In line with this suggestion, Brekke *et al.* (2003) implement moral motivation in their model by working with a social welfare function to determine the morally ideal effort, where individuals share a utilitarian moral philosophy. For simplicity, they assume that the labor supply and the income are exogenously fixed. In a next step, individuals maximize their utility in a benefit-cost environment, trading the benefits of maintaining a self-image as socially responsible individuals against the costs. The desire to improve self-image induces an improved effort towards upholding beliefs that are perceived to be morally right.

Keeping in mind the theoretical work outlined above, we examine the motivation for environmental participation by developing a model of volunteering. One might suggest that we could have presented such a theoretical model on voluntary participation in environment organizations much earlier. However, our key aim here is to extend a "traditional economic model" with environmental social norms and attitudes. Thus, it is useful to visualize such a theoretical framework in this chapter. Now, we assume that an individual's utility function is given by

$$U_i = U(x_i, l_i, G, \lambda_i) \tag{7a}$$

where is x_i individual i's consumption of private goods, l_i represents leisure (hours spent), G is the public good of increasing environmental quality, and λ_i the utility from participating voluntarily in an environmental organization.

Voluntary work is time-consuming and subject to opportunity costs. Thus, v_i represents the hours spent for voluntary work in an environmental organization. Individuals' consumption can therefore be written as an income constraint, defined by the product of the wage rate w and the working hours $T - l_i - v_i \geq 0$, where T is the time constraint (available time):

$$x_i = w_i(T - l_i - v_i) \tag{7b}$$

The total amount of public good (environmental quality) depends on the public provision G_p and private provision $\sum_i g_i$, assuming identical individuals N:

$$G = G_p + \sum_i g_i \tag{7c}$$

where

$$g_i = \alpha v_i \tag{7d}$$

is individual *i*'s production function that depends on the level of voluntary participation in an environmental organization and an efficiency parameter α. Such an efficiency parameter can take into account the stock of social capital within a society and within the environmental group. The quality of this stock may reduce transaction costs and facilitate the efficiency of social interactions (see Chapter 2). Since we have identical individuals $\sum_i g_i$ is equal to Ng_i. Therefore, we can write:

$$G = G_p + N\alpha v_i \tag{7e}$$

The utility from participating in a voluntary environmental organization (λ_i) has the following form:

$$\lambda_i = m_i v_i - (m_i - v_i)^2 \tag{7f}$$

where m_i is a factor that measures an individual's motivation to contribute to the environment ($m_i \geq 0$). It measures what the individual believes to be the morally ideal environmental involvement. Thus, participating in voluntary organizations is correlated with individuals' motivation towards contribution and this enhances an individual's utility function (see first term in Equation 7f). On the other hand, if the voluntary participation in the environmental organization is lower than that aspired to and regarded as morally acceptable, ($v_i < m_i$), individuals also experience moral or psychic costs (see second term). This induces a substantial feeling of guilt and shame due to deviations from their moral standards, which is visible in the squared difference. Despite the fact that the volunteering is "voluntary" we assume that deviating from moral standards by not contributing enough or not at all leads to psychic costs. Such an assumption may be not be that unrealistic, taking into account environmental organizations' proclivity for using large campaigns to trigger individuals' psychic costs.

We also assume that the utility function is additively separable in x_i, l_i, G, and λ_i despite the fact that the units of the influences are originally not identical. The utility function thus becomes:

$$U_i = x_i + l_i + G + \lambda_i \tag{7g}$$

Considering (7b) to (7f) leads to the following utility function:

$$U_i = w_i\,(T - l_i - v_i) + l_i + (G_p + N\alpha v_i) + m_i v_i - (m_i - v_i)^2 \tag{7h}$$

An individual maximizes utility (7.8) subject to their voluntary involvement in an environmental organization (v_i). Setting the first order condition $U_i' = \delta U_i / \delta v_i$ equal to 0 leads to the following condition for the optimal effort engagement:

$$v_i = \frac{-w_i + N\alpha + 3m_i}{2} \tag{7i}$$

Equation (7i) suggests that environmental participation will increase with an increase in individual's motivation to contribute. Thus, we can develop the following main hypothesis:

> Hypothesis 1: A higher level of environmental motivation due to higher environmental moral standards leads to a stronger voluntary involvement in environmental organizations.

Moreover, Equation (7i) also indicates that an increase in the wage rate changes the allocation of time. An increase leads to a decline of voluntary work in environmental organizations. However, such a negative effect is reduced with a higher level of efficiency in contributing to the private provision of the public good, α multiplied by the number of individuals in the society. It should be noted that we have implemented a consumer model. One may argue that individuals are also volunteering to accumulate human capital with the intention of increasing future income through the acquisition of certain types of skills and through creating and developing networks that enhance their human capital (Hackl *et al.* 2007). This would require the use of an investment model with a dynamic structure. However, we believe that our consumer model is useful and appropriate when exploring moral values.

Empirical model and variables

In line with data used in Chapters 5 and 6, we consider two variables that measure involvement in a voluntary environmental organization, namely membership and doing unpaid work:

> Please look carefully at the following list of voluntary organizations and activities and say which, if any, you are currently doing unpaid voluntary work for: conservation, the environment, ecology, animal rights (1 = yes).

> Please look carefully at the following list of voluntary organizations and activities and say which, if any, you belong to: conservation, the environment, ecology, animal rights (1 = mentioned, 0 = not mentioned).

This is an extension of the argument initiated in Chapter 5, where we focused only on active environmental participation. To check the robustness of results, we use three independent variables that measure different aspects of pro-environmental attitudes. However, one should note that our proxies are mainly defined in financial terms and are open to the criticism that such proxies are extremely narrow. The first two variables measure environmental preferences in the following way:

> I would give part of my income if I were certain that the money would be used to prevent environmental pollution (0 = strongly disagree, 3 = strongly agree).
>
> I would agree to an increase in taxes if the extra money were used to prevent environmental pollution (0 = strongly disagree, 3 = strongly agree).

Although we are not conducting a contingent valuation study (CV), these two questions offer the chance to investigate environmental preferences. However, the question is not free of problems. The statement is relatively vague: "environmental pollution" is not clearly specified, and neither is the level of improvement. Similarly, the degree of income to be spent and the tax increase are not clarified. Therefore the respondents are not aware of how much they would hypothetically have to contribute.[1] The consequences of taxation are not mentioned and no information is provided regarding the extent to which income tax, value added tax, or other taxes are supposed to increase. Thus, it is not clear who will bear the highest tax burden. Such questions alluding to unspecified payment schemes will increase the variance in responses but, on the other hand, may influence the willingness to contribute (Witzke and Urfei 2001).

Nevertheless, an unspecified statement still helps to measure preferences and values and to reduce strategic behavior via influencing the quantity or quality of environmental goods – people might intentionally indicate false values for their willingness to contribute in order to match their own preferences (Hidano *et al.* 2005). When neither specific goods nor quantitative values are used, the attributes of the environmental goods in question do not have to be thoroughly explained to be sure that respondents understand and respond with the appropriate willingness to spend income and accept an increase in taxes.[2] By asking "would you" pay more for goods if it helps the environment, we are capturing a real intention and not a financial transaction or an assessment of an individual's willingness to pay.

In a next step we will explore a variable that measures environmental attitudes, but takes into account the possibility that people may have an incentive to free-ride (profit without incurring costs). We predict that such a variable would lead to contradictory results (compared to the previous two variables):

> The Government has to reduce environmental pollution but it should not cost me any money (0 = strongly disagree, 3 = strongly agree).

Once again, a vector of control variables has been considered in this analysis, in a similar way to those included in the exercise carried out in Chapters 5 and 6. These variables are related to several socio-economic features, such as age, gender, marital status, education, and economic and employment issues. Additionally, we now also control for a parent effect (child).[3] Having children may make the future "a far more tangible concept," and causes individuals to reconsider present behavior in light of future consequences (Dresner *et al.* 2007). Since parents act both for themselves and their children when engaging in pro-environmental behavior, we can thus expect that the state of parenthood would heighten commitment to environmental issues when compared to non-parents (Teal and Loomis 2000). The parental effect can also be expected to influence the gender effect – even though men generally exhibit less tendency towards protecting the environment, concern over the wellbeing of their offspring will alter their perceptions of natural resource value (Wilson *et al.* 1996). Finally, we also differentiate again between western and eastern Europe countries. All variables are fully described in the Appendix (Table A7.1).

Table 7.1 presents the findings regarding being a member in an environmental organization. In the first three specifications we explore our key attitudinal questions separately. In the fourth specification we include all the three variables in the specification. The first three specifications indicate that all the attitudinal variables are statistically significant, and report the predicted sign. The first two have a positive impact, the third a negative one.

The negative coefficient in specification (3) is consistent with our prediction regarding individuals' interest in free-riding. A higher willingness to free-ride is negatively correlated with environmental engagement. The variable "willingness to give income" has the strongest effect. An increase in the scale by one unit from the average raises the probability of participating in an environmental organization by 2.5 percent. The importance of this variable is also visible once we include all three variables in the regression. The coefficient is still statistically significant at the 1 percent level with a marginal effect of 1.9 percent. On the other hand, the coefficient for the variable "willingness to increase taxes" is only statistically significant at the 10 percent level, and also shows a decrease in the marginal effects. Overall, these first results indicate that environmental attitudes or environmental motivation matter.

Looking at the control variables we can see that women are more likely to be members in an environmental organization. Age is also positively correlated with membership. Overall, the age group 50–59 shows the strongest level of environmental participation (largest marginal effects). Having a child is negatively correlated with environmental participation. The time restriction may act as barrier to any involvement in environmental organizations. Education and political interest, measured as "political discussion," have a positive impact on the probability of being a member in an environmental organization. The time restriction argument is also visible when focusing on the marital status. Never married people and people who are separated have the highest probability of participating in environmental organizations. Moreover, looking at the employment status, we observe that part-time employees are most likely to be members. There is also the tendency that self-employed individuals are more active in environmental organizations, possibly due to the opportunity to improve their networks. On the other hand, unemployed and retired people are less likely to be members, which is consistent with the literature reviewed in Chapter 3. Finally, we also observe that people in western Europe are more engaged in environmental organization through membership participation, a result that is also consistent with

Table 7.1 Determinants of being a member of environmental organizations

	Weighted probit											
	(1)			*(2)*			*(3)*			*(4)*		
	Coeff.	*z-Stat.*	*Marg.*	*Coeff.*	*z-Stat.*	*Marg.*	*Coeff.*	*z-Stat.*	*Marg.*	*Coeff.*	*z-Stat.*	*Marg.*
Environmental attitudes												
Willingness to give income	0.313***	19.07	0.025							0.250***	11.97	0.019
Willingness to increase taxes				0.223***	14.81	0.019				0.032*	1.70	0.002
Contribute at no costs							–0.246***	–17.43	–0.020	–0.177***	–11.79	–0.014
Demographic FACTORS												
Age 30–39	0.056	1.22	0.004	0.048	1.07	0.004	0.065	1.44	0.005	0.056	1.19	0.004
Age 40–49	0.115**	2.38	0.010	0.087*	1.82	0.008	0.110**	2.28	0.010	0.112**	2.25	0.009
Age 50–59	0.237***	4.65	0.022	0.216***	4.31	0.021	0.251***	4.93	0.024	0.243***	4.62	0.022
Age 60–69	0.189***	2.97	0.017	0.175***	2.77	0.016	0.212***	3.32	0.020	0.198***	3.02	0.018
Age 70+	0.238***	3.23	0.022	0.198***	2.68	0.019	0.213***	2.89	0.020	0.227***	2.96	0.021
Woman	0.054**	1.97	0.004	0.067**	2.47	0.006	0.059**	2.15	0.005	0.056**	1.99	0.004
Child	–0.104*	–1.90	–0.008	–0.120**	–2.19	–0.009	–0.117**	–2.15	–0.009	–0.108*	–1.91	–0.008
Formal and informal education												
Education	0.025***	12.02	0.002	0.025***	12.40	0.002	0.025***	12.18	0.002	0.022***	10.24	0.002
Political discussion	0.142***	7.01	0.011	0.151***	7.53	0.013	0.134***	6.64	0.011	0.114***	5.45	0.009
Marital status												
Widowed	–0.103*	–1.69	–0.007	–0.159***	–2.60	–0.012	–0.143**	–2.37	–0.011	–0.133**	–2.08	–0.009
Divorced	–0.062	–1.25	–0.005	–0.065	–1.31	–0.005	–0.072	–1.44	–0.006	–0.062	–1.20	–0.005

Separated	0.010	0.10	0.001	0.001	0.01	0.000	0.030	0.31	0.002	0.040	0.39	0.003
Never married	0.123***	3.24	0.010	0.121***	3.24	0.011	0.135***	3.58	0.012	0.128***	3.29	0.011
Employment status												
Part-time employee	0.141***	3.09	0.012	0.159***	3.54	0.015	0.158***	3.45	0.015	0.151***	3.22	0.013
Self-employed	0.085	1.63	0.007	0.087*	1.67	0.008	0.086	1.63	0.008	0.096*	1.81	0.008
Unemployed	–0.099**	–1.97	–0.007	–0.091**	–1.82	–0.007	–0.076	–1.51	–0.006	–0.068	–1.32	–0.005
At home	–0.114**	–2.19	–0.008	–0.105**	–2.06	–0.008	–0.087*	–1.69	–0.007	–0.094*	–1.76	–0.007
Student	–0.041	–0.66	–0.003	–0.007	–0.12	–0.001	–0.037	–0.60	–0.003	–0.061	–0.96	–0.005
Retired	–0.252***	–3.96	–0.016	–0.227***	–3.61	–0.016	–0.206***	–3.30	–0.014	–0.219***	–3.37	–0.014
Other	0.138	1.48	0.012	0.170*	1.85	0.016	0.166*	1.80	0.016	0.151	1.59	0.013
Region												
Western Europe	0.595***	20.91	0.047	0.554***	19.90	0.046	0.454	16.38	0.037	0.522***	17.99	0.040
Pseudo R2	0.101			0.086			0.093			0.114		
Number of observations	36086			36052			36237			34428		
Prob > chi2	0.000			0.000			0.000			0.000		

Notes: The reference group consists of man, age<30, not have children, married, full-time employee, Eastern Europe. The symbols *, **, *** represent statistical significance at the 10%, 5% and 1% levels, respectively. Robust standard errors.

the empirical evidence reported in Chapter 5 working with the WVS. The marginal effects are quite large (more than 4 percent).

In Table 7.2 we explore a second aspect, namely doing unpaid work for environmental organizations. The results are quite similar. All the attitudinal questions in specifications (5) to (7) are statistically significant. The strongest effects are again observable for the variable "willingness to give income." However, it should be noted that compared to Table 7.1 we find lower quantitative effects. Thus, it seems that the environmental attitudes have a stronger effect on membership participation. Specification (8) also shows that the coefficient for the variable "contribute at no cost" is no longer statistically significant.

Looking at the control variables we find that, compared to previous results, there is a negative correlation between environmental participation and being a woman. Thus, women are more likely to be a member in an environmental organization, but are less likely to do unpaid work.

The age effect is now less visible, but we still observe that the age group 50–59 has the highest probability of being involved in unpaid work. The parental effect is also less visible. On the other hand, similar to the results obtained previously, education and political interest have a significant and positive impact on environmental engagement. Moreover, we also observe that individuals who have never married are the most active individuals in environmental organizations. On the other hand, only retired people are significantly less willing than the full-time employed individuals to be active in environmental organizations through unpaid work. Finally we also observe that western European citizens are more likely to be engaged in voluntary work. However, the effect is not as strong as that previously observed and the coefficient is no longer statistically significant in all specifications.

In the next two tables we extend the previous regression to include individuals' economic situation with two dummy variables. It should be noted that the number of observations in Tables 7.3 and 7.4 diminished dramatically once we control for individuals' *economic situation*. The results indicate that a higher economic level leads to a higher probability of being a member and doing unpaid work in environmental organizations. It seems that wealthier citizens have a higher demand for a clean environment and less environmental damage and thus a stronger incentive to actively contribute to the environment by participating in a voluntary organization despite higher opportunity costs. Such a result is also consistent with the literature reviewed in Chapter 3.

In sum, we can conclude that the previous results remain robust. In particular, it should be noted that environmental attitudes have a strong impact on the probability of being engaged in environmental organizations.

Table 7.5 explores potential endogeneity problems and searches for causality relationships. Here, as discussed in the previous chapter, we have to be careful with such an analysis. Our investigation at the micro level with such a cross-sectional analysis does not convincingly solve the causality problem. We would like to remind the reader again that we prefer to interpret our results as correlations or relationships rather than effects, although for simplicity we frequently use the notion of "effect." As an instrument we use an index of perceived level of social non-compliance with well-known societal rules.[4] In previous studies we have seen that the perceived level of compliance affects individuals' intrinsic motivation to contribute and cooperate (Frey and Torgler 2007, Torgler *et al.* 2009, Dong *et al.* 2008). The extent to which others comply with social rules systematically influences the individual willingness and motivation to contribute. Additionally, Owen and Videras (2006) found a positive and significant relationship between civic cooperation and/or allowing free-riding behaviors and environmental attitudes and intentions. They concluded that civic cooperation was a key factor to improving pro-environmental attitudes, especially in low-income countries.

For simplicity, we only report the results on membership involvement in Table 7.5, including the results of two-stage least squares (2SLS) estimations together with the first stage regressions. The results indicate that pro-environmental attitudes still have a strong and statistically significant impact on environmental involvement.

Finally, we test whether the impact of the attitudinal variables on environmental involvement is driven by a subset of countries and present the results for the coefficients for environmental attitudes in Table 7.6 and Table 7.7. We use the same specifications as was used in the first two tables (without controlling for the economic situation). Each table is a summary of 96 regressions conducted on data from 32 countries. Table 7.6 focuses on membership participation, while Table 7.7 explores unpaid work as a dependent variable. In general we observe differences between the countries. Table 7.6 shows that the coefficient of the variable "willingness to give income" is statistically significant in 25 out 32 cases. The strongest effect is observed for the Netherlands. An increase in the willingness to give income by one unit increases the probability of being a member of an environmental organization by almost 10 percent. A strong quantitative effect is also observed in Austria, Belgium, Denmark, and Greece. In general, the effects are lower among Eastern European countries. We find a similar result for the variable "willingness to increase taxes. The coefficient is statistically significant in 24 out 32 cases. The strongest effect can also be found in the Netherlands (9.1 percent), followed by Denmark (4.4 percent) and Greece (3.4 percent).

The results are less strong when focusing on willingness to free-ride. However, here we also observe the strongest negative impact for the Netherlands (8.9 percent), followed by Denmark (4.2 percent) and Belgium (4.2 percent). Looking at Table 7.7, and therefore at unpaid work, we find that the relationship is less strong when using unpaid work as a dependent variable. Thus, environmental attitudes help to substantially increase the number of memberships, but are less strong when individuals are required to do unpaid work for environmental organizations. The coefficient for the variable "willingness to give income" is now only statistically significant in 18 out 32 regressions. The quantitative effects are also substantially smaller. Greece reports the strongest effect with a marginal effect of 3.5 percent. Moreover, it should be noted that the same picture can be found for the other two attitudinal questions.

Table 7.2 Determinants of unpaid work in environmental organizations

	Weighted probit											
	(5)			*(6)*			*(7)*			*(8)*		
	Coeff.	*z-Stat.*	*Marg.*	*Coeff.*	*z-Stat.*	*Marg.*	*Coeff.*	*z-Stat.*	*Marg.*	*Coeff.*	*z-Stat.*	*Marg.*
Environmental attitudes												
Willingness to give income	0.233***	10.45	0.009							0.204***	7.47	0.008
Willingness to increase taxes				0.162***	7.89	0.007				0.045*	1.83	0.002
Contribute at no costs							–0.091***	–4.83	–0.004	–0.028	–1.39	–0.001
Demographic factors												
Age 30–39	0.017	0.30	0.001	0.018	0.31	0.001	0.029	0.52	0.001	0.019	0.33	0.001
Age 40–49	0.094	1.58	0.004	0.077	1.32	0.003	0.090	1.54	0.004	0.081	1.34	0.003
Age 50–59	0.126*	1.96	0.005	0.127**	2.02	0.006	0.141**	2.22	0.006	0.116*	1.77	0.005
Age 60–69	0.123	1.51	0.005	0.096	1.18	0.004	0.116	1.42	0.005	0.110	1.30	0.005
Age 70+	0.101	0.92	0.004	0.055	0.50	0.002	0.035	0.31	0.001	0.049	0.42	0.002
Woman	–0.100***	–2.79	–0.004	–0.085**	–2.40	–0.004	–0.092**	–2.61	–0.004	–0.094**	–2.55	–0.004
Child	–0.106	–1.22	–0.004	–0.115	–1.35	–0.004	–0.101	–1.19	–0.004	–0.082	–0.94	–0.003
Formal and informal education												
Education	0.019***	7.13	0.001	0.020***	7.40	0.001	0.021***	7.90	0.001	0.019***	6.71	0.001
Political discussion	0.110***	3.98	0.004	0.119***	4.37	0.005	0.115***	4.28	0.005	0.099***	3.53	0.004
Marital status												
Widowed	–0.023	–0.28	–0.001	–0.062	–0.74	–0.002	–0.060	–0.72	–0.002	–0.049	–0.56	–0.002
Divorced	–0.100	–1.50	–0.004	–0.091	–1.40	–0.003	–0.102	–1.56	–0.004	–0.103	–1.53	–0.004

Separated	0.160	1.22	0.007	0.148	1.15	0.007	0.161	1.25	0.008	0.181	1.36	0.009
Never married	0.139***	2.92	0.006	0.138***	2.95	0.006	0.144***	3.07	0.007	0.144***	2.96	0.006
Employment status												
Part-time employee	0.064	0.99	0.003	0.071	1.13	0.003	0.080	1.28	0.004	0.065	0.99	0.003
Self-employed	–0.036	–0.50	–0.001	–0.028	–0.39	–0.001	–0.041	–0.57	–0.002	–0.034	–0.46	–0.001
Unemployed	–0.114	–1.60	–0.004	–0.095	–1.35	–0.004	–0.103	–1.46	–0.004	–0.096	–1.31	–0.004
At home	–0.163**	–2.13	–0.006	–0.137*	–1.85	–0.005	–0.140*	–1.88	–0.005	–0.161**	–2.07	–0.005
Student	0.073	1.02	0.003	0.119*	1.69	0.005	0.100	1.43	0.005	0.068	0.94	0.003
Retired	–0.310***	–3.79	–0.009	–0.310***	–3.82	–0.010	–0.317***	–3.90	–0.010	–0.299***	–3.59	–0.009
Other	0.139	1.14	0.006	0.146	1.21	0.007	0.140	1.16	0.007	0.157	1.27	0.007
Region												
Western Europe	0.092***	2.69	0.004	0.069**	2.04	0.003	0.024	0.69	0.001	0.069*	1.93	0.003
Pseudo R2	0.053			0.043			0.037			0.055		
Number of observations	36086			36052			36237			34428		
Prob > chi2	0.000			0.000			0.000			0.000		

Notes: The reference group consists of man, age<30, not have children, married, full-time employee, Eastern Europe. The symbols *, **, *** represent statistical significance at the 10%, 5% and 1% levels, respectively. Robust standard errors.

Table 7.3 Income and membership of environmental organizations

	Weighted probit											
	(9)			*(10)*			*(11)*			*(12)*		
	Coeff.	*z-Stat.*	*Marg.*	*Coeff.*	*z-Stat.*	*Marg.*	*Coeff.*	*z-Stat.*	*Marg.*	*Coeff.*	*z-Stat.*	*Marg.*
Environmental attitudes												
Willingness to give income	0.295***	12.87	0.023							0.264***	9.15	0.020
Willingness to increase taxes				0.196***	9.44	0.016				0.008	0.31	0.001
Contribute at no costs							–0.205***	–10.37	–0.017	–0.141***	–6.77	–0.011
Demographic factors												
Age 30–39	–0.058	–0.88	–0.004	–0.055	–0.85	–0.004	–0.043	–0.66	–0.003	–0.059	–0.88	–0.004
Age 40–49	0.011	0.16	0.001	–0.014	–0.20	–0.001	0.002	0.03	0.000	0.013	0.19	0.001
Age 50–59	0.141*	1.93	0.012	0.120*	1.65	0.011	0.154**	2.09	0.014	0.148*	1.95	0.012
Age 60–69	0.000	0.00	0.000	0.002	0.02	0.000	0.033	0.37	0.003	0.012	0.13	0.001
Age 70+	–0.051	–0.45	–0.004	–0.102	–0.89	–0.008	–0.108	–0.93	–0.008	–0.099	–0.82	–0.007
Woman	0.083**	2.02	0.006	0.090**	2.22	0.007	0.084**	2.07	0.007	0.085**	2.03	0.007
Child	–0.044	–0.54	–0.003	–0.044	–0.54	–0.004	–0.039	–0.47	–0.003	–0.030	–0.35	–0.002
Formal and informal education												
Education	0.026***	7.54	0.002	0.026***	7.78	0.002	0.027***	7.95	0.002	0.024***	6.79	0.002
Political discussion	0.147***	4.99	0.012	0.155***	5.29	0.013	0.138***	4.70	0.011	0.123***	4.06	0.009
Marital status												
Widowed	–0.067	–0.75	–0.005	–0.122	–1.35	–0.009	–0.095	–1.06	–0.007	–0.104	–1.09	–0.007
Divorced	–0.079	–1.06	–0.006	–0.094	–1.27	–0.007	–0.108	–1.43	–0.008	–0.088	–1.14	–0.006

Separated	0.015	0.10	0.001	0.016	0.11	0.001	0.050	0.36	0.004	0.048	0.33	0.004
Never married	0.001	0.01	0.000	0.002	0.04	0.000	0.017	0.29	0.001	0.013	0.23	0.001
Economic situation												
Upper class	0.142***	2.65	0.012	0.163***	3.06	0.015	0.156***	2.89	0.014	0.125**	2.26	0.010
Middle class	0.087**	2.04	0.007	0.092**	2.19	0.008	0.083*	1.95	0.007	0.079*	1.79	0.006
Employment status												
Part-time employee	0.088	1.21	0.007	0.108	1.53	0.010	0.093	1.29	0.008	0.091	1.22	0.007
Self-employed	0.059	0.75	0.005	0.055	0.72	0.005	0.063	0.81	0.005	0.074	0.95	0.006
Unemployed	–0.029	–0.42	–0.002	–0.027	–0.38	–0.002	–0.017	–0.24	–0.001	–0.013	–0.18	–0.001
At home	–0.176**	–2.40	–0.012	–0.158**	–2.20	–0.012	–0.146**	–2.01	–0.011	–0.172**	–2.27	–0.012
Student	–0.108	–1.22	–0.008	–0.056	–0.65	–0.004	–0.105	–1.21	–0.008	–0.128	–1.42	–0.009
Retired	–0.041	–0.50	–0.003	–0.028	–0.34	–0.002	–0.022	–0.27	–0.002	–0.036	–0.43	–0.003
Other	0.092	0.64	0.008	0.093	0.65	0.008	0.101	0.71	0.009	0.116	0.79	0.010
Region												
Western Europe	0.355***	8.06	0.026	0.301***	7.02	0.023	0.254***	5.93	0.019	0.334***	7.39	0.023
Pseudo R2	0.070			0.066			0.070			0.094		
Number of observations	18862			18887			18877			18155		
Prob > chi2	0.000			0.000			0.000			0.000		

Notes: The reference group consists of man, age<30, lowest class, not have children, married, full-time employee, Eastern Europe. The symbols *, **, *** represent statistical significance at the 10%, 5% and 1% levels, respectively. Robust standard errors.

Table 7.4 Income and unpaid work in environmental organizations

	Weighted probit											
	(13)			*(14)*			*(15)*			*(16)*		
	Coeff.	*z-Stat.*	*Marg.*	*Coeff.*	*z-Stat.*	*Marg.*	*Coeff.*	*z-Stat.*	*Marg.*	*Coeff.*	*z-Stat.*	*Marg.*
Environmental attitudes												
Willingness to give income	0.231***	8.06	0.010							0.212***	5.98	0.009
Willingness to increase taxes				0.153***	5.77	0.007				0.008	0.26	0.0003
Contribute at no costs							–0.138***	–5.44	–0.006	–0.084***	–3.18	–0.003
Demographic factors												
Age 30–39	0.011	0.14	0.000	0.009	0.11	0.000	0.027	0.34	0.001	0.015	0.18	0.001
Age 40–49	0.006	0.06	0.000	–0.007	–0.08	0.000	0.005	0.06	0.000	0.001	0.01	0.000
Age 50–59	0.099	1.09	0.004	0.088	0.99	0.004	0.111	1.23	0.005	0.089	0.95	0.004
Age 60–69	0.040	0.36	0.002	0.016	0.15	0.001	0.038	0.34	0.002	0.030	0.26	0.001
Age 70+	0.052	0.35	0.002	0.012	0.08	0.001	–0.030	–0.19	–0.001	–0.013	–0.08	–0.001
Woman	–0.158***	–3.04	–0.007	–0.144***	–2.80	–0.006	–0.145***	–2.80	–0.006	–0.155***	–2.90	–0.006
Child	–0.042	–0.35	–0.002	–0.039	–0.33	–0.002	–0.016	–0.14	–0.001	–0.005	–0.04	0.000
Formal and informal education												
Education	0.022***	5.43	0.001	0.023***	5.62	0.001	0.023***	5.68	0.001	0.021***	4.85	0.001
Political discussion	0.064*	1.68	0.003	0.066*	1.78	0.003	0.055	1.48	0.002	0.039	1.01	0.002
Marital status												
Widowed	0.029	0.25	0.001	–0.006	–0.05	0.000	0.011	0.09	0.000	–0.007	–0.06	0.000
Divorced	–0.077	–0.85	–0.003	–0.085	–0.94	–0.003	–0.106	–1.16	–0.004	–0.095	–1.03	–0.004

Separated	0.082	0.45	0.004	0.075	0.42	0.004	0.102	0.56	0.005	0.104	0.55	0.005
Never married	0.052	0.76	0.002	0.056	0.83	0.003	0.071	1.02	0.003	0.069	0.99	0.003
Economic situation												
Upper class	0.237***	3.58	0.012	0.254***	3.91	0.014	0.255***	3.83	0.013	0.241***	3.54	0.012
Middle class	0.153***	2.79	0.007	0.156***	2.88	0.007	0.161***	2.93	0.007	0.166***	2.95	0.007
Employment status												
Part-time employee	0.038	0.40	0.002	0.062	0.69	0.003	0.055	0.59	0.002	0.048	0.50	0.002
Self-employed	–0.015	–0.16	–0.001	–0.010	–0.11	0.000	–0.024	–0.25	–0.001	–0.018	–0.19	–0.001
Unemployed	–0.071	–0.77	–0.003	–0.063	–0.69	–0.003	–0.054	–0.58	–0.002	–0.058	–0.61	–0.002
At home	–0.160	–1.62	–0.006	–0.141	–1.48	–0.006	–0.144	–1.49	–0.006	–0.158	–1.57	–0.006
Student	0.002	0.02	0.000	0.024	0.23	0.001	0.007	0.07	0.000	0.000	0.00	0.000
Retired	–0.209*	–1.90	–0.007	–0.203*	–1.87	–0.007	–0.204*	–1.86	–0.007	–0.199*	–1.76	–0.007
Other	0.224	1.42	0.012	0.222	1.42	0.012	0.229	1.46	0.012	0.252	1.56	0.013
Region												
Western Europe	0.119**	2.32	0.005	0.087*	1.71	0.004	0.057	1.12	0.002	0.110**	2.07	0.004
Pseudo R2	0.063			0.053			0.053			0.070		
Number of observations	18862			18887			18877			18155		
Prob > chi2	0.000			0.000			0.000			0.000		

Notes: The reference group consists of man, age<30, lowest class, not have children, married, full-time employee, Eastern Europe. The symbols *, **, *** represent statistical significance at the 10%, 5% and 1% levels, respectively. Robust standard errors.

Table 7.5 2SLS focusing on environmental membership

Weighted 2SLS	*2SLS*	*(17)*	*First stage regression*	*2SLS*	*(18)*	*First stage regression*		*2SLS*	*(19)*	*First stage regression*		
	Coeff.	*t-Stat.*	*Coeff.*	*t-Stat.*	*Coeff.*	*t-Stat.*	*Coeff.*	*t-Stat.*	*Coeff.*	*t-Stat.*	*t-Stat.*	*Coeff.*
Environmental attitudes												
Willingness to give income	0.353***	3.61										
Willingness to increase taxes					0.232***	4.65						
Contribute at no costs									–0.267***	–4.29		
Demographic factors												
Age 30–39	0.014*	1.78	–0.028	–1.51	0.010	1.53	–0.023	–1.23	0.016**	2.28	0.043**	2.17
Age 40–49	0.032***	3.28	–0.060***	–2.98	0.013**	1.97	–0.011	–0.55	0.017**	2.33	0.019	0.89
Age 50–59	0.048***	4.48	–0.065***	–2.95	0.031***	4.20	–0.029	–1.34	0.041***	4.89	0.055**	2.42
Age 60–69	0.044***	3.49	–0.060**	–2.17	0.030***	3.26	–0.035	–1.28	0.054***	4.58	0.119***	4.34
Age 70+	0.073***	3.86	–0.148***	–4.51	0.034***	3.12	–0.059*	–1.83	0.049***	3.85	0.109***	3.34
Woman	–0.019**	–2.09	0.075***	6.20	–0.005	–1.07	0.059***	4.92	0.001	0.16	–0.025**	–2.07
Child	–0.008	–0.89	–0.002	–0.11	–0.014*	–1.92	0.018	0.86	–0.023***	–2.90	–0.050**	–2.34
Formal and informal education												
Education	–0.002	–1.40	0.017***	15.84	0.000	–0.39	0.017***	15.26	–0.001	–0.99	–0.018***	–15.62
Political discussion	–0.033**	–2.27	0.143***	15.91	–0.013*	–1.76	0.131***	14.66	–0.022**	–2.24	–0.148***	–16.42
Marital status												
Widowed	0.024*	1.77	–0.093***	–3.92	0.004	0.47	–0.065***	–2.79	0.001	0.17	0.043*	1.89
Divorced	0.024**	2.03	–0.079***	–3.50	0.013	1.61	–0.073***	–3.27	0.013	1.49	0.064***	2.92

Separated	–0.004	–0.19	0.020	0.48	0.007	0.45	–0.014	–0.32	0.022	1.33	0.069	1.62
Never married	0.025***	3.25	–0.029*	–1.65	0.022***	3.61	–0.032*	–1.89	0.021***	3.27	0.021	1.16
Employment status												
Part-time employee	0.009	0.89	0.030	1.34	0.016*	1.96	0.019	0.87	0.014	1.62	–0.024	–1.03
Self-employed	–0.013	–1.13	0.071***	3.10	0.001	0.09	0.045*	1.93	–0.006	–0.59	–0.062**	–2.52
Unemployed	0.013	1.11	–0.074***	–3.24	0.002	0.27	–0.065***	–2.89	0.016	1.59	0.105***	4.67
At home	–0.009	–1.00	–0.001	–0.04	–0.001	–0.20	–0.038*	–1.75	0.016*	1.69	0.096***	4.32
Student	–0.040***	–2.85	0.082***	2.97	–0.015	–1.55	0.032	1.15	–0.034***	–2.92	–0.092***	–3.16
Retired	0.021	1.48	–0.114***	–4.86	0.005	0.66	–0.105***	–4.71	0.025**	2.05	0.163***	7.54
Other	0.022	1.21	–0.004	–0.08	0.016	1.00	0.037	0.86	0.012	0.73	–0.049	–1.11
Region												
Western Europe	0.111***	6.25	–0.177***	–15.69	0.073***	11.40	–0.106***	–9.42	–0.024	–1.37	–0.271***	–23.66
Instrument:												
Perceived level of dishonesty			–0.009***	–4.06			–0.014***	–6.20			0.012***	5.30
Test of excluded instruments			16.45***				38.50				28.10***	
Anderson canon. Cor. LR statistic	21.552***				47.697***				32.857***			
Anderson-Rubin test	43.86***				41.73***				40.040***			

Notes: The reference group consists of man, age<30, not have children, married, full-time employee, Eastern Europe. The symbols *, **, *** represent statistical significance at the 10%, 5% and 1% levels, respectively. Robust standard errors.

Table 7.6 The impact of environmental attitudes on membership participation in single countries

96 regressions	*Weighted ordered probit estimations*			*Weighted ordered probit estimations*			*Weighted ordered probit estimations*		
Variable:	*Willingness to give income (32 regressions)*			*Willingness to increase taxes (32 regressions)*			*Contribute at no costs (32 regressions)*		
Western Europe									
Germany	0.586***	4.47	0.012	0.365***	3.24	0.011	–0.244**	–2.47	–0.008
Austria	0.299***	4.51	0.041	0.193***	3.29	0.028	–0.175***	–3.03	–0.025
Belgium	0.263***	5.36	0.046	0.159***	3.33	0.029	–0.241***	–5.05	–0.042
Great Britain	1.119***	3.51	0.001	0.887***	4.51	0.003	–0.030	–0.14	–0.001
Denmark	0.207***	3.12	0.041	0.224***	3.63	0.044	–0.234***	–3.56	–0.046
Finland	0.402***	3.60	0.027	0.259**	2.44	0.021	–0.187*	–1.90	–0.016
France	0.269***	3.02	0.008	0.141*	1.74	0.005	–0.017	–0.20	–0.001
Iceland	0.161	1.29	0.013	0.291**	2.25	0.022	–0.077	–0.65	–0.006
Ireland	0.316*	1.88	0.007	0.102	0.79	0.002	–0.116	–1.02	–0.003
Italy	0.422***	4.15	0.022	0.273***	3.64	0.017	–0.267***	–3.89	–0.016
Luxembourg	0.211***	3.06	0.035	0.137**	2.11	0.023	–0.116*	–1.88	–0.019
Malta	0.060	0.56	0.003	–0.078	0.66	–0.004	–0.023	–0.20	–0.001
Netherlands	0.240***	4.03	0.095	0.232***	4.06	0.091	–0.227***	–3.34	–0.089
Northern Ireland	0.538***	2.65	0.021	0.692***	3.17	0.018	–0.075	–0.50	–0.004
Portugal	2.473***	4.22	0.000	0.095	0.39	0.000	0.148	0.72	0.000
Spain	0.481***	3.77	0.010	0.237**	2.14	0.006	–0.306**	–2.38	–0.007
Sweden	0.237***	2.73	0.040	0.074	0.98	0.013	–0.133*	–1.86	–0.022

Eastern Europe									
Belarus	0.229	1.39	0.005	0.335***	2.38	0.007	–0.109	–0.84	–0.003
Bulgaria	0.633***	3.86	0.009	0.437***	2.83	0.008	–0.190	–1.34	–0.005
Croatia	0.146	1.10	0.004	–0.006	–0.03	0.000	–0.122	–0.91	–0.004
Czech Republic	0.234***	2.79	0.028	0.141**	2.07	0.017	–0.107*	–1.66	–0.013
Estonia	0.608***	3.89	0.015	0.312*	1.78	0.011	–0.216	–1.65	–0.008
Greece	0.309***	3.94	0.049	0.225***	3.35	0.037	–0.044	–0.70	–0.007
Hungary	0.435***	3.17	0.010	0.360***	2.98	0.011	–0.274***	–3.28	–0.010
Latvia	0.312*	1.74	0.001	0.427***	2.65	0.010	–0.502**	–1.97	–0.010
Lithuania	1.078***	4.08	0.002	0.520***	3.13	0.007	–0.254	–1.21	–0.003
Poland	0.312**	2.15	0.004	0.362**	2.06	0.004	–0.048	–0.39	–0.001
Romania	–0.116	–0.82	–0.003	0.032	0.21	0.001	0.216	1.37	0.010
Russia	0.422***	3.99	0.005	0.135	0.91	0.002	0.307**	2.34	0.004
Slovak Republic	0.365***	3.57	0.015	0.347***	3.95	0.016	–0.173**	–2.22	–0.009
Slovenia	0.152	0.90	0.010	0.021	0.16	0.001	0.111	1.21	0.007
Ukraine	0.120	0.62	0.001	0.386**	2.08	0.002	–0.167	–1.16	–0.001

Notes: Only the attitudinal coefficient is reported in the Table. Regressions without the economic situation. The symbols *, **, *** represent statistical significance at the 10%, 5% and 1% levels, respectively. Robust standard errors.

Table 7.7 The impact of environmental attitudes on unpaid work in single countries

96 Regressions	*Weighted ordered probit estimations*			*Weighted ordered probit estimations*			*Weighted ordered probit estimations*		
Variable:	*Willingness to give income (32 regressions)*			*Willingness to increase taxes (32 regressions)*			*Contribute at no costs (32 regressions)*		
Western Europe									
Germany	0.650***	3.40	0.004	0.607***	4.14	0.005	–0.330**	–2.13	–0.005
Austria	0.164*	1.71	0.007	0.044	0.52	0.002	–0.117	–1.56	–0.006
Belgium	0.107*	1.68	0.006	0.073	1.13	0.004	0.006	0.08	0.000
Great Britain	0.229**	2.11	0.024	0.110	1.04	0.012	–0.171*	–1.68	–0.017
Denmark	0.193	1.61	0.007	0.058	0.60	0.002	–0.181	–1.52	–0.007
Finland	0.198	1.07	0.007	0.254	1.40	0.007	–0.156	–1.27	–0.005
France	0.226**	2.03	0.003	0.150	1.30	0.002	–0.085	–0.79	–0.001
Iceland	0.339	1.35	0.009	0.328	1.56	0.009	0.019	0.12	0.001
Ireland	–0.132	–0.65	0.000	–0.038	–0.21	0.000	0.154	0.77	0.000
Italy	0.410***	3.16	0.013	0.270***	2.90	0.009	–0.352***	–3.94	–0.012
Luxembourg	0.211**	2.10	0.016	0.099	1.01	0.008	–0.106	–1.18	–0.008
Malta	0.193	1.22	0.011	–0.053	–0.37	–0.003	–0.014	–0.11	–0.001
Netherlands	0.117	0.90	0.007	0.240*	1.84	0.013	0.154	1.06	0.009
Northern Ireland	1.513**	2.34	0.000	0.576***	3.15	0.001	–0.263	–0.80	0.000
Portugal	9.210	1.28	0.000	–0.382	–1.30	0.000	0.032	0.12	0.000
Spain	1.141***	3.76	0.001	0.391***	3.01	0.004	–0.406**	–2.40	–0.004
Sweden	0.346**	2.13	0.013	0.178	1.37	0.007	–0.151	–1.60	–0.006

Eastern Europe									
Belarus	0.118	1.27	0.003	0.060	0.63	0.001	0.178**	2.04	0.005
Bulgaria	0.479***	3.50	0.007	0.277**	2.01	0.005	–0.174	–1.25	–0.003
Croatia	0.167	1.15	0.003	–0.063	–0.31	–0.001	–0.039	–0.26	–0.001
Czech Republic	0.130	1.39	0.008	0.156*	1.72	0.009	–0.162*	–1.77	–0.009
Estonia	0.746***	3.99	0.000	0.249	1.10	0.000	–0.288	–1.60	0.000
Greece	0.226***	2.72	0.035	0.111	1.64	0.018	0.049	0.74	0.008
Hungary	0.362***	3.42	0.011	0.211*	1.86	0.008	–0.137	–1.46	–0.005
Latvia	0.009	0.06	0.000	0.008	0.07	0.000	0.226	0.23	0.001
Lithuania	0.886***	3.87	0.003	0.741***	3.55	0.006	0.009	0.03	0.000
Poland	1.010***	3.48	0.000	0.028	0.13	0.000	–0.367**	–2.40	0.000
Romania	–0.127	–0.73	–0.001	0.076	0.50	0.001	0.318	1.12	0.003
Russia	0.337***	2.80	0.003	0.309*	1.85	0.004	0.189	1.19	0.003
Slovak Republic	0.358***	2.63	0.013	0.341***	3.08	0.013	–0.197**	–2.29	–0.009
Slovenia	0.126	0.71	0.008	0.016	0.12	0.001	0.007	0.07	0.070
Ukraine	0.175	0.62	0.000	0.586***	2.84	0.000	–1.183***	–4.74	0.000

Notes: Only the attitudinal coefficient is reported in the table. Regressions without the economic situation. The symbols *, **, *** represent statistical significance at the 10%, 5% and 1% levels, respectively. Robust standard errors.

Conclusions

Chapter 7 has investigated whether environmental motivation or environmental attitudes affect environmental behavior. We use both terms as substitutes, although we are aware that there might conceptual differences. Such an approach is empirically driven. We first presented a very simple micro model exploring the relationship between environmental motivation/attitudes and volunteering, and then empirically tested the hypothesis generated by that theoretical model. The chapter investigated the differences between active environmental engagement and membership in general. Thus, while we have discovered several similarities, especially in education issues and economic situation, we have identified some dissimilarity related to socio-demographic features. A significant difference exists between the contribution of women from an economic point of view, and the willingness to contribute with unpaid work in environmental organizations. We attribute this effect to the higher restrictions faced by women regarding the free time available for active volunteering. Differences in the effects of age have also been found. We used three different proxies for environmental attitudes, two of which measure pro-environmental attitudes, namely the willingness to give part of one's own income to prevent environmental pollution, and whether the respondent would agree to an increase in taxes if the extra money is used to prevent environmental pollution. We are aware of the potential limitations of such proxies and we discuss their shortcomings in this chapter, but without neglecting their advantages. In addition, we have explored a variable that measures people's incentive to free-ride (profit without incurring costs). The motivation behind such a study is the observation that deterrence models fail to predict the relatively high level of compliance in various situations where a private cost is incurred in order to provide a public good. Previous literature on this paradox investigates other situations such as the high level of tax compliance despite the low chance of being audited, and the situation investigated in Chapter 6 regarding not littering despite the low probability of getting caught and penalized. Similarly, a high level of cooperation can also be found in experiments. According to Ochs and Roth (1989) and Roth (1995), many ultimatum experiments have shown that the modal offer is (50, 50), that the mean offer is somewhere around (40, 60), and that the smaller the offer, the higher the probability that the offer will be rejected. Moreover, according to Ledyard (1995) and Davis and Holt (1993), public good experiments indicate that, on average, subjects contribute between 40 and 60 percent of their endowment to a public good. Baldry (1987) identifies a need to revise the theory rather than questioning the experimental method.

This chapter provides empirical support for the idea that environmental motivation and environmental attitudes indeed affect individuals' voluntary involvement in environmental organizations. By using a large micro data set covering not less than 32 different countries we are able to provide a comprehensive summary for every single country (almost 200 regressions). Environmental motivation or pro-environmental attitudes are necessary for an understanding of why some people are more involved in environmental protection. However, it should be noted that these social norms work more strongly towards membership of an environmental organization rather than doing unpaid work in these groups. Unpaid work is associated with higher opportunity costs which may help to explain such a difference.

The results of our analyses in this chapter add to those results from previous chapters, presenting an insight into voluntary participation and whose preferences are being served by voluntary provision of a public environmental good. Considering the difficulty and expense involved in regulating to protect the environment (and the political sensitivity of such actions), policymakers seeking the most effective ways to address the consequences of climate change and ecological degradation could find efficient solutions through crowding in these existing motivations.

These empirical findings are not only useful in the context of environmental issues, but can also be applied to voluntary participation and provision of public goods more generally. A very lengthy discussion of this dynamic can be found in Chapter 2. Ostrom (2000: 154) claims that the (pre-Mancur Olson) idea of collective action arising organically from groups in order to solve their own dilemmas was "not entirely misguided," and maintains that institutional, cultural, and biophysical contexts may play a role in determining which individuals join collective action groups. Ostrom also raises the uncomfortable point that past policy based on payoff structures appealing to the rational egoists could have been misdirected. In fact, this could have worked against the original intention of the policy, crowding out social norms that encourage cooperative behavior rather than encouraging collective action (Ostrom 2000).

With respect to environmental issues, by focusing on willingness to pay for environmental quality, past policy may have placed an inappropriate emphasis on financial values for the environment. Moreover, as pro-social behavior is both voluntary and conditioned by observed norms of behavior in society, there exists a stronger chance to crowd in these behaviors than to persist in seeking the appropriate monetary value for the environment based on an individually stated willingness to incur private costs in order to supply a public good. In seeking policy implications from the current study, we could look to policies supporting formation of new community-based organizations and partnerships with existing organizations. A partnership that matches community effort could increase the warm glow "g" for the purely egoistic contributor while also increasing the "G" for the purely altruistic contributor. If policies cease to be aimed at the rational egoist and instead are aimed at crowding in existing motivations and pro-social behaviors, environmental quality might be achieved at lower transaction and policing costs. Finally, it should be noted that further investigations are required to gain a better understanding of what shapes individuals' environmental motivation. This would provide a better foundation to derive policy implications to promote, encourage, and maintain a higher willingness to contribute to the environment.

Appendix

Table A7.1 Description of control variables

Variable	*Definitions*
Micro analysis	
Age	Age 30–39, age 40–49, age 50–59, age 60–69, age +70 (age –30 in the reference group)
Gender	Woman (man in the reference group)
Parent effect	Child (not having children in the reference group)
	Formal and informal education Education: What is the highest educational level that you have attained? 19. No formal education 20. Incomplete primary school 21. Completed primary school 22. Incomplete secondary school: technical/vocational type 23. Complete secondary school: technical/vocational type 24. Incomplete secondary: university-preparatory type 25. Completed secondary: university-preparatory type 26. Some university-level education, without degree 27. University-level education, with degree
	Political discussion: When you get together with your friends, would you say you discuss political matters? 1 Never 2 Occasionally 3 Frequently
Marital status	Widowed; divorced; separated; never married (married in the reference group)
Economic situation	People sometimes describe themselves as belonging to the working class, the middle class, or the upper or lower class. Would you describe yourself as belonging to the: Upper class, middle class (the rest, working class and lower class, in the reference group).
Employment status	Part-time employee, self-employed, unemployed, at home, student, retired, other (full-time employed in the reference group).

Table A7.2 Descriptive statistics micro-analysis

Variables	*Obs*	*Mean*	*Std. Dev.*	*Min*	*Max*
Key variables					
Environmental attitudes (income)	38877	1.620	0.885	0	3
Environmental attitudes (taxes)	38834	1.412	0.877	0	3
Environmental free-riding	39038	1.996	0.894	0	3
Member voluntary environmental organization	41125	0.049	0.216	0	1
Working voluntary environmental organization	41125	0.020	0.140	0	1
Control variables					
Age 30–39	40963	0.197	0.398	0	1
Age 40–49	40963	0.191	0.393	0	1
Age 50–59	40963	0.15	0.357	0	1
Age 60–69	40963	0.135	0.342	0	1
Age 70+	40963	0.102	0.302	0	1
Woman	41114	0.54	0.498	0	1
Children	41125	0.077	0.266	0	1
Education	39840	18.712	5.125	5	74
Political discussion	40713	1.886	0.654	1	3
Upper class	21335	0.136	0.343	0	1
Middle class	21335	0.338	0.473	0	1
Widowed	39861	0.097	0.295	0	1
Divorced	39861	0.07	0.256	0	1
Separated	39861	0.016	0.124	0	1
Never married	39861	0.228	0.42	0	1
Part-time employed	40919	0.068	0.252	0	1
Self-employed	40919	0.052	0.222	0	1
Unemployed	40919	0.229	0.42	0	1
At home	40919	0.095	0.293	0	1
Student	40919	0.061	0.24	0	1
Retired	40919	0.073	0.261	0	1
Other	40919	0.018	0.131	0	1
Instrument					
Perceived level of dishonesty	32903	13.098	2.496	5	20

Table A7.3 Countries macro-analysis

Albania	Lithuania
Argentina	Luxembourg
Austria	Malta
Bangladesh	Mexico
Belarus	Moldova
Belgium	Netherlands
Bulgaria	Peru
Canada	Philippines
Chile	Poland
China	Portugal
Croatia	Romania

continued

Table A7.3 Continued

Czech Republic	Russia
Denmark	Singapore
Estonia	Slovakia
Finland	Slovenia
France	South Africa
Germany	Spain
Greece	Sweden
Hungary	Tanzania
Iceland	Turkey
India	Uganda
Ireland	Ukraine
Italy	United Kingdom
Japan	United States
South Korea	Vietnam
Latvia	Zimbabwe

Notes

1 It has been shown that the preferences to protect the environment (regarding causes and consequences of environmental damages) depend on the level of information the questionnaire includes (Bulte *et al.* 2005).
2 For a detailed discussion regarding possible survey biases see Carson and Mitchell (1995).
3 We consider not having children as the reference group.
4 Aggregated index of the following questions: According to you, how many of your compatriots do the following: Claiming state benefits to which they are not entitled. Driving under the influence of alcohol. Speeding over the limit in built-up areas (each scale from 4 = almost all to 1 = almost none).

References

Ajzen, I. and Fishbein, M. (1977) "Attitude-behavior relations: a theoretical analysis and review of empirical research," *Psychological Bulletin*, 84: 888–918.

—— and —— (1980) *Understanding Attitudes and Predicting Social Behaviour,* Englewood Cliffs: Prentice-Hall.

Andreoni, J. (1988) "Privately provided public goods in a large economy: the limits of altruism," *Journal of Public Economics*, 35: 57–73.

—— (1990) "Impure altruism and donations to public goods: a theory of warm-glow giving," *Economic Journal*, 100: 464–77.

Bagozzi, R., Baumgartner, J., and Yi, Y. (1989) "An investigation into the role of intentions as mediators of the attitude-behavior relationship," *Journal of Economic Psychology,* 10: 35–62.

Bamberg, S. and Möser, G. (2007) "Twenty years after Hines, Hungerford, and Tomera: a new meta-analysis of psycho-social determinants of pro-environmental behaviour," *Journal of Environmental Psychology*, 27: 14–25.

Baldry, J.C. (1987) "Income tax evasion and the tax schedule: some experimental results," *Public Finance*, 42: 357–83.

Brekke, K.A., Kverndokk, S., and Nyborg, K. (2003) "An economic model of moral motivation," *Journal of Public Economics,* 87: 1967–83.

Bulte, E., Gerking, S., List, J.A., and De Zeeuw, A. (2005) "The effect of varying the causes of environmental problems on stated WTP values: evidence from a field study," *Journal of Environmental Economics and Management,* 49: 330–42.

Carson, R.T. and Mitchell, R.C. (1995) "Sequencing and nesting in contingent valuation surveys," *Journal of Environmental Economics and Management*, 28: 155–73.

Clark, C.F., Kotchen, M.J., and Moore, M.R. (2003) "Internal and external influences on pro-environmental behaviour: participation in a green electricity program," *Journal of Environmental Psychology*, 23: 237–46.

Davis, D.D. and Holt, C. (1993) *Experimental Economics*, Princeton, NJ: Princeton University Press.

Dong, B., Dulleck, U., and Torgler, B. (2008) "Conditional corruption: CREMA working paper series 2008–29," Basel: Center for Research in Economics, Management and the Arts (CREMA).

Dresner, S., McGeevor, K., and Tomei, J. (2007) *Public Understanding Synthesis Report: A report to the Department for Environment, Food and Rural Affairs*, London: Policy Studies Institute.

Frey, B.S. and Torgler, B. (2007) "Tax morale and conditional cooperation," *Journal of Comparative Economics*, 35: 136–59.

Hackl, F., Halla, M., and Pruckner, G.J. (2007) "Volunteering and income – the fallacy of the good samaritan?," *Kyklos*, 60: 77–104.

Hidano, N., Kato, T., and Aritomi, M. (2005) "Benefits of participating in contingent valuation mail surveys and their effects on respondent behaviour: a panel analysis," *Ecological Economics,* 52: 63–80.

Hines, J.M., Hungerford, H.R., and Tomera, A.N. (1986/87) "Analysis and synthesis of research on responsible environmental behaviour: a meta-analysis." *Journal of Environmental Education*, 18: 1–8.

LaPiere, R.T. (1934) "Attitudes vs. actions," *Social Forces,* 13*:* 230–37.

Ledyard, J. (1995) "Public goods: a survey of experimental results," in J. Kagel, H. Roth, and E. Alvin (eds), *The Handbook of Experimental Economics*. Princeton, NJ: Princeton University Press.

Lewis, A. (1982) *The Psychology of Taxation*, Oxford: Martin Robertson.

Nixon, J., Martín, J., McKeown, P., and Ranson, S. (1996) *Encouraging Learning: Towards a theory of the learning school,* Milton Keynes, Open University Press.

Ochs, J. and Roth, A.E. (1989) "An experimental study of sequential bargaining," *American Economic Review,* 79: 355–84.

Ostrom, E. (2000) "Collective action and the evolution of social norms," *The Journal of Economic Perspectives,* 14: 137–58.

Owen, A.L. and Videras, J. (2006) "Civic cooperation, pro-environmental attitudes, and behavioural intentions," *Ecological Economics*, 58: 814–29.

Roth, A.E. (1995) "Bargaining experiments," J. Kagel, H. Roth, and E. Alvin (eds), *The Handbook of Experimental Economics*. Princeton, NJ: Princeton University Press.

Teal, G. and Loomis, J.B. (2000) "Effects of gender and parental status on the economic valuation of increasing wetlands, reducing wildlife contamination and increasing salmon population," *Society and Natural Resources*, 13: 1–14.

Torgler, B. (2007) *Tax Compliance and Tax Morale: A theoretical and empirical analysis*, Cheltenham, Glos.: Edward Elgar.

—— and Valev, N. (2006) "Corruption and age," *Journal of Bioeconomics,* 8: 133–45.

—— and —— (2009) "Gender and public attitudes toward corruption and tax evasion," *Contemporary Economic Policy*, forthcoming.

——, Schaffner, M., and Macintyre, A. (2007) "Tax compliance, tax morale and governance quality," School of Economics and Finance Discussion Papers and Working Papers Series 225, School of Economics and Finance, QUT, Australia.

——, Frey, B.S., and Wilson, C. (2009) "Environmental and pro-social norms: evidence on littering," *The B.E. Journal of Economic Analysis & Policy*, 9: art. 18.

Wilson, M., Daly, M., Gordon, S. and Pratt, A. (1996) "Sex differences in valuations of the environment?" *Population and Environment: A journal of interdisciplinary studies*, 2: 143–59.

Witzke, H.P. and Urfei, G. (2001) "Willingness to pay for environmental protection in Germany: coping with the regional dimension," *Regional Studies*, 35: 207–14.

8 Environmental participation, environmental outcome, and international engagement

A macroeconomic perspective

> One of the best demonstrated theories is that contacts made in small intimate groups tend to produce favorable attitudes toward one another among the members . . . leads to "taking the role of the other," to put oneself in the other's shoes, and hence of sharing his values and aspirations to some degree.
>
> (Angell 1969: 30)

Introduction

Up until this point the book has been devoted to providing a solid empirical micro-foundation, even as we recognize that such a micro-foundation has its limitations. Therefore, we now extend the previous analyses by adding an investigation at the macro level that considers three main ideas regarding the relationship between environmental participation and macro-level factors. As discussed in previous chapters, it can be difficult to link environmental participation to environmental outcomes, so we first attempt to check whether the micro-level actions have any effect at the macro level.

Moreover, the descriptive analysis conducted in Chapter 4 only gave us information about the "raw effects" and not the "partial effects" of the associations between our variables. We then look at the determinants of environmental participation at the macro level. Just as we studied the determinants at the micro/individual level in Chapters 5 and 7, we now ask what sort of macro conditions are related to micro-level participation. In Chapter 7, we determined that environmental motivation or environmental attitudes affect environmental participation in a positive way. We are also keen to explore at the macro level whether people can better express their environmental preferences in the context of more transparent and accountable political environments. It is also interesting to see whether politicians, the government, and the administration help to translate environmental preferences into a stronger environmental commitment. In the final section of this chapter, we look at macro-level participation, and whether micro-level motivation encourages macro-level participation in intergovernmental organizations. This investigation may provide some indication as to whether the motivations and values of citizens are represented in the actions of the national government on the international stage.

Environmental participation and environmental outcome

We now exploit some large data sets to investigate whether the micro-level participation studied in previous chapters is indeed related to the macro-level outcomes. For those people volunteering their time in environmental organizations, it is of great interest as to whether their efforts have any effect. We use national measures of pollution and sustainability to check whether joining and volunteering in an environmental organization helps to improve the overall environmental conditions.

Variables

The descriptive analysis conducted in Chapter 4 only gave us information about the raw effects and not the partial effects of the associations between our variables. We are interested in exploring these relationships in a multivariate context, and Chapter 4 provided guidance on just which relationships are worth probing more deeply. For example, the initial results from that chapter indicated that environmental membership may help to deal with global externalities. We used the variable "CO2 emissions" (measured as CO2 emissions (kg per 2000 PPP $ of GDP) resulting primarily from fossil fuel combustion and cement manufacturing) and found a relatively strong and statistically significant correlation between decreased CO2 emissions and environmental membership.[1]

Moreover, our simple linear regression using CO2 emissions as a dependent variable indicated that environmental participation can explain 11 percent of the total variance of the variable CO2 pollution. Of course, this analysis is open to criticism, particularly as we are exploring global externalities, which makes it very difficult to identify a link with any certainty. In other words, any country's CO2 level is also affected by the behavior of other countries, not just by the behavior of the citizens, corporations or state bodies inside the geographical borders of the country in question. So, it is not fully clear why environmental participation should reduce the CO2 emissions at the country level. However, one should note that this variable does not measure the amount of carbon emissions actually in the atmosphere above a country, but rather how much greenhouse gas the country produces. Hence, we propose that a greater level of environmental participation at the individual level will bring greater pressure on industry to create less pollution, and to use alternative energy sources. On the other hand, it could also be argued that the more alternative energy sources and the "cleaner" are the industries in a country, the more likely there will be greater environmental participation, because shutting down or decreasing the activity of those industries for the sake of environmental quality will not cost as many jobs. One should also note that using environmental outcome variables as dependent variables can also lead to problems as they depend on a large range of factors (including natural endowments) that are difficult to control for in a regression analysis.

Control variables

GDP per capita growth (annual percentage)

We use GDP growth and GDP growth squared because a faster growing economy could produce greater environmental damage, and would be expected to display an attitude of "grow now and clean up later." These variables were originally proposed by Carlsson and Lundström (2003), and allow us to control for business cycle fluctuations. Di Vita (2007) uses this measure and finds that it is always positive in explaining carbon dioxide pollution. The use of this measure is based on variations of the Environmental Kuznets Curve (EKC), which suggests an inverted U-shaped relationship between emissions and per capita income.[2] Whether or not this relationship actually exists is a subject of much debate in the literature, as the empirical evidence is not consistent. Among others, Shafik (1994), Selden and Song (1994) and Grossman and Krueger (1995) report empirical evidence in favor of the EKC. However, results presented by Arrow *et al.* (1995) point out that this finding is not necessarily robust.[3] Generally speaking, the EKC relationship can be divided into three parts: scale, composition, and technique (Brock and Taylor 2005). If, as an economy grows, the *scale* of all activities increases proportionally, pollution will increase with economic growth. If growth is not proportional but is accompanied by a change in the composition of goods produced, then pollution may decline or increase with income. If richer economies produce proportionally fewer pollution-intensive products, because of changing tastes or patterns of trade, this composition effect can lead to a decline in pollution associated with economic growth. Finally, if richer countries use less pollution-intensive production *techniques*, perhaps because environmental quality is a normal good, growth can lead to falling pollution. The EKC summarizes the interaction of these three processes.

Agriculture, percentage share of GDP

Previous studies have considered several measures to indicate the composition of the economy. Borghesi (2000) includes the percentage of GDP related to industrial activities. Neumayer (2003) considered the share of GDP from manufacturing activities. In this exercise, we have included the percentage of GDP in agriculture to show the composition of the economy. Sustainability of the agricultural sector is one of the most significant topics on the agenda of many countries. It has been recognized that certain farming activities have a very important impact on different environmental areas, such as soil, water resources, air, even biodiversity and landscape. Thus, the environmental problems caused by those activities are diverse: the eutrophication of surface water, contamination of groundwater resources, evaporation as ammonia, or soil erosion. Pollution as a result of the agricultural production process is a critical issue, as it is in other economic sectors. By including the share of agriculture as a percent of GDP we control for the extent to which an agrarian economy will produce CO2 emissions. Thus, we expect a positive relationship between emissions and "agriculture as a share of GDP."

Exports of goods and services as a percentage share of GDP

This third control variable is included to represent the composition of the economy. If a country is more export-focused, it is more likely to incur environmental damage through exploiting natural resources. This reasoning takes into account the fact that resources are needed to create exports, and thus will be removed from the environment. We predict a positive relationship between the share of exports and CO2 emissions. Furthermore, it is worth considering that the more open an economy, the higher the level of opportunity for exports which, combined with the openness to free trade and cost pressures of competing on the world market, can lead to a lower level of regard for the environment. Some studies have included several trade intensity indexes (Antweiler *et al.* 2001, Cole and Elliot 2003, Cole 2004).

Methodology and results

The link between environmental outcome and environmental participation is also challenging to evaluate because it is difficult to estimate what sort of lag may exist between active environmental participation and its effect on environmental outcomes.

We are going to work with five-year averages to deal with the issue of lags between activity and outcomes. Using the five-year averages for all variables also takes into account that surveys in each wave were not always conducted in the same year. The preliminary results obtained in Chapter 4 are interesting enough that we will now take the analysis a step further and explore whether this relationship is still visible once we control for regional and economic conditions. The results have been obtained using a relatively simple model, and are presented in Table 8.1. To maximize the number of observations we use recent data and include further WVS waves. The inclusion of regional dummies controls for regional invariant factors.[4] We also control for a range of other factors, as outlined in the remainder of this section.

We are interested in the relative importance of the variables employed, thus it should be noted that we report beta or standardized regression coefficients. To obtain robust standard errors in these estimations, we use the Huber/White/Sandwich estimators of standard errors. We are also providing the elasticity of y with respect to x equivalent to evaluated at the multivariate point of means of the data.

The results presented in Table 8.1 indicate that the coefficient for membership participation is always statistically significant at the 5 percent level. We first estimate a simple regression using only time and regional fixed effects (specification (1)). In a second stage (specification (2)) we report a regression including all the control variables. The beta coefficient indicates that the impact of membership is comparable to the impact of the composition of the economy. The strongest effect is observable for economic growth, exhibiting a non-linear relationship that is consistent with some of the empirical work that extended the Environmental Kuznets Curve (as discussed earlier in the chapter). Thus, our results indicate that

Table 8.1 Environmental participation and CO2 pollution

Dep variable: CO2 pollution	*(1)*			*(2)*		
	Beta	*t-statistics*	*Elasticities*	*Beta*	*t-statistics*	*Elasticities*
Membership of environmental organization	–0.281**	–2.34	–0.148	–0.284**	–2.32	–0.154
Economic CONDITIONS						
GDP growth				–0.985***	–2.91	–0.616
(GDP growth)^2				0.873***	2.98	0.149
Composition of the economy						
Agriculture (% of GDP)				0.244*	1.75	0.153
Exports of goods and services (% of GDP)				0.341**	2.45	0.397
Regions	yes			yes		
Years	yes			yes		
Prob > F	0.000			0.000		
R^2	0.169			0.400		
No. of observations	73			71		

Notes: Robust standard errors. Beta/standardized coefficients reported. The symbols *, **, *** represent statistical significance at the 10%, 5% and 1% levels, respectively. Regions: Dummies using the common differentiation (Europe, Latin America, North America, North Africa, Sub-Saharan Africa, the Pacific, Asia, the Caribbean and Australia).

economic growth leads to environmental improvement, but at a decreasing rate. After the optimal level is achieved, an increase in economic growth leads to an increase in environmental pollution. The economic growth effect is four times larger than the effect of other factors. All variables exhibit elasticity values below 1, indicating an inelastic relationship between CO2 emissions and the independent variables economic growth, share of agriculture, and share of exports (Table 8.1). Not surprisingly, there is a positive correlation between export and CO2 pollution and agriculture and CO2 pollution.

Next, we are interested in exploring further environmental outcome variables. From the descriptive statistics presented in Chapter 4, the relationship between environmental participation and the local environmental outcome remains unclear. We speculate that we might observe an incentive for voluntary action when the environmental situation is more critical at the local level, and local externalities are the focus of the analysis. The results of the micro analyses conducted in Chapters 5, 6, and 7 seem to suggest that we indeed observe a stronger willingness to take some pro-environmental actions if the situation is perceived to be more severe or the government is not perceived to be able to cope with it.

To explore this question, we first run the same model presented in Table 8.1 and use a measure of local environmental outcome (PM10 levels) as the dependent variable (see specification (3) and (5)). In specification (4) and (6) we instead use environmental participation as dependent variable and environmental pollution the independent variable. Based on the countries for which data is available, we are not able to add several WVS waves, so we report a cross-sectional analysis. One should note that this approach is not intended to solve the causality issue. The issue remains open and we doubt that we are able to solve the problem based on the data structure (this remains the case, even when considering an instrumental approach). The results of the cross-sectional analysis are presented in Table 8.2. We observe a stronger effect running from the level of pollution to the environmental involvement than the other way round (see specification (4) and (6) compared to (3) and (5)). The beta coefficient in regression (6) shows a relative impact comparable to that of economic growth, while estimation (5) reports a substantially lower effect. This difference is also observable when comparing the elasticities. We observe an elastic relationship in specification (4) and (6) with values higher than 1, while the relationship in specification (3) and (5) seems to be inelastic. The difference is also visible when looking at the level of statistical significance. Pollution is statistically significant at the 1 percent level, yet environmental participation is on the border of being statistically significant. Thus, these findings offer convincing support for the argument that higher local environmental pollution induces a stronger commitment through voluntary participation.

Determinants of environmental participation

We are now interested in conducting a broad exploration of the factors that contribute to environmental participation. Having investigated this question at the micro level in previous chapters, we now examine whether the previous results

Table 8.2 Interaction between environmental participation and environmental outcome

Dep variable: CO2 pollution	*PM10 pollution*			*Work in environmental organization*			*PM10 pollution*			*Work in environmental organization*		
	(3)			*(4)*			*(5)*			*(6)*		
Work in environmental organization	0.369*	1.85	0.173				0.356*	1.77	0.170			
PM10 pollution				0.521***	3.49	1.110				0.500***	3.00	1.049
Economic conditions GDP growth							–0.335	–1.34	–0.209	0.665**	2.24	0.870
(GDP growth)2							0.223	1.02	0.041	–0.596**	–2.36	–0.227
Composition of the economy Agriculture (% of GDP)							0.181	1.42	0.113	0.145	0.72	0.188
Exports of goods and services (% of GDP)							–0.067	–0.81	–0.074	–0.084	–0.73	–0.193
Regions	YES			YES			YES			YE		
Prob > F	0.000			0.000			0.000			0.000		
R^2	0.570			0.392			0.625			0.472		
No. of observations	56			56			55			55		

Notes: Robust standard errors. Beta/standardized coefficients reported. The symbols *, **, *** represent statistical significance at the 10%, 5% and 1% levels, respectively. Regions: Dummies using the common differentiation (Europe, Latin America, North America, North Africa, Sub-Saharan Africa, the Pacific, Asia, the Caribbean and Australia).

remain robust at the macro level. In the micro-level studies, we determined that environmental motivation or pro-environmental attitudes affect environmental participation in a positive manner. These investigations are useful from a policy perspective. The link between policy strategies or institutions and environmental outcomes is likely to be weaker as a substantial number of factors outside a government's control will have an impact on outcomes. As explained in previous chapters (particularly in Chapter 2), policy devices and the strength of institutions should have a direct impact on environmental commitment, which is itself less likely to be influenced by many of the outside factors that affect environmental outcomes. Similarly, environmental morale is also less likely to be affected by the possibility of externalizing the problem upon the future and outside a country's frontier (Neumayer 2002). Thus, one can justify moving our "focus away from environmental outcomes and towards environmental commitment" (Neumayer 2002: 145).

We extend the number of countries in the dataset beyond that implemented in the micro-level work (using the latest 2000 WVS data). We do not recode the original environmental motivation variables, which means that higher values are related to lower environmental motivation for the first two variables (willingness to give income and willingness to increase taxes). In other words, we measure the non-willingness to give income or increase taxes.

We report beta or standardized regression coefficients to reveal the relative importance of the variables employed. To obtain robust standard errors in these estimations, we also use the Huber/White/Sandwich estimators previously mentioned. As control variables we use a proxy for institutional quality, the growth rate, the level of urbanization and the population size age >65. Institutional quality has been measured using the political risk rating from the *International Country Risk Guide*. It is an index that measures government stability, internal and external conflicts, corruption, law and order, democratic accountability, bureaucracy quality, ethnic and religious tensions, and the military in politics; as well as the socioeconomic and investment conditions. Higher values are correlated with better institutions. The idea is that in better political environments people are able to express their environmental preferences. Moreover, politicians and government have an incentive (and the administration has enough resources) to translate it into a stronger environmental commitment. Such preferences are also more likely to be honored within society (Neumayer 2002). In addition, citizens may be better informed about environmental problems and have more effective channels to express their environmental concerns and demands which will put pressure on those setting the policy agenda to take action domestically and at the international level (Payne 1995, Neumayer 2002). On the other hand, countries with lower institutional quality may try to ignore the costs of environmental degradation by concentrating on and drawing attention to other problems (Chadwick 1995). A state with well-functioning institutions may have a political incentive to incorporate the longer term in policy instruments which would lead to a stronger environmental commitment (e.g., stricter environmental regulations). Authoritarian regimes have a highly uncertain career path and may only be in office for a relatively short time. They are also less risk averse and have higher marginal costs of pollution control (Congleton 1992). Previously, we have obtained results at the micro level indicating that if people perceive the government is not able to be trusted (measured by perceived corruption), individuals try to achieve environmental goals on their own. Thus, perceived weak and dysfunctional governance can induce people to pursue their goals via the non-governmental sector, perhaps cooperating through environmental organizations. On the other hand, we also found that rapid collapse of institutional structures produced a vacuum in the country and crowded out environmental participation. The empirical work in this chapter uses a political-risk rating proxy that covers a large set of different factors at the institutional and governance level. Such a proxy is much broader than just "perceived corruption" or use of country dummy variables. Implementing a set of institutional factors that have their foundation also at the *constitutional level* reduces the connection to individuals' perceptions of the *current politicoeconomic* situation. We are utilizing a better measurement of institutional stability, which may be linked to how the relationship between the state and its citizens is established. Hence we predict a positive relationship between our political-risk rating variable and environmental participation.

We also control for the level of economic development and urbanization. A higher level of urbanization may provide a larger potential subject pool, but on the other hand it also increases the level of anonymity among individuals. It could be argued that this higher degree of anonymity would lead to higher transaction costs when forming a voluntary organization. Controlling for economic development may also be useful in order to better isolate the effect of institutional quality. As discussed at length in previous chapters (especially Chapter 3), a well-established system with a functioning rule of law and high levels of regulatory quality would support economic development and would put some pressure on the environment (Desai 1998, Neumayer 2002). We also control for the age structure (in line with the micro-analysis), as it is expected that the number of individuals who are actively involved in environmental organizations decreases as age increases. The intuition is that older people will not live to enjoy the benefits of preserving resources for the coming years. However, as discussed previously, it is also possible to expect the opposite effect (Torgler 2007). Table 8.3 presents the results using both environmental participation variables. We observe that environmental motivation is correlated with environmental participation, which is in line with the results of the micro-level analysis. The coefficients for the two first proxies are always statistically significant, reporting relatively large beta coefficients on the political factors. Similarly, the calculated elasticities demonstrate that these two environmental motivation regressors are elastic, with a decrease in environmental motivation having an effect on environmental participation that is more than four times as large. However it should be noted that the coefficient on the third proxy is not statistically significant.

Looking at the control variables we observe that there is a positive relationship between institutional/governance quality (proxied by political risk factor) and participation in environmental organizations. However, this proxy is more relevant

Table 8.3 Macro-evidence focusing on environmental motivation

Dep variable	*Membership*			*Work*		
	(7)	*(8)*	*(9)*	*(10)*	*(11)*	*(12)*
Environmental motivation						
Non-willingness to give income	–0.392***			–0.236*		
	–2.96			**–1.84**		
	–4.130			*–2.657*		
Non-willingness to increase taxes		–0.406***			–0.369***	
		–4.25			**–3.16**	
		–5.080			*–4.950*	
Against contribute at no costs			0.258			0.058
			0.93			**0.27**
			2.069			*0.498*
Political factor						
Political risk factor	0.562**	0.501*	0.410*	0.228*	0.163	0.204
	2.00	**1.78**	**1.76**	**1.83**	**1.40**	**1.00**
	4.160	*3.709*	*3.037*	*1.805*	*1.295*	*1.621*
Further factors						
GDP growth	–0.111	–0.142	–0.050	0.155	0.112	0.188
	–0.82	**–1.08**	**–0.37**	**1.05**	**0.82**	**1.16**
	–0.198	*–0.253*	*–0.089*	*0.297*	*0.214*	*0.358*
Urbanization	–0.042	–0.039	–0.129	–0.422	–0.390*	–0.478**
	–0.21	**–0.21**	**–0.61**	**–1.87***	**–1.91**	**–2.03**
	–0.166	*–0.154*	*–0.512*	*–1.799*	*–1.662*	*–2.035*
Population (age > 65)	–0.481*	–0.462	–0.425	–0.107	–0.071	–0.119
	–1.67	**–1.57**	**–1.46**	**–0.48**	**–0.32**	**–0.39**
	–1.436	–1.381	–1.269	–0.343	–0.226	–0.380
Regions	YES	YES	YES	YES	YES	YES
Prob > F	0.004	0.000	0.024	0.056	0.010	0.074
R^2	0.369	0.375	0.302	0.456	0.513	0.418
No. of observations	52	52	52	52	52	52

Notes: Robust standard errors. Beta/standardized coefficients reported. t-values in bold and elasticities in italics. The symbols *, **, *** represent statistical significance at the 10%, 5% and 1% levels, respectively. Regions: Dummies using the common differentiation (Europe, Latin America, North America, North Africa, Sub-Saharan Africa, the Pacific, Asia, the Caribbean and Australia).

when dealing with membership participation. Looking at the other variables we observe a negative relationship between urbanization and environmental participation, yet the coefficient is only statistically significant when focusing on unpaid work. Interestingly, the variables on economic growth and population structure are hardly statistically significant.[5]

In Tables 8.4 and 8.5 we also present 2SLS regressions. As an instrument we use "child qualities: tolerance and respect for other people."[6] It measures individuals' willingness to educate their children on social norms, and we predict a statistically significant correlation between this variable and our environmental motivation variables. Additionally, tolerance and other related attitudes are features of affective education clearly linked to cooperation and interaction which promotes children's abilities in areas that reinforce social capital (Nixon *et al.* 1996). This relationship is confirmed when looking at the first stage regressions in Tables 8.4 and 8.5. We also conduct the Anderson's likelihood-ratio test, as a failure to reject the null hypothesis would call into question the identification status of the estimated equation. The results presented in Tables 8.4 and 8.5 show that it is possible to reject the null hypothesis that our specified instrument is redundant. In general, the results obtained in the six 2SLS estimations indicate that our previous findings on the key hypothesis remain robust. We observe a relatively robust relationship between environmental motivation and environmental participation although one should be cautious in interpreting the results as fully consistent estimates (see previous discussions in Chapters 1 and 7).

Intergovernmental engagement

Our previous analysis has mainly focused on environmental engagement at the local level. In historical terms, intergovernmental organizations constitute a relatively new phenomenon (Frey 1997). Globalization tendencies have led to a situation where intergovernmental institutions are becoming more prominent. Figure 8.1 shows five indicators of environmental involvement (Frank *et al.* 2000), namely the cumulative number of national parks and protected areas, chapters of international environmental associations, state membership in international non-government environmental organizations, environmental impact assessment laws, and national environmental ministries. As we can see in Figure 8.1 there has been a distinct increase in environmental involvement over time, especially after the 1960s. It seems that substantial investments have been made to build up environmental regimes after the UN Stockholm Conference on Human Environment in 1972 (Ward 2006). Since the 1980s, environmental IGOs have created networks based on a broad set of different issues (Keck and Sikkink 1998).

Importance of cooperation at this level

Beckfield (2008: 419) stresses that "the global network of states and intergovernmental organizations (IGOs), which comprises a central part of the *world polity*, is shifting the balance of sovereignty among national and global actors, and

Table 8.4 2SLS focusing on membership participation

Dep. variable: membership	*IV (2SLS) estimation*	*First stage regression*	*IV (2SLS) estimation*	*First stage regression*	*IV (2SLS) estimation*	*First stage regression*
	(13)		*(14)*		*(15)*	
Environmental motivation						
Non-willingness to give income	–0.310*					
	–1.95					
Non-willingness to increase taxes			–0.262**			
			–2.17			
Against contribute at no costs					0.280*	
Political factor						
Political risk factor	0.003**	0.0003	0.002*	–0.001	–0.002	0.015
	2.15	*0.08*	*1.81*	*–0.38*	*–0.45*	*2.92*
Further factors						
Gdp growth	–0.005	–0.014	–0.006	–0.019	–0.0002	–0.003
	–1.15	*–1.00*	*–1.38*	*–1.47*	*–0.03*	*–0.19*
Urbanization	0.0003	0.004	0.0002	0.004	–0.0004	–0.002
	0.33	*1.36*	*0.24*	*1.60*	*–0.37*	*–0.56*
Population (age > 65)	–0.004	0.007	–0.005	0.005	0.0003	–0.023
	–0.81	*0.43*	*–1.14*	*0.31*	*0.03*	*–1.24*
Regions	yes	yes	yes	yes	yes	yes
Instrument:						
Child qualities: tolerance and respect for other people	–0.836*		–0.990**		0.924*	
	–1.92		*–2.47*		*1.78*	
Test of excluded instruments		3.67*		6.09**		3.16*
Identification/IV relevance test:						
Anderson canon. corr. LR statistic	4.479**		7.232***		3.881**	
Weak identification statistics:						
Anderson-Rubin test	4.26**		4.26**		4.26**	

Notes: t-values in italics. The symbols *, **, *** represent statistical significance at the 10%, 5% and 1% levels, respectively. Regions: Dummies using the common differentiation (Europe, Latin America, North America, North Africa, Sub-Saharan Africa, the Pacific, Asia, the Caribbean and Australia).

Table 8.5 2SLS focusing on unpaid work

Dep. variable: unpaid work	*IV (2SLS) estimation*	*First stage regression*	*IV (2SLS) estimation*	*First stage regression*	*IV (2SLS) estimation*	*First stage regression*
	(16)		*(17)*		*(18)*	
Environmental motivation						
Non-willingness to give income	–0.187*					
	–1.73					
Non-willingness to increase taxes			–0.158**			
			–2.11			
Against contribute at no costs					0.169	
					1.46	
Political factor						
Political risk factor	0.001	0.0003	0.0003	–0.001	–0.002	0.015***
	0.64	*0.08*	*0.34*	*–0.38*	*–0.87*	*2.92*
Further factors						
Gdp growth	0.001	–0.014	0.001	–0.019	0.004	–0.003
	0.30	*–1.00*	*0.22*	*–1.47*	*1.19*	*–0.19*
Urbanization	–0.001	0.004	–0.001*	0.004	–0.001*	–0.002
	–1.26	*1.36*	*–1.70*	*1.60*	*–1.77*	*–0.56*
Population (age > 65)	0.001	0.007	0.0005	0.005	0.004	–0.023
	0.29	*0.43*	*0.18*	*0.31*	*0.71*	*–1.24*
Regions	YES	YES	YES	YES	YES	YES
Instrument:						
Child qualities: tolerance and respect for other people		–0.836*		–0.990**		0.924*
		–1.92		*–2.47*		*1.78*
Test of excluded Instruments		3.67*		6.09**		3.16*
Identification/IV relevance test:						
Anderson canon. corr. LR statistic	4.479**		7.232***		3.881**	
Weak identification statistics:						
Anderson-Rubin test	3.71*		3.71*		3.71*	

Notes: t-values in italics. The symbols *, **, *** represent statistical significance at the 10%, 5% and 1% levels, respectively. Regions: Dummies using the common differentiation (Europe, Latin America, North America, North Africa, Sub-Saharan Africa, the Pacific, Asia, the Caribbean and Australia).

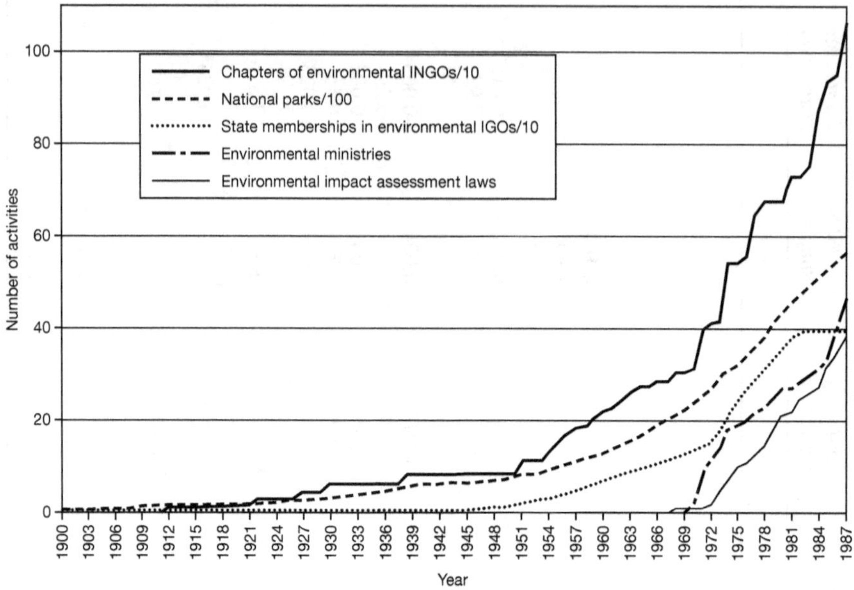

Figure 8.1 Environmental engagement over time

Source: Frank *et al.* (2000: 98).

as such represents a central public concern and social issue." As we face environmental problems of a global nature, the solutions will require global cooperation and, indeed, many current problems would benefit from global cooperation. The discussion about the importance of civil society networks and the functions of intergovernmental organizations in dealing with regional and global environmental problems may produce important insights on how to deal with future environmental challenges. The theories at the individual level about social capital and networking positions may also apply at the international level. In an empirical study by Ward (2006), it was found that the general network position of a country reinforces and supports the way it is located in the environmental regime network. The results indicated an increase in sustainability for an increase in the centrality within the network. We could argue that this is an example of the positive effect of the network dimension of social capital, as discussed extensively in Chapter 2. Such social capital can be brought to bear on states in the network, which may result in agreements to promote peace, and may also build up trust and norms of reciprocity (Dorussen and Ward 2008). Rey and Barkdull (2005: 386) emphasize the idea that "shared membership in intergovernmental organizations (IGOs) is the third leg of the 'Kantian triangle' of factors leading to more peaceful relations between democratic dyads." Shanks *et al.* (1996: 595) also stress that, with regard to IGOs, "like biological populations, organizational populations acquire dynamic properties affecting their development; these are related to, but not entirely dependent on, their environments." However, Biermann and Bauer (2004) point out that

> in analysing international environmental co-operation, most studies have focused on states as actors of international relations (IR) and on international institutions as constraints that place limits on state action. Scholars have also reached beyond the traditional focus of interstate relations and have examined the role of non-state actors and of public-private partnerships. Intergovernmental organisations, however, have largely stayed outside the mainstream debate in IR discourse. Apart from a small literature of descriptive and taxonomic studies that are informed by international law, diplomatic history, and the accounts of practitioners, few scholars have yet attempted to systematically examine the effectiveness of international organisations as actors in their own right
>
> (Biermann and Bauer 2004: 189–90)

In light of the points made above, we feel that it may be interesting to take the analysis in this chapter one step further and examine whether societies with stronger voluntary engagement at the individual level are also more engaged at the intergovernmental level. It should be noted that we are not analyzing empirically the effectiveness or efficiency of the intergovernmental activism, but rather we suggest that stronger pro-environmental preferences and activities at the local level places pressure on countries to also be active at the international level through intergovernmental organizations (IGOs). Moreover, leaders become aware of strong environmental preferences at the local level (norms and rules within their society) and apply it to their execution of intergovernmental relationships. Governments will join IGOs in order to respond to popular demands for environmental engagement. In other words, we now aim to explore the determinants of membership participation in intergovernmental environmental organizations. Najam (2003: 380) cites a report by Turiq Banuri and Erika Spanger-Siegfried that recommends the establishment of deeper linkages with civil society actors. Najam also stresses the "need to begin viewing civil society not just as stakeholders in but as motors of global environmental governance."

Functions of IGOs: winners, losers, and future relevance

Shanks *et al.* (1996: 593) define IGOs as "those associations established by governments or their representatives that are sufficiently institutionalized to require regular meetings, rules governing decision making, a permanent staff, and a headquarters."[7] IGOs in general help to reduce transaction costs, provide information and may help to make promises more credible, but they are also vulnerable to outside pressure such as interest groups (e.g., large business interests), bureaucrats and political leaders (Keohane 2002). The "hope" is that IGOs provide the conditions for greater cooperation and interdependence among nations (McCormick 1980).

Intergovernmental organizations are active where national interests collide and where global public good problems and externalities lead to winners and losers. The existence of such a forum alerts the interest of national governments (mainly the losers), allowing them to put matters on the international negotiating table. IGOs are therefore seen as being useful in the regulation of collective goods (Simmons and Martin 2002) such as the environment, with the incentive to solve a range of collective action problems (Keohane 1984). They can affect the efficiency of collective activities and can help in negotiating the environment and the states' interests. The management of the coastal zone is an interesting example. The rising sea level is producing many problems for island communities, and there are considerable costs involved in rebuilding sea defenses and ship-handling facilities. Tourism, exploitation, and pollution affect the biodiversity in the oceans (e.g., coral reefs). Thus, local problems can become regional ones (leaving aside the argument that rising sea levels are caused by a global problem of climate change; in this case, an international problem has become a local one). When local problems require regional or international solutions, intergovernmental organizations can play an advisory or catalytic role to bring about the changes required (Holland 1998). Several UN agencies have been involved in coastal zoning questions (for example, World Health Organization, United Nations Environment Program, International Maritime Organization). Since the 1960s we have observed interactions between intergovernmental and scientific organizations to deal with problems around marine affairs (Wooster 1973).

Relevance

The subfield of international environmental law is one of the fastest growing areas in international law. UN agencies actively set agendas dealing with issues such as desertification, biodiversity, and climate change and they are involved in negotiating global regimes in the area of ozone depletion, endangered species, hazardous waste, seas, and pollutants (Najam 2003). We could take this as an indication that the relevance of IGOs is not going to decrease over time.

However, it is unclear whether their activities lead to real outcomes. The public choice literature has made some strong statements to the effect that IGOs are an extreme example of waste effected by a lack of democracy. On the other hand, some economists acknowledge their relevance in an increasingly interdependent world characterized by external effects, economies of scale, and the development of political and administrative units at the regional and international level (Frey 1997). Moreover, IGOs have been criticized due to their lack of authority and efficacy regarding enforcement of both norms and laws, as this means they have minimal influence on state behavior (Mearsheimer 1994–95). Interestingly, while the network of states is becoming more interconnected and less centralized, IGOs demonstrate a tendency to become more centralized (Beckfield 2008). Such a centralization process may also breed further inefficiencies, as the public choice literature has shown (e.g., bureaucratic incompetence and wastefulness, lack of transparency).

IGOs vary strongly in regards to their functions, structure, and capacities; this causes problems when we try to explore their efficiency in general. Some studies have suggested that IGOs can provide a forum for attitude changes, socialization through interpersonal contacts within IGOs, and internalization of norms among member nations (McCormick 1980, Pentland 1976, Coplin 1971). Beyers (2005) develops the idea behind socialization as

> the organization of social interactions (that is, institutional conditions and informal/formal rules that structure social life) and/or the logic of these interactions (that is, instrumental bargaining, role playing, or suasion) affect which behavioral practices, norms about appropriateness, and preferences about outcomes are internalized by individual actors. More importantly, these practices, norms, and preferences are not only internalized by individual actors, but, because they are shared by many, also characterize and shape the identity of large social aggregates (that is, a bureaucratic agency, a political party, a country and so on).
>
> (Beyers 2005: 900)

Problems with IGOs

The level of transparency of IGOs is also an important issue (Grigorescu 2007). For example, government pressure for confidentiality reduces transparency (Keohane 2005). In addition, the behavior of IGO delegates may systematically deviate from the wishes of national voters. There have been various cases where intergovernmental organizations have attracted scrutiny. For example, World Bank officials have been under investigation for skimming millions of dollars from an African job creation program; UN peacekeepers in Congo were involved in rape, pedophilia, and prostitution; an official at the World Meteorological Organization stole $3 million; and the UN scandal regarding the Oil-for-Food Program saw large profits distributed to Saddam Hussein ($2 billion), hundreds of foreign companies and several UN officials (Grigorescu 2008). Certainly, fraudulent activities are not confined to IGOs: this kind of behavior happens in all institutions and organizations. However, the visibility and reach of IGOs mean that such cases raise discussions about the accountability of intergovernmental organizations. Engagement at the international level may also blur the division of responsibility between IGOs and the national government. Moreover, the common actions of large international organizations makes it impossible for voters to compare alternative policies (there are no competing international organizations), which reduces the incentives to monitor their own effectiveness and enhances the discretionary power of the organization (Frey 1997). Interestingly, Grigorescu (2007) finds that organizations made up of democratic states tend to establish policies and put further policies into action that emphasize transparency, ensuring public access to information about the actions of the IGO.

Benefits to member countries

Nevertheless, even in the face of these criticisms, there are several researchers who have re-emphasized the importance of international organizations (Minnich 2005). The positive side of IGOs is that they have the capacity to operate as agents who are "neutral in managing interstate disputes and conflicts" (Abbott and Snidal 1998: 5). A study shows that for the years 1885–1992, rising indicators of democracy, economic interdependence, and involvement in international organizations have corresponded to a reduction in the incidence of militarized interstate disputes. The benefits of membership participation in intergovernmental organizations were less strong but still significant for important dyads (Oneal and Russett 1999). A key (material) benefit of participating in IGOs is the opportunity to play a role in influencing the institutional design and shape of international environmental regimes. Participation may help to generate concessions at the country level and secure national loopholes that serve national interests and reduce compliance costs. In addition, it may help to increase the international image of global environmental responsibility regardless of its true intentions or motivations (Wu 2009). Also, networking has been perceived as a benefit (Dorussen and Ward 2008), as it promotes similarity of interest and mutual understanding. Involvement in networks also decreases incomplete information and provides certainty regarding participants' preferences, which helps to build trust, establish credibility, and achieve bargaining solutions instead of conflicts. Bearce and Bondanella (2007) argue that

> states that are joint members of more IGOs should show greater interest convergence than states with less joint IGO membership. Indeed, if regular sustained contact/interactions within IGOs socialize states in the international system, then more socialization opportunities should lead to even greater interest convergence.
>
> (Bearce and Bondanella 2007: 708)

Their empirical results show that joint membership leads indeed to an increase in common interests. Repetition can also provide incentives to mediate in an honest manner despite potential pre-existing biases. IGOs may have a stronger incentive to preserve a reputation for honesty due to their long-term function as mediators of conflict resolutions (Kydd 2006), since a reputation for trustworthiness is essential for many relationships (Keohane 1984). Archer (2001) neatly summarizes some of the key issues surrounding the existence of IGOs:

> Are they one of the many participants jostling in transactions with other groups, with political leaders and states' representatives? Are they the mere instruments of the other players, being used as tools to gain advantages or as a means of communications between interlocutors? Or are they part of the scenery itself, plinths for speeches, forums for meetings, common grounds for gatherings?
>
> (Archer 2001: 65)

Data and variables

To establish the factors involved in a country's intergovernmental activism, we use the ESI data set from 2001 that provides an index of the number of memberships in environmental intergovernmental organizations. In line with Minnich (2005) we stress that it is important to take into account the characteristics at the domestic level in order to uncover the sources of international behavior. The nature of constraints at the domestic level affects the creation, entering, and maintenance of memberships at the international level (Putnam 1988). This requires an exploration of a large set of institutional variables.

The process of deciding whether to join an intergovernmental organization is affected by governmental decisions. Countries with a higher level of governance and institutional quality have more resources available for operations as a member of an IGO and to monitor and deal with international activities and problems. Previous studies have stressed that stability is positively correlated with membership in international institutions (Shanks *et al.* 1996). Thus, we will also explore the importance of governance and institutional quality. To measure this factor, we are going to use the *Quality of Governance Index* from 2000 (Kaufmann *et al.* 2003), which has been mentioned in previous chapters. This index reports the mean value of six governance dimensions and we implement each of the variables from the index, exactly as described below. It is based on several hundred variables that measure perceptions of governance, and is derived from 25 different data sources. Kaufmann *et al.* (2003) classify the six governance indicators into three groups as follows:

1 Process by which governments are selected, monitored and replaced.
   - Voice and accountability: measures political process, civil liberties, and political rights.
   - Political stability and absence of violence: measures perceptions of the likelihood that the government will be destabilized/overthrown.
2 Capacity of the government to effectively formulate and implement sound policies.
   - Government effectiveness: inputs required for the government to be able to produce and implement good policies and deliver public goods.
   - Regulatory quality: focuses more on policies, such as incidence of market/unfriendly policies, perceptions of the burdens imposed by excessive regulation.
3 Respect of citizens and the state for the institutions that govern economic and social interactions.
   - Rule of law: several indicators measuring the degree of agents' confidence in and compliance with the rules of society. According to Kaufmann *et al.* (2003: 4) these indicators "measure the success of a society in developing an environment in which fair and predictable rules form the basis of economic and social interactions."
   - Control of corruption: measures the perceived corruption (exercise of public power for private gain).

All scores estimated by Kaufmann *et al.* (2003) lie between –2.5 and 2.5, with higher scores corresponding to better institutions (outcomes). Thus, we predict that a more legitimate and responsive state appears to be an essential precondition for a stronger involvement at the intergovernmental level. As far as we know, such a large set of institutional factors has not been explored before in the literature. Minnich (2005) conducted a study in which he investigated the effect of a variety of democratic institutions on the international behavior of states. He stresses that constitutional structure and electoral design shapes countries' membership participation in international organizations. Similarly, Shanks *et al.* (1996) found that democratic states increased their IGO memberships over time, when compared to poor and unstable states that had decreased their participation.

Controls

Moreover, it has been established that capitalist and wealthy states are more likely to support international cooperation through membership in international institutions (Minnich 2005). We therefore use proxies such as trade level (trade percentage of GDP) and GDP growth to control for such effects. Jacobson *et al.* (1986) also found that for poor country members in IGOs, membership is associated with enhanced economic performance and a lower proneness to war. Rey and Barkdull (2005) took a closer look at the question as to why some democratic countries are more likely to join IGOs than others and found that consensus democracies are more likely to join IGOs than majoritarian democracies. This is interesting insofar as the creation of many new democracies has led to an increase in institutional differences among democracies.

We are considering several control factors: not only the *economic conditions* and the *composition of the economy*, but also *geographic power* proxied by the surface area (surface area km^2). Countries with larger surface areas may have higher incentives to cooperate in order to protect their land mass, and it may be the case that smaller states have fewer resources available to be allocated for IGO activities. For the same reason we also control for regional fixed effects. Regional dummies take into account the fact that geography determines a country's neighbors. Since many IGOs are regional, location also indicates how often a country might be invited to join IGOs (Shanks *et al.* 1996). Moreover, in the past, developing countries have tended to have a strong influence in shaping the structure and operation of IGOs.

Results

The results are reported in Tables 8.6 and 8.7. Table 8.7 looks more deeply into the relationship between intergovernmental involvement and governance quality, increasing the number of countries included in the analysis by leaving out our membership variable. Table 8.6 shows that there is a strong link between voluntary membership in environmental organizations at the individual level and intergovernmental involvement in environmental agreements. The coefficient is statistically significant in all the reported estimations, and registers relatively large beta coefficients. We first explore the membership variable without controlling for governance quality and then in the following regressions we analyze each single governance factor independently. To check the robustness of the findings, we implement alternative measure of governance, namely the political risk rating that we have used in the previous section (political risk factor from the ICRG).

It is also evident that all the governance quality factors are statistically significant at the 5 or 1 percent level. Thus, we can state that governance quality matters, as it seems to produce a stronger intergovernmental involvement. If we look at each of the different factors independently, we can see that government effectiveness induces the strongest effect, followed by rule of law and lack of corruption. Thus, countries that are organized effectively are inclined to be environmentally active at the intergovernmental level. Governance conditions provide a good basis for dealing with intergovernmental engagement. Such a result is consistent with Neumayer (2002), who found that democracies exhibit stronger international environmental commitment than non-democracies. The results remain relatively robust among the large number of dependent variables implemented in this study (including signing and ratification of multilateral environmental agreements, membership in environmental intergovernmental organizations, extent to which complies with reporting requirements for the Convention on International Trade in Endangered Species of Fauna and Flora, percentage of a country's land area under protection status, existence of a National Council on Sustainable Development in a country, and the availability of environmentally relevant information concerning a country).

Interestingly, we also find that geographic power proxied by the surface area matters, indicating that the larger the surface area of a country, the stronger the incentives to be environmentally active at the intergovernmental level. On the other hand, economic openness is negatively correlated with intergovernmental involvement. Similarly, as expected, a stronger agriculture sector is also related to less involvement in intergovernmental agreements with respect to the environment.

Conclusions

This chapter began by using a multivariate context to explore the relationship between environmental participation and environmental outcome. We observe that the preliminary findings from Chapter 4 remain robust after controlling for factors such as economic development, composition of the economy, or regional factors. First, we use a global externality (namely CO2 emissions) to investigate the relationship between environmental participation and environmental outcome, and discover a positive correlation. In a next step, we explore the relationship between environmental participation and local environmental outcome, based on the premise that people will be more likely to cooperate when the environmental threats are at the local level. In the descriptive statistics from Chapter 4 we observed a negative relationship between these variables. We noted that caution should be used in this analysis, as it is not clear whether environmental outcome

Table 8.6 Membership of voluntary organizations and intergovernmental involvement

Dep. variable: membership of environmental intergovernmental organizations	*(19)*	*(20)*	*(21)*	*(22)*	*(23)*	*(24)*	*(25)*	*(26)*
Voluntary participation								
Membership of voluntary environmental organization	0.326*** *3.66*	0.217** *2.63*	0.280*** *3.46*	0.214** *2.50*	0.272*** *3.37*	0.258*** *3.00*	0.221*** *3.01*	0.231*** *2.81*
Governance quality								
Kaufmann *et al.*								
Government effectiveness		0.627*** *3.55*						
Political stability			0.409*** *3.15*					
Control of corruption				0.587*** *3.17*				
Voice and accountability					0.470*** *2.74*			
Regulatory quality						0.387** *2.31*		
Rule of law							0.656*** *3.60*	

Institutional quality (ICRG)								
Political risk factor								0.579***
								3.41
Further factors								
Surface area (sq. km)	0.147*	0.289**	0.237***	0.322***	0.285***	0.307**	0.316***	0.326***
	1.93	*2.62*	*2.46*	*3.16*	*3.11*	*2.48*	*3.37*	*2.74*
GDP growth	0.012	–0.144	–0.016	–0.061	–0.041	–0.116	–0.053	–0.077
	0.10	*–1.65*	*–0.16*	*–0.70*	*–0.39*	*–1.03*	*–0.73*	*–0.75*
Trade (% of GDP)	–0.359**	–0.315***	–0.349**	–0.272**	–0.308**	–0.308**	–0.273**	–0.343**
	–2.45	*–2.68*	*–2.49*	*–2.04*	*–2.17*	*–2.12*	*–2.33*	*–2.39*
Agriculture (% of GDP)	–0.723***	–0.223	–0.485***	–0.294	–0.390**	–0.451**	–0.225	–0.346**
	–4.92	*–1.32*	*–3.33*	*–1.62*	*–2.29*	*–2.65*	*–1.34*	*–1.99*
Manufacturing (% of GDP)	–0.235**	–0.082	–0.163	–0.157	–0.112	–0.102	–0.093	–0.104
	–2.11	*–0.65*	*–1.28*	*–1.35*	*–0.88*	*–0.72*	*–0.79*	*–0.74*
Regions	YES	YES	YES	YES	YES	YES	YES	YES
R^2	0.598	0.734	0.658	0.707	0.650	0.654	0.739	0.683
Prob > F	0.000	0.000	0.000	0.000	0.000	0.000	0.000	0.000
No. of observations	54	54	54	54	54	54	54	52

Notes: standardized/beta coefficients. t-statistics in italics. *, ** and *** denote significance at the 10%, 5% and 1% level, respectively. Regions: Dummies using the common differentiation (Europe, Latin America, North America, North Africa, Sub-Saharan Africa, the Pacific, Asia, the Caribbean and Australia).

Table 8.7 Voluntary organizations and intergovernmental involvement and governance quality

Dep. variable: membership of environmental intergovernmental organizations	*(27)*	*(28)*	*(29)*	*(30)*	*(31)*	*(32)*	*(33)*	*(34)*
Governance quality								
Kaufmann *et al.*								
Government effectiveness		0.526*** *3.74*						
Political stability			0.160 *1.60*					
Control of corruption				0.501*** *4.03*				
Voice and accountability					0.398*** *3.47*			
Regulatory quality						0.483*** *5.27*		
Rule of law							0.644*** *5.20*	

Institutional Quality ICRG)								0.386***
Political risk factor								*2.92*
Further factors								
Surface area (sq. km)	0.122**	0.216***	0.140***	0.234***	0.175***	0.274***	0.248***	0.188***
	2.46	*3.51*	*2.70*	*3.95*	*3.70*	*3.89*	*4.27*	*2.71*
GDP growth	–0.011	–0.122	–0.018	–0.056	–0.020	–0.134	–0.048	–0.039
	–0.15	*–1.68*	*–0.23*	*–0.80*	*–0.29*	*–1.83*	*–0.77*	*–0.48*
Trade (% of GDP)	–0.236**	–0.227**	–0.257**	–0.201**	–0.270**	–0.233**	–0.201**	–0.275**
	–2.11	*–2.35*	*–2.27*	*–2.00*	*–2.40*	*–2.22*	*–2.18*	*–2.24*
Agriculture (% of GDP)	–0.602***	–0.200	–0.508***	–0.278**	–0.340**	–0.237*	–0.141	–0.263*
	–4.74	*–1.30*	*–4.14*	*–2.13*	*–2.61*	*–1.90*	*–1.10*	*–1.91*
Manufacturing (% of GDP)	–0.194*	–0.052	–0.158	–0.097	–0.074	–0.025	–0.067	–0.093
	–1.76	*–0.46*	*–1.38*	*–0.86*	*–0.66*	*–0.24*	*–0.61*	*–0.76*
Regions	YES	YES	YES	YES	YES	YES	YES	YES
R^2	0.428	0.531	0.440	0.520	0.482	0.530	0.569	0.438
Prob > F	0.000	0.000	0.000	0.000	0.000	0.000	0.000	0.000
No. of observations	118	118	118	118	118	118	118	107

Notes: standardized/beta coefficients. t-statistics in italics. *, ** and *** denote significance at the 10%, 5% and 1% level, respectively. Regions: Dummies using the common differentiation (Europe, Latin America, North America, North Africa, Sub-Saharan Africa, the Pacific, Asia, the Caribbean and Australia).

affects environmental participation or the other way round. In this regard the causality issue is quite a challenge and we are aware that we are not able to solve the problem by working with the available data sets. However, to get a better idea about the direction of the effect we explored both factors, environmental participation and environmental outcome, as a dependent variable. This allows us to see whether the impact of the environmental situation exerts a stronger effect on environmental participation than environmental participation does on the environmental outcome. The result of our analysis indicates that we observe a stronger effect running from the level of pollution to the environmental involvement than the other way round. Thus, these findings provide some support for the argument that higher local environmental pollution induces a stronger commitment through voluntary participation. In other words, individuals have an incentive to be active in voluntary environmental organizations when the *local* environmental situation is more critical.

The empirical work in this chapter provides support for the idea that environmental motivation and pro-environmental attitudes indeed affect individuals' voluntary involvement in environmental organizations. Such a result was also found in Chapter 7 at the micro level; however we now use a macro data set to check if the relationship is also observable at the macro level. Environmental motivation seems to be a key factor in understanding environmental engagement of individuals and societies. Our results also indicate that political stability and institutional quality that has its foundation at the *constitutional* level – measuring how the relationship between the state and its citizens is established – has a positive influence on environmental participation. Well-functioning institutions provide a good foundation for environmental commitment, but individuals also organize when they perceive that the *current* politicoeconomic system is not achieving their environmental goals.

This chapter also attempts to explore countries' environmental engagement at the intergovernmental level. In this analysis, we are broadening the scope from an engagement at the voluntary level to investigate involvement at the intergovernmental level. We have explored whether societies with a stronger voluntary engagement at the individual level are also more engaged at the intergovernmental level, and the results indeed support such a relationship. Thus, we observe that there is some sort of culture of environmental participation within a country that is visible at the local and also at the intergovernmental level. We were therefore (naturally) keen to explore the determinants of intergovernmental environmental participation. In particular, we focused on the importance of governance and institutional quality, relying on the process by which governments are selected, monitored, and replaced; the capacity of the government to effectively formulate and implement sound policies; and the respect of citizens and the state for the institutions that govern economic and social interactions. The results indicate that governance quality matters. Interestingly, the strongest effects can be found for government effectiveness, rule of law, and lack of corruption. Thus, there is a strong positive relationship between how effectively the countries are organized and the intergovernmental involvement in environmental issues. It seems that governance quality is a key requirement for a sustainable intergovernmental environmental program.

Notes

1 See variable descriptions in Chapter 4 for more details.
2 See Sahu (2002) for a review of empirical studies about Environmental Kuznets Curve.
3 Several authors have proposed an inverted N-shaped or even an N-shaped relationship. See for instance Holtz-Eakin and Selden (1995), Cole *et al.* (1997) or Moomaw and Unruh (1997). However, often the additional turning-point is out-of-sample.
4 We differentiate between Europe, Latin America, North America, North Africa, Sub-Saharan Africa, the Pacific, Asia, the Caribbean and Australia.
5 It should be noted that the impact of economic growth does not change when neglecting the political institutions in the regressions.
6 Question: Here is a list of qualities that children can be encouraged to learn at home. Which, if any, do you consider to be especially important? Please choose up to five. Tolerance and respect for other people (0 = Not mentioned, 1 = Important).
7 For a detailed classification and identification see Volgy *et al.* (2008).

References

Abbott, K.W. and Snidal, D. (1998) "Why states act through formal international organizations," *Journal of Conflict Resolution*, 42: 3–32.

Angell, R.C. (1969) *Peace on the March: Transnational participation*, New York: van Nostrand Reinhold.

Antweiler, W., Copeland, B.R., and Taylor, M.S. (2001) "Is free trade good for the environment?" *American Economic Review*, 91: 877–08.

Arrow, K., Bolin, B., Constanza, R., Dasgupta, P., Folke, C., Holling, C.S., Jansson, B.O., Levin, S., Maler, K.G., Perrings, C., and Pimental, D. (1995), "Economic growth, carrying capacity and the environment," *Ecological Economics*,15: 91–95.

Archer, C. (2001) *International Organizations*, New York: Routledge.

Bearce, D.H. and Bondanella, S. (2007) "Intergovernmental organizations, socialization, and member-state interest convergence," *International Organization*, 61: 703–33.

Beckfield, J. (2008) "The dual world polity: fragmentation and integration in the network of intergovernmental organizations," *Social Problems*, 55: 419–42.

Beyers, J. (2005) "Multiple embeddedness and socialization in Europe: the case of council officials," *International Organization*, 59: 899–936.

Biermann, F. and Bauer, S. (2004) "Assessing the effectiveness of intergovernmental organisations in international environmental politics," *Global Environmental Change*, 24: 189–93

Borghesi, S. (2000) "Income inequality and the Environmental Kuznets Curve," Fondazione Eni Enrico Mattei, Nota di Lavoro 83.2000.

Brock, W. and Taylor, M.S. (2005) "Economic growth and the environment: a review of theory and empirics," in S. Durlauf and P. Aghion (eds, *The Handbook of Economic Growth*, Amsterdam: North Holland.

Carlsson, F. and Lundström, S. (2003) "The effects of economic and political freedom on CO2 emissions," Working Paper in Economics 29, Göteborg University.

Chadwick, B.R. (1995) "Fisheries, sovereignities and red herrings," *Journal of International Affairs*, 48: 559–84.

Cole, M.A. (2004) "Trade, the pollution haven hypothesis and the environmental Kuznets curve: examining the linkages," *Ecological Economics*, 48: 71–81.

—— and Elliott, R.J.R. (2003) "Determining the trade-environment composition effect: the role of capital, labor and environmental regulations," *Journal of Environmental Economics and Management*, 46:363–83.

——, Rayner, A.J., and Bates, J.M. (1997) "The environmental Kuznets curve: an empirical analysis," *Environment and Development Economics*, 2: 401–16.

Congleton, R.D. (1992) "Political institutions and pollution control," *Review of Economics and Statistics*, 74: 412–21.

Coplin, W.D. (1971) "International organization in the future international bargaining: a theoretical projection," *Journal of International Affairs*, 55: 287–301.

Desai, U. (1998) "Environment, economic growth, and government," in U. Desai (ed.), *Ecological Policy and Politics in Developing Countries*. Albany, NY: State University of New York Press.

Di Vita, G. (2007) "Legal families and environmental protection: is there a causal relationship?" Fondazione Eni Enrico Mattei, Working Paper 2007–78.

Dorussen, H. and Ward, H. (2008) "Intergovernmental organizations and the Kantian peace: a network perspective," *Journal of Conflict Resolution*, 52: 189–212.

Frank, D.J., Hironaka, A., and Schofer, E. (2000) "The nation-state and the natural environment over the twentieth century," *American Sociological Review*, 65: 96–116.

Frey, B.S. (1997) "The public choice of international organizations," in D.C. Mueller (ed.), *Perspectives on Public Choice*. Cambridge: Cambridge University Press.

Grigorescu, A. (2007) "Transparency of intergovernmental organizations: the role of member states, international bureaucracies and nongovernmental organizations," *International Studies Quarterly*, 51: 625–48.

—— (2008) "Horizontal accountability in intergovernmental organizations," *Ethics & International Affairs*, 22: 285–308.

Grossman, G.M. and Krueger, A.B. (1995) "Economic growth and the environment," *Quarterly Journal of Economics*, 110: 353–77.

Holland, G.L. (1998) "The role of intergovernmental organizations in coastal zone management," *Ocean & Coastal Management*, 39: 25–31.

Holtz-Eakin, D. and Selden, T. (1995) "Stoking the fires? CO2 emissions and economic growth," *Journal of Public Economics*, 57: 85–101.

Jacobson, H.K., Reisinger, W., and Mathers, T. (1986) "National entanglements in international governmental organizations," *American Political Science Review*, 80: 141–59.

Kaufmann, D., Kraay, A., and Mastruzzi, M. (2003) *Governance Matters III: Governance Indicators for 1996–2002*, World Bank.

Keck, M.E. and Sikkink, K. (1998) *Activists beyond border: advocacy networks in international politics*. Ithaca, NY: Cornell University Press.

Keohane, R.O. (1984) *After Hegemony*, Princeton, NJ: Princeton University Press.

—— (2002) "Intergovernmental Organizations and Garbage Can Theory," *Journal of Public Administration Research and Theory*, 12: 155–50.

—— (2005) "Abuse of Power," *Harvard International Review*, 27: 48–53.

Kydd, A. (2006) "When can mediators build trust?" *American Political Science Review*, 100: 449–62.

McCormick, J.M. (1980) "Intergovernmental organizations and cooperation among nations," *International Studies Quarterly*, 24: 75–98.

Mearsheimer, J. (1994–95) "The false promise of international institutions," *International Security*, 19: 5–49.

Minnich, D.J. (2005) "Veto players, electoral incentives and international commitments: the impact of domestic institutions on intergovernmental organization membership," *European Journal of Political Research*, 44: 295–325.

Moomaw, W. and Unruh, G. (1997) "Are environmental Kuznets curves misleading us? The case of CO2 emissions," *Environment and Development Economics*, 2: 451–64.

Najam, A. (2003) "The case against a new international environmental organization," *Global Governance*, 9: 367–84.

Neumayer, E. (2002) "Do democracies exhibit stronger international environmental commitment? A cross-country analysis," *Journal of Peace Research*, 39: 139–64.

—— (2003) "Are left-wing party strength and corporatism good for the environment? Evidence from panel analysis of air pollution in OECD countries," *Ecological Economics*, 45: 203–20.

Nixon, J., Martín, J., McKeown, P., and Ranson, S. (1996) *Encouraging Learning: Towards a theory of the learning school.* Milton Keynes, Open University Press.

Oneal, J.R. and Russett, B. (1999) "The Kantian peace: the pacific benefits of democracy, interdependence and international organizations, 1885–1992," *World Politics*, 52: 1–37.

Payne, R.A. (1995) "Freedom and the environment," *Journal of Democracy*, 6: 41–55.

Pentland, C. (1976) "International organizations," in J.N. Rosenau, K.W. Thompson, and G. Boyd (eds), *World Politics*, New York: Free Press.

Putnam, R.D. (1988) "Diplomacy and domestic politics: the logic of two-level games," *International Organization*, 42: 427–60.

Rey, D. and Barkdull, J. (2005) "Why do some democratic countries join more intergovernmental organizations than others?" *Social Science Quarterly*, 86: 386–402.

Sahu, N.C. (2002) "The environmental Kuznets curve: a critique in the Indian perspective," in N. Rajalakshmi (ed.) *Environmental Costs of Economic Evaluation.* New Delhi: Manak.

Selden, T.M. and Song, D. (1994) "Environmental quality and development: is there a Kuznets curve for air pollution emissions?" *Journal of Environmental Economics and Management*, 27: 147–62

Shafik, N. (1994) "Economic development and environmental quality: an econometric analysis," *Oxford Economic Papers*, 46: 757–73.

Shanks, C., Jacobson, H.K., and Kaplan, J.H. (1996) "Inertia and change in the constellation of international governmental organizations, 1981–92," *International Organization*, 50(4): 593–627.

Simmons, B. and Martin, L. (2002) "International organizations and institutions," in W. Carlsnaes, T. Risse, and B. Simmons (eds), *Handbook of International Relations*, London: Sage.

Torgler, B. (2007) *Tax Compliance and Tax Morale: A theoretical and empirical analysis*, Cheltenham, Glos.: Edward Elgar.

Volgy, T.J., Fausett, E., Grant, K.A., and Rodgers, S. (2008) "Identifying formal intergovernmental organizations," *Journal of Peace Research*, 45: 837–50.

Wooster, W.S. (1973) "Interactions between intergovernmental and scientific organizations in marine affairs," *International Organization*, 27: 103–13.

Ward, H. (2006) "International linkages and environmental sustainability: the effectiveness of the regime network," *Journal of Peace Research*, 43: 149–66.

Wu, J.S.Y. (2009) "Towards a model of international environmental action: a case study of Japan's environmental conversation an participation in the climate change environmental regime," *Review of Policy Research*, 26: 267–87.

Index

Note: Page numbers in *italic* indicate tables. Those in **bold** indicate figures.

For Product Safety Concerns and Information please contact our EU representative GPSR@taylorandfrancis.com
Taylor & Francis Verlag GmbH, Kaufingerstraße 24, 80331 München, Germany

www.ingramcontent.com/pod-product-compliance
Lightning Source LLC
LaVergne TN
LVHW011121300926
849160LV00008B/465
* 9 7 8 0 4 1 5 5 1 6 8 9 1 *